A DICTIONARY OF HERALDRY
AND RELATED SUBJECTS

A DICTIONARY OF
HERALDRY
AND
RELATED SUBJECTS

by

COLONEL A. G. PUTTOCK

ARCO PUBLISHING, INC.
New York

© 1985 Arco Publishing, Inc.
215 Park Avenue South, New York, N.Y. 10003

Library of Congress Cataloging in Publication Data
Puttock, A. G.
A dictionary of heraldry and related subjects.

Bibliography: p.
1. Heraldry—Dictionaries.   I. Title.
CR13.P8   1985   929.6′03′21   85-7363
ISBN 0-668-06572-9

This edition published by arrangement with
Blaketon Hall Limited, London under licence
from the author Colonel A. G. Puttock.

Reproduced, printed and bound in Great Britain

DEDICATION

To my grandsons Andrew, James and David.

I hope that they will find as much interest in, and obtain as much joy from the study of Heraldry and its Related Subjects as I have.

CONTENTS

AUTHOR'S PREFACE

HERALDRY IS a subject about which one never stops learning. My own introduction to the subject was a little over forty years ago when I was still at school, and though I did not work at it seriously during my years in the army, yet it was always in the back of my mind and now, though I am engaged in both Heraldry and Genealogy in a professional capacity, I still have a great deal to learn.

This book represents the fruits of a considerable amount of research, and as it is research which can be of considerable help to others I have tried to set out in these pages what I think will be of assistance to them.

Many people look on Heraldry and Genealogy as being dry subjects which would possibly be of interest to nobody but a snob, but how far this is from the truth, and I am glad to say that the last fifteen or twenty years have produced a terrific crop of students, by no means all of whom are themselves armigerous, who are anxious to learn about and enjoy the fascinations of Heraldry. Furthermore, though there has always been a considerable number of people keen to find out something of their own family history, yet the last few years seem to have brought out even more than usual.

Throughout the years I have gained a great deal from such works as *Shield and Crest* by Julian Franklyn, *Boutells Heraldry* as revised by C. W. Scott-Giles and J. P. Brooke-Little, *Scots Heraldry* by Sir Thomas Innes of Learney, to say nothing of the many and varied titles by Leslie Pine. All of these I commend to my readers, yet I feel that a Dictionary of Heraldry and Related Subjects, such as this, can be used as a quick reference by any and everybody, and for this reason I have grouped the four parts together.

To my wife I give my thanks for her encouragement, particularly in the early days of my research, and in recent months for her criticism of the illustrations.

To my secretary Glynis Kirkbride I give my thanks for the patient way she has taken dictation, then typed the manuscript.

Finally I hope my readers will obtain as much joy from reading the pages of this book as I have experienced in putting it together.

A. G. PUTTOCK.

PART ONE
HERALDRY

HERALDRY

As A keen Heraldist for many years I have always hoped for the publication of an up-to-date Dictionary of Heraldry, as the last one was published over 100 years ago and, though still extremely useful, is of course out of date in many ways. However, nothing seems to materialise from any of the many Heraldic writers and so eventually I decided to write one myself.

A Dictionary of Heraldry if properly used can be an extremely valuable book. It is never designed to give exhaustive information on any one particular subject but to provide sufficient information at least to give its user enough general information about a particular subject for his immediate needs. After all, if one is at a loss to know the meaning of a word in every-day life one makes reference to one of the standard dictionaries. One does not expect to get a complete explanation of all the whys and wherefores about it, but enough information to know its general meaning.

Heraldry is an extremely fascinating subject which is playing a much wider part in all our lives today than at almost any time in history. During the Middle Ages probably a greater use was made of armorial bearings, in that, though all who possessed them displayed them more widely, their use was restricted almost entirely to the Nobility. Today, however, personal arms can be used by almost anybody, providing he is a straightforward and decent living citizen. Furthermore, arms are used by cities, towns, hospitals, schools and many other well known institutions, and even some of the larger and well established industrial companies.

This means that almost everybody both male and female owes a loyalty to one or more persons or bodies bearing arms.

During World Wars I and II a great many members of the community served with the forces and bear a loyalty to a particular unit or formation. In the case of the Navy it would have been a ship's badge; if it was the Army there would have been a regimental or corps badge together with a formation sign; in the case of the Royal Air Force there were the squadron badges, many of which became exceedingly famous. All this is Heraldry and though service badges may be treated as one of the Related Subjects yet it is still part of the Heraldic study.

Royal Heraldry though lightly touched upon in these pages is again a definite study of its own and a particularly interesting one, too.

Much of the information I have gathered in compiling this work of reference has been obtained from or verified in those excellent books on Heraldry by C. W. Scott-Giles and Julian Franklyn, to whom I gladly give fullest acknowledgement.

Finally I hope that all students of Heraldry will find this reference of value. We are all students of Heraldry however knowledgeable we may be, because it is a subject in which one can never learn everything and that, too, is one of its great fascinations.

A

Abased, abaissé – An expression used when a chevron, fess or other ordinary is placed lower than its usual position.

Abatements – Sometimes known as rebatements are marks of disgrace applied to arms in early Heraldry on account of some dishonourable act of the bearer. There were nine in number viz.
1. Delf
2. Inescutcheon reversed.
3. Point dexter.
4. Point in point.
5. Point champaine.
6. Plain point.
7. Gore sinister.
8. Gusset dexter.
9. Gusset sinister.
These marks must be in one of the old tinctures, namely sanguine or tenné as in any other tincture they may very occasionally be found as a normal charge.

There is another mark of disgrace which is due only to the traitor; this consists of reversing the entire coat.

There is considerable speculation as to whether these abatements were ever used. Guillim describes them as 'these whimsical abatements', but as the marks only applied to the unfortunate bearer of the arms and they were designed to keep him out of public life, this they must successfully have done and it is probable that they were used.

Abatements were imposed for such 'crimes' as the following:
1. Revoking one's own challenge.
2. Deserting one's sovereign's banner.
3. Discourteously treating either maiden or widow against their will.
4. Boasting of one's prowess.
5. Killing one's prisoner.
6. Telling lies to one's sovereign.
7. Cowardice.
8. Drunkenness.
Special Heraldic marks of bastardy have sometimes been called abatements because they abate or reduce the status of the arms to is not in the direct legitimate line the extent of showing that the bearer of succession. This use of the word abatement does not imply dishonour in any way whatsoever.

Abbreviations – The following abbreviations are commonly used in Heraldry:
1. Arg – argent.
2. Az – azure.
3. Erm – ermine.
4. Gu – gules.
5. Or – Or.
6. Ppr – proper.
7. Pur – purpure.
8. Sa – sable.
9. Ve – vert.
Other tinctures, furs etc. are not abbreviated.

In the case of tricking arms in order to save space and avoid any chance of error the abbreviations *ar* and *B* are used for silver and blue (azure) instead of those listed above.

Abeyance – This is the state of a peerage which is vested in two or more co-heirs both or all of whom appear to have an equal claim. When there are several equal claimants e.g. descendants of the daughters and co-heiresses of the deceased peer none is in a position to maintain a claim against the others and a peerage remains in abeyance. It is not therefore held by any of them until by death of the other claimants only one remains and he then has the right to claim the peerage.

á Bouche – An expression which describes a shield of the older type with a notch for the lance to rest in.

Abouté – Placed end to end.

Accessories – An achievement contains the coat of arms which is emblazoned on the shield, together with certain accessories. These include he!m, wreath, crest, mantling, supporters, compartment, motto, coronet, cap of estate, etc.

Accolade – The ceremony of conferring Knighthood by embrace, placing hand on neck or by a light blow on the shoulder or neck with the flat of a sword (sometimes known as ' dubbing ').

Accollé – This word has two meanings:
1. It is synonymous with *gorged and collared* and occasionally with *wreathed or entwined*.
2. It also denotes the position of two shields joined side by side; a practice that was sometimes adopted prior to the introduction of impaling.

Accompanied or **accompagné** – An expression often found in older Heraldry instead of the word *between*

which is in use today e.g. a cross accompanied by four mullets.

Accosted – An expression used when charges are placed on each side of another charge, e.g. a pale accosted by four crescents. Another application of the word is to two beasts walking or running side by side. Unless they are *accosted passant counter passant* the more distant should be shown a little in advance of the other.

Achievement – This is the correct name given to armorial bearings which include the shield and all appropriate accessories (q.v.). Unfortunately there is considerable misinterpretation of the expressions as frequently an achievement is called a coat of arms, particularly by journalists and other writers.

In early Heraldry the expression achievement was applied particularly to the decorative plaques prepared on the death of an armiger for erection outside his house and in his church. These plaques fol!owed the general rules of Heraldry and today are generally described as funeral hatchments (q.v.).

Acorné – Means having horns or attires.

Acorned – The expression used in connection with an oak tree to denote that it is bearing acorns. The expression fructed is however more generally used.

Addorsed, adorsed, endorsed – An expression used of two animals, etc., placed back to back. It may also be used in connection with keys, wings, etc. e.g. a falcon wings elevated and adorsed.

Adorned – Where a chapeau or other article of clothing is charged

Arms of Cardinal Godfrey

with a particular charge it is said to be *adorned* with such a charge.

Adze – An old Heraldic expression for the common axe.

Aeroplane – A modern charge which has found its place in Heraldry in the last 40 years. If flying, it is described as volant.

Eagle Wings elevated and adorsed

Affronté – Facing the viewer, thus showing its full face.

Agnus Dei – The Holy Lamb emblem of St. John the Baptist. See Paschal Lamb.

Aiguisé – Sharply pointed. In modern Heraldry urdé is generally used.

Ailettes – The term given to square appendages emblazoned with the wearer's arms and fastened upright on the shoulders. These are found in some of the early 14th century effigies.

Ainent – Running, applied to beasts but seldom used in modern Heraldry.

Lion Affronté

Aislé – Winged.

á la Cuisse – At the thigh. This indicates the point at which the leg is cooped or erased. The expression is taken from the piece of armour covering that part of the body.

Aland – A mastiff with short ears. The dexter supporter of the arms of Lord Dakar, though generally called a wolf, appears to have been meant for an aland.

Albany Herald – One of the Scottish officers of arms (q.v.).

17

Albert Medal – One of the decorations awarded by the Sovereign which may be suspended from the shield by its appropriate ribbon.

Alisé – Rounded or globular.

Allerion – An old Heraldic term for eagle which when so blazoned was generally depicted without beak or legs and with the points of the wings downward.

Allumé – Describes a beast's eyes when flecked with colour.

Altar – A tall circular pedestal generally borne inflamed. Seldom found in modern Heraldry.

Ambulant – Walking.

Amphiptère – A winged serpent.

Amphisien Cockatrice – A basilisk (q.v.).

Anchor – The anchor is frequently found as a charge, particularly in the case of naval personnel. It may also symbolise hope. In some cases the ring and flukes (points) are blazoned of a different tincture.

Ancré, anchory – An expression used on occasions, particularly in old Heraldry, of a cross of which the arms end in the flukes of an anchor.

Andrew, St. – The patron saint of Scotland. The saltire is said to be derived from the shape of the cross on which St. Andrew was crucified.

Angels – Figures sometimes used as supporters.

Angenne – A six-leaved flower, sometimes used instead of a sexfoil.

Angled – One of the lines of partition (q.v.) seldom seen in modern Heraldry.

Angles – A pair of rods each bent in a right angle, entwined saltirewise having rings at each end.

Angles

Animé – With fire issuing from mouth and ears.

Annodated – Bowed, embowed or bent in the form of the letter ' s '.

Annulet – A plain ring which may be found singly or in multiples. Sometimes they are entwined, in which case they are blazoned as annulets conjoined.

The annulet is a mark of cadency for the fifth son.

Annulet

Annulettée, annuly – Ringed at the ends.

Antelope – The natural animal which is occasionally found in Heraldry and which must not be confused with the Heraldic antelope, which is a mythical animal dealt with under monsters (q.v.)

18

Anthony, St. – cross of – A type of cross more generally known as the tau cross.

Antique Crown – Sometimes known as the eastern crown (q.v.)

Anvil – Sometimes found as a charge, represented normally.

Apaumé – Describes a hand or gauntlet which is open to show the palm.

Apple of Granada – The pomegranate, as seen in the arms of Queen Mary I and Katherine of Aragon.

Arbalest – The cross bow.

Arch – This may be single or double, springing from two or three pillars.

Arched – In the form of an arch. May also be used of an ordinary embowed.

Argent – Silver. As silver paint does not reproduce well and rapidly tarnishes argent is represented in all Heraldry as white. If on white paper the section which is to be argent is left blank, if on coloured paper the argent section is painted white. In the doubling of mantling it may be called white rather than argent because, in that case the metal is not used, but in ancient Heraldry it was customary to use the skin of a small animal called a lituite.

Arm – The human arm is frequently found as part of a crest though seldom as a charge in armorial bearings. The blazon must state whether it is dexter or sinister, erect, embowed or counter embowed, vested, vambraced or naked as the case may be. If cooped care must be taken to describe where. When cooped at the

elbow it is known as a cubit-arm.

Armed – The expression used with regard to beasts, monsters and birds with reference to teeth, talons, horns and claws.

It may also be used with reference to the heads of arrows.

(a) Cubit Arm
(b) Arm embowed in armour

Armed at all points, armed cap á pie – This applies to a man entirely covered with armour except his face.

Armiger – A person legally entitled to bear arms.

Armigerous – Refers to a man who is entitled to bear arms.

Arming Buckle – Refers to a buckle (q.v.) of lozenge shape.

Armorial Bearings, Arms – Armorial bearings correctly apply to the coat of arms or what is displayed upon the shield. The expression has,

19

however, loosely come to be applied to the Achievement.

There are two main types of arms, namely:

1. Private or personal arms which have been granted to a man for himself and for the use of all his heirs male, and by courtesy to his heirs female of the next generation only.

2. Corporate arms which have been granted to institutions whether public or ecclesiastic, civic bodies and industrial concerns.

3. Attributed arms. These are bearings which have been attributed either to Kings and Queens and to famous people who lived before the inception of Heraldry or to mythical characters.

An example of attributed arms can be seen in the famous coat of Edward the Confessor, *azure a cross patonce between five martlets Or.* This coat was frequently quartered by King Richard II. It may also be found in the arms of Westminster.

Reference is also made to other types of arms which strictly fall into one or other of the above categories. These include:

1. Arms of Dominion which are those borne by Sovereign Princes, not the arms of their families but those of the states over which they reign.

2. Arms of Pretension, which are arms of dominion borne by sovereign princes who have no actual authority over the states to which such arms belong, but quarter them to express their right thereunto; thus the Kings of England quartered the arms of France from the time of Edward II to 1801.

3. Arms of Succession which are those borne by the holder of certain lord-ships or estates thus Earls of Derby as Lords of Man quartered the arms of that island.

4. Arms of Assumption. In early days, if a man captured a prisoner, who was armigerous, in battle, he was entitled to assume the arms of that prisoner, either adding them to his own or bearing them alone.

5. Arms of Adoption where the last survivor of a family bearing arms has no issue he may, with Royal consent, adopt a stranger to bear his name and arms and to possess his estates.

6. Canting arms which are sometimes known as allusive or punning arms. These are bearings which contain charges which allude to the name of the bearer.

Armorial Display – Armigerous persons may well display their arms in one or more of the following places: A Heraldic banner; wall plaques and paintings for use in the house; on the side of a vehicle; on decorative scroll work either on gates or on furniture; table silver and table mats; cigarette boxes; cigarette cases; lighters; cuff links; rings; stationery, seals and bookplates.

Armory – The early name given to the study of armorial bearings. This name was used more particularly in the early days when the word Heraldry applied to all the duties of a Herald. It must not be confused with 'armoury' which is the name given to the place where small arms are stored.

Armour – The defensive covering used by fighting men. Generally it was made of iron or steel but records are in existence whereby other tough materials have been used.

Arrache – Erased.

Arrondi – Rounded or curved.

Arrow – The ordinary position of an arrow is in pale with the point downwards but to avoid possibility of error the blazon should state the position. Arrows are emblazoned as 'barbed' or 'armed' of the colour of their points and 'flighted' or 'feathered' with that of their feathers. A sheaf or bundle of arrows consists of three, unless more are specified, one erect and the others crossing in saltire tied together in the centre. The term 'banded' is used to describe that tie.

Ascendant – Said of rays, flames etc. issuing upwards.

Aspectant – Respecting (looking at) one another.

Assurgent – Rising out of.

Astral Crown – The type of crown (q.v.) allocated to corporations or private individuals who have connection with the air.

At Gaze – The expression describing a stag who would otherwise be known as statant gardant.

Attire – The antlers of a stag. The beast is said to be attired.

Attires

Avellane Cross – Formed of four hazel nuts placed crosswise.

Averdant – Covered with green herbage chiefly applied to a mount in base or to the compartment.

Aversant – Said of a hand of which the back only is seen.

Augmentation – In mediaeval times there were no such things as Orders, Decorations and Medals which the King could bestow upon such of his subjects who had distinguished themselves in battle.

The Order of the Garter was instituted by Edward III 1348 but the recipients were limited in number, and then it was only awarded to the greater members of the Nobility.

Stories exist of the crusades from which it would appear that several Esquires and Gentlemen were Knighted on the battlefield in recognition of some particularly spectacular achievement in battle against the Saracens, and there are records of cases where armorial bearings were granted to some of the Knights who did not already possess them. In this connection even in the time of Henry V he is said to have legalised any armorial bearings which had, presumably, been previously assumed by those of his followers present at the battle of Agincourt who had not borne arms previously.

John Phillipot, a 17th century writer on Heraldry, tells a story of which the veracity is extremely suspect, to the effect that the two round buckles with straps borne in the Pelham family arms were granted to Sir John Pelham in recognition of his brilliant services when he captured the French King at the battle of Poitiers.

Whatever the origin, however, during the later part of the Middle Ages it was a custom for the Sovereign to bestow additional quarters or charges upon those of his subjects who warranted such an honour. These came to be known as Augmentations of Honour. On occasions

21

these augmentations took the form of an additional quarter added to the armorial bearings and which became an integral part of them. At other times they consisted merely of an additional charge or group of charges which were added to the arms.

Examples of additional quarters being added to the arms can very easily be seen amongst the wives of Henry VIII. For example, when Anne Bullen became Marchioness of Pembroke, immediately prior to her marriage to the King, he granted her three additional quarters as augmentations. These were: 1. England with a label of three points azure charged on each point with as many fleurs-de-lis Or (for Lancaster). 2. France with a label of three points gules (for Angoulême). 3. *Gules a lion passant gardant Or* (for Guinne).

Jane Seymour, however, only received an addition of one quarter which was *Or six fleurs-de-lis sable two, two and two a pile gules thereon three lions passant gardant in pale Or.*

Henry had no use whatsoever for his fourth wife, Anne of Cleeves, and she did not survive long enough for an augmentation even to be considered.

Katherine Howard, possibly as a result of Henry's relief at being rid of Anne, was granted two additional quarters. These were: 1. *Azure three fleurs-de-lis in pale Or between two flaunches ermine each charged with a rose gules barbed and seeded proper.* 2. *Azure two lions passant gardant Or between four demi fleurs-de-lis of the last.*

Katherine Parr received one such coat as follows: *Or on a pile between six roses argent.*

There are many cases of additional charges etc. being given. Perhaps the most famous being that known as the Howard augmentation given after the Battle of Flodden, in which the King of Scotland met his death. The Earl of Surrey who later became Duke of Norfolk and who led the English forces in this battle, received as augmentation an escutcheon charged with a demi-lion pierced in the mouth with an arrow within a double tressure flory counter flory. This was, of course, virtually taken from the Scottish arms.

John Churchill, first and most famous Duke of Marlborough, whose military achievement saved Europe, was awarded an augmentation consisting of an escutcheon argent charged with the cross of St. George thereon another azure with three fleurs-de-lis Or. This addition was placed on the palar line in the chief of his quartered shield and today, though the quarterings have changed, the augmentation may be seen in a similar position in the arms of the 10th Duke of Marlborough whose second cousin Sir Winston Churchill K.G. bore the same arms.

The human heart so well known in the arms of Douglas is an augmentation commemorating his stalwart attempt to carry out the wishes of King Bruce that on his death his heart should be carried to the Holy Sepulchre.

During the time of Cromwell both Charles I and Charles II had nothing else to bestow on loyal friends and a few such augmentations are well worth recording.

At the battle of Naseby after Edward Lake had been wounded sixteen times and with his left arm useless he fought on with his reigns gripped in his teeth. His feat was recognised by a quarter of augmentation *gules a dexter arm embowed in armour holding in the hand a sword erect all proper there to affixed a banner argent charged with a cross between sixteen escutcheons of the field, on the cross a lion of England.*

At the battle of Worcester despite the King's magnificent Generalship and great valour, when failure was certain, his escape was due to the loyal courage of Colonel Newman whose arms were augmented by *an inescutcheon gules charged with a portcullis imperially crowned Or.*

During the wanderings of Charles II his companion Colonel Careless afterwards called Carlos, who was hiding with the King in the famous Oak tree at Boscobel, was non-armigerous. The story is told that they discussed a Coat of Arms for the Colonel which would be granted if and when the King eventually came to the throne. This great, *Or, issuing from a mount in base vert an oak tree proper over all on a fess gules three imperial crowns also proper.*

Later when the chase had cooled slightly the King reached the house of the Lane family where he was disguised as a servant and travelled with Mistress Jane Lane, riding behind her on a strawberry roan horse, to the coast where he took ship for France. On his restoration the family received the highest honour of any which was a Canton of England. In addition they were awarded a crest of augmentation consisting of a strawberry roan horse cooped at the flanks holding on its foot the Royal Crown.

There is an interesting outcome to this augmentation because when, during the reign of Queen Victoria, the armorial bearings tax was imposed a clause was introduced excluding Royal armory. Consequently, when the local tax inspector called at the Lane household, he was advised to observe the Canton of England whereupon he went away empty handed and the Lanes never paid a penny piece.

A number of interesting augmentations were bestowed during the late 18th century and early 19th century particularly to members of the services. Colonel Clark-Kennedy who captured the eagle of the 105th French regiment at the battle of Waterloo was granted a chief with a representation of this crossed with a sword and, in addition, a crest of a demi dragon holding aloft the same flag.

The Duke of Wellington was granted an escutcheon charged with the union flag. These arms can be seen today on the gates of Wellington College, Berkshire.

On some occasions augmentations were granted beyond the realm of common sense so that the original arms became virtually impossible to see, an example of this can be seen in the arms of Lord Nelson, which were originally *Or a cross flory sable.* His first augmentation consisted of *a bend gules surmounted by another engrailed Or charged with three bombs fired proper.* This was granted on the 2nd October 1797. A year later, in honour of his triumph in the battle of the Nile he was after augmented with *a chief undulatory argent thereon waves of the sea from which a palm tree issuant between a disabled ship on the dexter and a ruinous battery on the sinister all proper.*

After the hero's death his brother the Reverend William Nelson, who became Earl Nelson of Trafalgar and Merton, was given a further augmentation *on a fess wavy azure the word Trafalgar in text letters Or.* This last augmentation finally removed all traces of the cross in the original arms.

An example of two augmentations which were placed well enough to provide a coat of arms which if a little crowded were not unsightly were those of Lord Kitchener of

23

Khartoum, the blazon of whose arms is *gules between three bustards close proper a chevron argent surmounted by another azure in the centre chief point a bezant* to which were added the first augmentation *a pile Or thereon two flag staves salterwise flowing to the dexter the union flag of Great Britain and Ireland and to the sinister a representation of the Egyptian flag all proper enfiled by a mural crown gules the rim inscribed 'Khartoum' in letters of gold* and the second augmentation *a chief argent thereon a pale gules charged with a lion passant gardant Or between on the dexter an eagle displayed sable and on the sinister on a mount vert an orange tree fructed proper.*

Aulned – Bearded. Used when ears of corn are spoken of.

Axe – There are various types of axe which apply in Heraldry, and of which details must be carefully blazoned.

1. 'Axe' makes reference to the common hatchet.

2. 'Battle axe' has a broad splayed out curved blade and which has a point at the back of the blade.

3. 'Danish axe' has a blade like a battle axe but the helve is curved.

4. 'Pickaxe' is similar to the normal workman's pickaxe.

Ayet – Sometimes known as sea swallows or Cornish Choughs.

Azure – The tincture blue.

B

Badger – Sometimes called 'brock', one of the animals occasionally seen used as a charge.

Badges – Marks of distinction somewhat similar to the crest but not placed on a wreath nor worn on the helmet. In early days it was generally embroidered upon the sleeves of servants and followers.

In modern days badges are used extensively by ships of the Navy, regiments of the Army, squadrons of the Air Force, schools and many of the employees of hospitals, industrial concerns, etc.

Some of the better known badges were the following: The House of Plantagenet. The Planta Genista or Broome plant.

Planta Gerista (Plantagenets)

King Stephen. A sagittary, and ostrich feathers in plume with the motto 'utrumque'.

Richard I. A star issuing from between the horns of a crescent. With Richard's association with the crusades this may have been symbolic of the ascendancy of Christianity over Mahommedanism. An armed arm holding a shivered lance.

Edward I. A rose Or stalked proper.

Edward II. A hexagonal castle with a tower thereon. This is an allusion to his descent from the house of Castile.

Edward III. The sun's rays descending from clouds proper, an ostrich feather and also a falcon. It is from this badge that the Herald of that name appointed by this King was called.

Richard II. The sun in splendour and also a white hart couchant on a mount under a tree proper gorged with a crown and chained Or.

White Hart (Richard II)

The House of Lancaster. A red rose.

Henry IV. A genet and an eagle displayed Or.

Henry V. A beacon Or inflamed proper and an antelope gorged with a crown and chained.

Henry VI. Two feathers in saltire the sinister argent surmounted of the dexter Or.

The House of York. A white rose.

Edward IV. A falcon displayed argent within a closed fetterlock. Or and a bull sable.

Cypher (Henry VII)

Richard III. A rose within the sun.

The House of Tudor. The red and white roses variously united sometimes per pale, sometimes quarterly but generally one within the other, also a portcullis.

Henry VII. A Hawthorn bush fructed and Royally crowned between the letters H.R. Or. Also a red dragon

Henry VIII. A white greyhound.

Queen Mary. The dexter half of a double rose proper impaled with a semi-circle therein a sheaf of arrows Or. The whole rayonnant and ensigned with a Royal Crown.

Rose and Pomegranate
(Mary I)

Queen Elizabeth I. A rose with the motto ' rosa sine spina '.

Great Britain and Ireland
(Elizabeth II)

25

The House of Stuart. Fleurs-de-lis. A rose and thistle impaled by dimidiation

The House of Brunswick. The roses, fleurs-de-lis, thistles and harps in various forms as used by their predecessors.

These devices are still used in varying forms by members of the Royal family today.

Bag of Madder – An ordinary sack corded with three bands each fess wise and palewise.

Madder is a dye and this charge is found in the arms in the Company of Dyers of London.

Bagpipes – These seldom apply in Heraldry but when they do they are generally associated with a hare which is seen to be playing them.

Bagwyn – An imaginary beast similar to the Heraldic antelope having the tail of a horse and long horns curved over the ears.

Bailloné – Gagged. This describes an animal, especially a lion, when holding a staff in its mouth.

Balance – A set of scales.

Bale – A package of merchandise rather similar to the Bag of Madder but less decoratively painted.

Bale fire – A beacon.

Banded – Encircled with a band cord or ribbon but when a different tincture is to be used for the band the blazon must state particulars.

Banners – A square or oblong (the depth greater than the width) flag which is charged with the arms of its owner. In early days banners were borne by Knights banneret and by all the higher ranks of the nobil-

ity. To be more accurate, an esquire carried the banner of his lord. If

Banner of Nevill

an ordinary knight, who carried a pennon with two points, distinguished himself in battle it was customary for a member of the higher nobility, or the King to remove the two points turning the pennon into a small banner and thus promoting its bearer to knight banneret.

Banners of the Knights of the Garter hang in St. George's Chapel, Windsor during the lifetime of the knight concerned; so too, the banners of the Knights of the Bath hang in Westminster Abbey.

The flag which is flown over the Royal residences during their occupation by the reigning Monarch, which is generally known as the Royal Standard, should correctly be called the Royal Banner.

Banneret – The rank of the nobility between knight bachelor and baron.

Bar – An ordinary resembling the fess in form but of lesser width. It is seldom borne singly and consequently is not confined to the middle of the shield. It has two diminutives the closet (q.v.) and the barrulet (q.v.).

Barb – The name given to the sepals appearing between the petals of the Heraldic rose. In the case of an arrow it refers to the head.

Barded – Furnished with bardings. This refers to the caparison of a horse which, in early days, was frequently charged with armorial bearings.

Barnacle – An instrument used by farriers to curb unruly horses. It may occasionally be found extended i.e. horizontally. There is also a water fowl of this name sometimes found in Heraldry.

Baron – The fifth and lowest rank of the British Peerage. The word seems to have been introduced into England at an early period and was originally applied to all the nobility. Barons, according to Spelman, were first made by King's writ summoning them to Parliament in the reign of John. The first baron by patent was John Beauchamp of Holt who was raised to the peerage by King Richard II in the 11th year of his reign (10th October, 1387) under the title of Baron of Kidderminster.

Until after World War II when the system of life peerage was introduced the rank of baron was hereditory which it remains for all other than life peers.

Baroness – The wife of a Baron.

Baronet – Baronets of Great Britain. An order founded by King James I 1611 for the encouragement of plantations in the province of Ulster. The dignity is bestowed by patent and is hereditary but generally limited to the heirs male of the grantee. It was in the first instance bestowed upon knights and esquires (being duly qualified) each of whom undertook to maintain thirty foot soldiers in Ireland at 8 pence per day for the term of two years. Upon the establishment of the order it was decreed that the number of British Baronets should not exceed 200 and upon the extinction of a baronetcy no other should be created to fill the vacancy but these regulations were soon dispensed with and the number became unlimited.

The badge of baronetage (*argent a sinister hand erect, open and cooped at the wrist gules,* being the arms of the province of Ulster) was granted in 1612. It may be borne upon a canton or upon an inescutcheon which may be placed either upon the middle chief point or fess point it must never be placed upon an intersection of two or more coats quartered.

Baronets of Ireland. Established by King James I in 1619. Their qualification, privileges and badge were the same as those of the Baronets of Great Britain. None have been conferred, however, since the Union of 1801.

Baronets of Scotland and Nova Scotia. A similar order projected by James I but founded by Charles I in 1625 immediately after his accession. The object of this order was to encourage the plantation of Nova Scotia, in which colony each Baronet had granted to him by his patent eighteen square miles of land having a sea coast or at least the bank of some navigable river three miles in length and an extent of six miles inland.

These were authorised to add to their arms either on a canton or an inescutcheon argent *on a saltire azure an escucheon of the Royal Arms of Scotland,* which were the arms of the province of Nova Scotia.

Since the union of England and Scotland all new creations have been Baronets of the United Kingdom.

Barrulé – An expression used to describe a field divided horizontally into ten or any higher even number of equal parts. In modern Heraldry the term barry (q.v.) has more generally been used.

Barrulet – A diminutive of the bar of which it is approximately $\frac{1}{4}$ its width, that is to say approximately $\frac{1}{20}$ of the height of the shield.

Barry – An expression denoting that the field is horizontally divided into an even number of equal parts of which the number must be stated. In the case of barry it is customary for the metal to precede the tincture and thus take the senior position.

Barry bendy – An expression denoting that the field is divided fess wise and bend wise in equal proportions thus producing a number of diamond sections lying on their sides. The tinctures thus become counter changed. Barry bendy sinister may also be found.

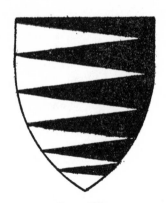

Barry Piley

Bars Gemel – These are bars voided or closets placed in couples.

Bars Gemelles

Bar wise – An expression denoting that charges on the shield are arranged horizontally one beside the other.

Base – The lower portion of the shield. It may refer to a portion of the base equal in width of a bar parted off by a horizontal line.

Basilisk – A monster resembling a wyvern but with a dragon's head at the end of the tail.

Basket – Several kinds of baskets may be used in Heraldry generally

Barry Bendy

Barry Piley – The field divided horizontally into a number of pile shaped pieces.

28

referring to the occupation or trade of the bearer. A basket may be covered.

Bastard – Illegitimate issue.

Baston – A single cotise used as an ancient mark of difference.

Bat – The creature which is sometimes found in Heraldry and generally blazoned as flittermouse or reremouse.

Baton – A bendlet cooped. The baton sinister is sometimes used as a difference for bastardy. A staff of office.

Battering Ram – A charge which seldom appears in modern heraldry depicting a cylindrical shaft fess wise with a ram's head on the dexter end and rings for suspension.

Battle axe – An axe with a curved edge and a spike on the back of the blade, which is mounted on a straight helve headed by a spike.

Battle Axe

Baudric – A sword belt which was looked upon as one of the distinctions of a knight. It is thought to have been a prototype of the bend.

Bayeux Tapestry – A well known piece of embroidery constructed by the sewing ladies of Matilda wife of William the Conqueror, probably at the request of Odo, Bishop of Bayeux, brother of William the Conqueror. It is some 230 feet long by 20 inches wide containing eighty-one scenes which tell the story of events leading up to and during the battle of Hastings.

It is of particular interest to students of Heraldry because the shields and banners of the many personalities who can be identified do not bear Heraldic emblems, thus proving that the inception of Heraldry was after the Norman conquest.

Beacon – An iron cage or trivet mounted on a long pole and provided with a step ladder, which was used originally to guide travellers across unfrequented tracks of country or to alarm the neighbourhood in event of invasion or rebellion.

Beacon

29

It is more frequently found as a crest than as a charge and is invariably emblazoned with the fire burning.

Beaked – Refers to the beaks of birds or monsters.

Bear – Found in several positions in Heraldry most frequently in conjunction with the ragged staff. One may also find the bear's head and a bear's gamb.

Bear and Ragged Staff

Bearer – An expression used in Scottish Heraldry in lieu of supporter.

Bearing – Any Heraldic device or figure borne upon the shield. When used in the plural it has come to mean the whole of the Coat of Arms.

Beaver – The animal which may be found, but infrequently, as a charge: an example being in the arms of Beverley, Yorkshire.

Bee – When used as a charge frequently denotes industry.

Bee Hive – Occasionally used on its own or may be blazoned 'beset with bees diversely volant' as in the arms of Earl Beatty.

Bell – There are two types of bell used in Heraldry unless stated otherwise a Church bell is intended, the alternative is a hawk's bell which must be blazoned in full.

Belled – An expression sometimes found in the blazon in conjunction with the falcon e.g. 'belled and jessed'. In modern Heraldry, however, it has come to be assumed automatically that the falcon is belled and jessed. The term applies to the bell fixed to one leg.

Bellows – A rarely found charge, but if used they are emblazoned in the traditional form.

Bend – An ordinary being a diagonal strip from dexter chief to approximately $\frac{2}{3}$ of the way down on the sinister side, which, according to Leigh and many earlier Heraldic writers, should occupy $\frac{1}{3}$ of the field when charged and $\frac{1}{5}$ when plain. The latter proportion is, however, generally adopted whether the bend is charged or not, the exact proportion being left entirely to the Heraldic artist.

The bend may be decorated with any one of the lines of division which must, of course, be stated in the blazon.

Bend sinister – Similar in every respect to the bend but running from sinister chief to the dexter base side of the shield.

Bendlet, bendlet sinister – A diminutive of the bend or bend sinister, not more than half the width of the bend, though normally narrower. Bendlets are occasionally enhanced.

Bendwise – An expression used to to describe the position of a number of charges placed in bend.

Bendy – Describes a field or charge divided bendwise into an even number of parts. The number required must be so stated in the blazon.

Bengal Tiger – The traditional tiger which appears occasionally in Heraldry more particularly perhaps as a crest or supporter.

Beson – A bird bolt.

Bevilled – A line of partition occasionally found in Heraldry commencing from the dexter side it runs approximately 7/12 horizontally towards the dexter then backwards and upwards at an angle of 45° approximately ⅙ of the width of the shield then, at an angle of 45°, it continues horizontally across to the sinister.

Bezant – A roundlet Or. It represents the old coin of Byzantium and should therefore, unlike most of the other roundlets, be emblazoned as a flat object. It was introduced into English Heraldry by the crusaders.

Bezanté – An expression describing a field which is strewn with bezants.

Bi-corporate – Having two bodies but only one head.

Bill – An instrument used by woodmen for the purpose of lopping trees. The head alone is more frequent as a charge than the entire instrument.

Bill Hook – Rather similar to the bill (q.v.) but with a short handle and therefore generally emblazoned complete.

Billet – A small oblong figure generally supposed to represent a letter; its proportion being two squares.

Billetté – Semé of billets.

Bird bolt – A blunt headed arrow used in early days for shooting birds. As the number of heads varies the blazon should mention if more than one are required.

Birds – There are numerous different species of birds used as charges, but by far the most important is the eagle which may be portrayed in a number of different positions, for example, an eagle displayed is one with his wings, legs and talons outstretched on either side of his body which is affronté and his head faces the dexter. He may be displayed with two heads. He may be shown in flight, in which case he is 'volant'. He may be standing with his wings closed, as an 'eagle close', or if he stands with wings partly opened he is an 'eagle rising'.

One will occasionally find an eagle's head either cooped or erased and as a diminutive the word eaglets will be applied when there are more than one or if they are to be white in colour they will be known as ospreys.

As with the lion, the eagle may be armed and langued, or his legs may be said to be 'membered' of a different tincture.

Another bird which is frequently seen is the falcon, and this is understandable because the sport of hawking was adopted by so many of the mediaeval knights. The falcon is generally shown on a perch with his wings close but they may be elevated and addorsed and whatever the position, the falcon is always belled and jessed which term refers to the bell and straps used in the old time sport. Other birds to be found include the Pelican which is generally shown standing above its nest and vulning or wounding its breast to nourish its young from the drops of blood which can be seen dripping down. The martlet, as found in the arms attributed to Edward the Confessor, is particularly popular in parts of Sussex. There is also the swan, the ostrich, which is usually shown with a horse-shoe in its beak, the crane, the heron, the stork, the shell-drake, the raven, the peacock, which is always ' in his pride ', the dove, the parrot, which in Heraldry is the popinjay, the kite and the cock which on occasions is blazoned as the dunghill cock, which is in fact nothing more than the farmyard rooster.

Birds may be blazoned as ducally gorged and on occasions chained and not infrequently they are themselves charged with some other charge.

Bishop – The armorial bearings of a bishop are normally impaled with the arms of the See in all official documents.

Various references to his office appear as charges and in crests, namely the mitre, the crozier, and the ordinary which is known as a pall was adopted from the ecclesiastical pallium.

Bit – The horses bit is occasionally to be found as a charge but the type must be specified in blazon.

Blackamore's Head – A number of heads have been used both as a charge and as a crest of which that of a blackamore is one.

Bladed – An expression used when the stalk of any grain is tinctured differently from the ear.

Blasted – Leafless, may sometimes be applied to trees.

Blazon – A word derived from the German ' blasen ' meaning to blow a trumpet or horn. It signifies the description of an achievement in general, and a coat of arms in particular, in such detail that an accurate drawing may be made from the description. In order to do so a knowledge of the points of the shield is particularly necessary. (See ' Points of the Shield ')

1. Emblazoning the coat of arms the first thing to be mentioned is the field, whether it be of one tincture, party of two, or of any of the patterns frequently found. Examples: (a) *Gules,* (b) *per fess argent and gules,* (c) *gyronny Or and sable,* (d) *bendy of eight argent and azure,* (e) *Azure semi-de-lis.*

2. The first charges which should be noticed are those laid immediately upon the field and normally occupying the central and most commanding position. These include the principal ordinaries. Examples: (a) *argent a lion rampant gules,* (b) *azure a bend Or,* (c) *argent a chevron engrailed sable.*

3. Any secondary charges resting on the surface of the shield. Example: *gules a bend Or between three crescents argent.*

4. Objects placed on one of the charges already mentioned. Example: *argent on a fess gules between three garbs azure two crosses patté Or.*

5. Important charges resting on the surface of the shield but not occupying the central position: viz. a chief, canton, bordure etc. Example: *gules on a bend sinister between three water bougets Or as many ogresses, a canton argent.*

6. Objects placed on the charges mentioned in number 5. Example: *sable on a fess Or between three*

Barry Bendy

Barry Piley

Annulet

Bars Gemelles

Lily as in
Arms of Eton College

Planta Genista
(Plantaganets)

Great Britain and Ireland
(Elizabeth II)

plates as many fleurs-de-lis of the first, on a chief argent a lion passant azure armed and langued gules.

7. Marks of cadency etc., if any. Examples: (a) *gules on a bend sinister between three water bougets Or as many ogresses, on a canton argent a baronets badge a crescent for difference.* (b) *sable on a fess Or between three plates as many fleur-de-lis of the first on a chief argent a lion passant azure armed and langued gules a label of five points.*

It can be noticed from the examples that where a similar number of charges appear on say the field and one of the ordinaries instead of repeating the number a second time the expression 'as many' is used, and similarly, where a tincture is repeated, rather than repeating the name of the tincture the expression 'of the first', 'of the second' or 'of the field' are used according to where that tincture has been used previously.

In the case of a quartered coat of arms the blazon of each quarter is given separately and on occasions where any particular charge is superimposed over the whole shield particulars of this are given at the end.

Blue bottle – The Heraldic name given to the common blue corn flower.

Boar's Head

Bluemantle Pursuivant – one of the English Officers of Arms (q.v.).

Boar and Boar's Head – The wild boar may be found in one of several postures as a Heraldic charge or as a crest but the most common form is the boar's head either cooped or erased. It is of particular significance in Scottish Heraldry.

Body heart – The heart, generally blazoned as 'body heart', and frequently surmounted by a crown, is used as a charge, particularly in the arms of Douglas. It is emblazoned in a manner similar to the heart seen on a playing card.

Bomb – Sometimes blazoned as 'grenade' is shown as a ball with flames issuing from the top, an example may be found in the arms of Lord Nelson.

Bone – Bones, generally human, are occasionally found as charges but the blazon must specify the type of bone required. They have also been used held in the mouth of an animal as a part of crest. A complete skeleton may be found in the arms of Londonderry.

Bonnet – The velvet cap within a coronet.

The electoral bonnet, which is also a cap of crimson velvet turned up ermine, was borne superimposed over the arms of Hanover until the elevation of that state into a kingdom in 1814 when the crown of Hanover was substituted.

Books – Books are borne in arms either open as in the arms of the University of Oxford or closed as in those of the University of Cambridge. The blazon must state full particulars with regard to their position and the tinctures of the binding, clasps, etc., and inscriptions.

Bordure = The Heraldic name for

33

border. It is frequently used in Scottish Heraldry as a mark of cadency but in English Heraldry it is sometimes seen as a charge. The bordure may be subject to decoration as for the lines of partition and may itself be charged in which case the number of minor charges is always eight unless otherwise specified.

Botonné or Treflé – Refers specifically to a type of cross implying that each arm ends in three round knobs.

Bouget, budget – The water bouget is a charge resembling a yolk from which are suspended two waterskins. It is frequently found in the arms of families which have a crusading ancestor.

Bouchier Knot – A device frequently repeated on the tomb of Archbishop Bouchier. See Knots.

Bourdon – A palmer's staff.

Bow – A long bow must be shown unless a cross bow is specified. It is normally shown bent and strung. If the strings are of a different tincture from the frame the blazon must so state.

Bowen's Knot – A continuous piece of rope set out in a square with a loop at each corner.

Braced – An early Heraldic word for interlaced.

Branch – If unfructed a branch should correctly consist of three slips. If fruit is included four leaves are generally considered sufficient.

Brass – Engraved monumental plate generally found in churches.

Breathing – An early Heraldic word applied to the stag which has the same meaning as 'at gaze'.

Bretesse – Embattled on both sides.

Brick – A charge resembling a billet but showing its thickness in perspective.

Bridge – When a bridge is given in blazon the number of its arches and all other particulars such as masoning, etc., must be given.

British Empire, Order of – A decoration (q.v.).

Brisure – A mark of cadency.

Broad arrow – A charge similar to the pheon but the inner edges of the barbs are not engrailed.

Buckles

Broche – An instrument used by embroiderers and borne as a charge by their company.

Brock – Another name for badger (q.v.).

Buck – An animal of the stag variety borne as such in blazon on some occasions.

Bucket – Several varieties of bucket have been used in Heraldry but unless specified a common well bucket is inferred. The blazon may state an addition of feet, hoops and handle which are generally tinctured differently from the bucket.

Buckle – From a very early period buckles have been marks of honour and authority. There are various forms used and the blazon must mention the shape. An arming buckle for example refers to one of lozenge shape.

In some examples the tongues are turned to the dexter or to the sinister.

Other shapes include oval, round and square. An alternative name which is sometimes found is 'fermail'.

Bugle horn, or hunting horn – A curved horn with the mouth piece to the sinister generally shown suspended by ribbons or strings which are tied in a knot above it; in which case they will be blazoned as stringed of the tincture required if

Bugle Horn

different from that of the horn. When decorated with bands of a different tincture it will be 'garnished' or 'viroled' of that tincture.

Bull – The animal of that name which appears in Heraldry, particularly in the Arms of Cole.

Burgeonée – Description of a fleur-de-lis with petals closed in the form of a bud.

Burling Iron – An instrument used by weavers. It occurs in the arms of their company at Exeter.

Butt – A fish of the flounder type.

Butterfly – This insect is generally borne volant with its four wings expanded. The harvest fly is similar but has two wings only.

Buzzard – An alternative name for the kite (q.v.).

C

Cable – A chain or rope attached to an anchor. It must not be included unless the blazon specifically states that it is there.

Caboshed – An expression used when applied to an animal's head (except leopard) to indicate that it is cut off so as to show part of the neck.

Cadency – The system showing the position of members or branches of the family in relation to its head.

Marks of cadency are sometimes known as brisures or differences and are applied differently in English and Scottish Heraldry.

England. In England the differences now in use may be divided into two classes, those used by the Royal family and those which should be borne by others. The sons and daughters of the sovereign all bear labels of three points argent. That of the Prince of Wales is plain but those of the other Princes and Princesses are charged with crosses, fleur-de-lis, hearts, roses, anchors, etc. for the sake of distinction. Princes and Princesses, being the sons and daughters of the above, are distinguished by labels of five points charged in a similar manner. These differences as well as those which follow should be borne on the arms, crest and supporters.

Differences now in use for all families except that of the Sovereign are as follows: First House. First son during the life of his father, a label of three points. Second son a crescent. Third son a mullet. Fourth son a martlet. Fifth son an annulet. Sixth son a fleur-de-lis. Seventh son a rose. Eighth son a cross moline. Ninth son a double quatrefoil. The first son of the first son of the first house bears a label of five points and the second a label charged with a crescent and so on for all other sons of this branch.

Second House. First son, a crescent charged with a label of three points. Second son, a crescent charged with a crescent and so on for the remainder but it is not usual to bear double differences. There are no differences for sisters (except in the Royal family) as they are all equal but they should bear the differences which pertain to their fathers.

Charges used as differences should be drawn smaller than usual to distinguish them from ordinary charges. They may be placed upon any part of the arms which is most convenient but will generally be found in the centre chief or the dexter chief. There is no rule respecting their tinctures except that they may not be argent which is reserved for the Royal family.

Unfortunately in English Heraldry the system of differencing is not strictly applied as it should be. *Scotland*. In Scotland automatic lineal descent of armorial bearings is only to the eldest son and to the eldest son of the eldest son. All other sons must matriculate with Lord Lyon, King of Arms, the Scottish Heraldic authority before possessing an entitlement to bear arms.

An appropriate difference will be allocated to each son thus matriculating, which will be retained by him as the arms of his particular cadet branch. Differences in Scotland very largely consist of the bordure in one of its forms together with frequent changes of tincture.

Caduceus – The staff of Mercury consisting of a ball headed rod, winged and entwined by two serpents.

Caerlaverock – A famous siege which took place in 1300 in the reign of Edward I between the English and the Scots. It is noteworthy as it was one of the early occasions at which the Heralds produced a roll of arms.

Calf – The young of the cow from which it is chiefly distinguished in Heraldic drawing by the absence of horns.

Calopus – A monster similar to a wolf but with horns.

Caltrap – A four pointed trap used in early battles when fighting against horsemen. It was so formed that which ever way it fell one point was in the air and thus it formed a trap against horses.

Caltrap

Cap of Estate

Calvary Cross – A passion cross elevated upon three steps which are said to represent the three graces, Faith, Hope and Charity.

Camel – The animal of that name which appears on infrequent occasions as a charge.

Camelopard – The Heraldic giraffe. If it is blazoned as camelopardel it is then depicted with two long curved horns.

Canon – The name given to the ancient muzzle loader unless another type is specified.

Canting Arms – Arms which contain an allusion to the name of the bearer.

Canton – A subordinary resembling the quarter in form but of smaller dimension. Its size is not fixed but it is generally about ⅓ of the chief. Cantons are always placed in the dexter chief unless on the very rare occasions the sinister chief is given in the blazon. Cantons are generally but not always charged.

Cap of Estate – Sometimes called chapeau or cap of maintenance. A cap generally of crimson velvet turned up ermine with two long points of the brim to the sinister. It is sometimes used to form the basis of a crest in lieu of the wreath.

Caparison – The embroidered covering of a horse which was often charged with the arms of the knight to whom the horse belonged. Originally made of leather for battle, light cotton material was used for tournaments and ceremonial.

Carbuncle – See Escarbuncle.

Carrick Pursuivent – One of the Scottish Officers of Arms (q.v.).

Castle – The word castle used alone generally signifies either a single tower or two towers with a gate between them. A castle triple towered is a tower with three turrets thereon.

Other castles which occur may be blazoned triangular or square which are seen in perspective. Frequently the blazon will say that the castle is masoned of another tincture and the same may apply to domes, ports and flags.

Castle

Cat – The wild cat which is blazoned catamountain. He may be shown in one of several positions which must be stated.

The alternative is the Cornish cat which is but infrequently found and which is of a sandy tabby type with a very short tail.

37

Catherine Wheel – A wheel consisting of eight spokes extending to a number of short curved blades along the rim. If an alternative number of spokes is required, it must be given in blazon.

Celestial Crown – A type resembling the eastern crown.

Centaur – Alternatively known as sagittarius or sagittary, is the man horse of mythology represented with bow and arrow and said to have been the emblem of King Stephen.

Centre Point – An alternative name for the fess point.

Chafant – An expression applied to the wild boar meaning enraged.

Chaffinch – The bird of that name sometimes blazoned as pinson.

Chains – Are often fixed to the collars of animals and on either side of a portcullis. They are also borne on occasions as distinct charges. They are usually shown with round or oval links unless square ones are specified.

Chalice – A cup without cover drawn on a pedestal with round or octagonal feet.

Chalice

Champion of England – An office probably created by William the Conqueror and retained for many years by the Marmion family. During the reign of Richard II, the title passed to their descendant Sir John Dymoke and has continued as an hereditary right in that family ever since. When the champion carried out his original duties, he rode into Westminster Hall, armed cap-á-pie, during the banquet following the coronation of a new Sovereign and publicly challenged to combat anyone who dared dispute the King's or Queen's title to the throne. The ceremony has not been carried out since the reign of George IV. Another honour of his office as champion granted to the head of the Dymoke family is to quarter with his own arms a silver sword on a black shield; and he also uses a motto 'rege dimico' thus combining a play on his surname with the office held by his family for so long.

Chamber Piece – A small piece of ordnance without a carriage.

Chapeau – See Cap of Estate.

Chaplet – A garland of leaves with four flowers spaced equally amongst them. The type of flower must be stated in blazon.

Charge – Anything borne on an escutcheon whether upon the field or upon an ordinary.

Charged – A term applying to a shield, crest, supporter or banner having any object depicted thereon. Also to any charge having another charge upon it.

Charger – A dish.

Chaussé – Wearing shoes.

38

Checky – An expression applied to a field or charge divided by perpendicular and horizontal lines into small equal sized squares of metal and colour alternately.

Chessrook – A charge represented by two wing-like projections issuing from the base of a chess piece.

Chessrook

Chester Herald – One of the English Officers of Arms (q.v.).

Chevalier – Literally a man on horseback but generally refers to a knight in armour which may be found in several cases as a charge.

Chevron – An ordinary said to have been derived from a pair of rafters and occupying approximately $\frac{1}{3}$ of the field. It has two diminutives, the chevronel and the couple-close.

Chevronel – A diminutive of the chevron generally about half its width. Seldom borne singly.

Chevronny – Divided into even number of equal portions chevronwise.

Chevronwise – An expression describing a number of charges which are placed upon shield in a position as if resting upon a chevron.

Chief – A sub-ordinary occupying $\frac{1}{3}$ to $\frac{1}{5}$ of the shield from the top downwards. Its line of partition with the rest of the field can be decorated with one of the lines of decoration.

Chinese Dragon – A wingless creature resembling a lizard.

Chivalry – An expression used extensively in the Middle Ages to describe the knightly system and covering the virtues and qualities which it inspired. It can also be used to mean the actual knightly ranks in the army in general.

Cinquefoil – A bearing derived originally from a plant of the clover type; however, in modern Heraldry, from its general shape, it is frequently looked upon as representing the Narcissus.

Civic Crown – A wreath of oak leaves and acorns which should not be confused with any other type of crown (q.v.).

Civic Heraldry – During the 14th and 15th centuries a few of the more important English cities and towns acquired unauthorised armorial bearings which were in due course recorded at the College of Arms, and thus became legal grants. From the 16th century onwards there has been a steady flow of grants to local authorities until to-day some 500 have been granted in Great Britain as a whole of which approximately three-quarters were granted during the last 100 years.

Clam – A word sometimes used by both English and Scottish Heralds for the escallop.

Clarion, claricord – A wind instrument depicted in two various forms as a Heraldic charge. In one of its forms it is similar to, but should not be confused with, a lance rest.

Clarion

Claymore – A type of sword particularly applicable to Scotland and frequently found in connection with supporters where a sword is carried.

Clenched – Describes a hand when closed.

Climant – An expression used in connection with one of the Heraldic positions of the goat which in beasts of prey would be described as rampant.

Close – An expression describing the wings of a bird in the natural position against the body.

Closet – A diminutive of the bar of which it is half the width.

Clouds – Occasionally found as charges, they are sometimes represented by a nebuly line and occasionally in the more orthodox manner.

Cloué – Studded or fastened with nails, a term frequently found in conjunction with the portcullis.

Clove – The spice so called which appears in the arms of the Grocers Company.

Coat of Arms – A term which refers to all the bearings placed upon a Heraldic shield. In modern times the term is frequently found loosely employed to mean the full achievement. The name ' coat of arms ' was derived from the surcoat (q.v.).

Cock – Generally refers to the normal farmyard rooster and may be incorrectly blazoned as dunghill cock, gamecock or moorcock though the later two have minor differences.

Cockatrice – A monster resembling a wyvern with the head of a cock and the tongue barbed. Normally it is born with wings elevated and adorsed but may be blazoned as displayed.

Co-heir, co-heiress –Where an armiger dies without male issue but leaves two or more daughters, all are considered equal and described as co-heirs or co-heiresses until the final survivor becomes the heiress.

Collar of S.S. – An ornamental collar constructed of a series of letter S's in gold which may be either entwined or set close together. It is worn by Kings of Arms and Heralds on state occasions.

College of Arms – Prior to 1484 the King and many of the nobility employed heralds to carry out duties in connection with Tournaments and as messengers in Peace and War. The senior heralds came to be called Kings of Arms. On the 23rd March 1484 King Richard III incorporated the Heralds by charter to form what was known at the time as the College of Heralds, and gave them a house named Coldharbour for their work. A year later his successor cancelled the Royal warrant and acquired the building used by the College for his own purposes. On 15th July 1555 Queen Mary I reformed the College with a new charter and gave them Derby House which is the site on which the present College of Arms now stands.

The College of Arms is a department of the Royal household operating under the Earl Marshal who has a number of officers of Arms (q.v.) to carry out all the duties in connection with issuing and recording armorial bearings in the United Kingdom. Until 1943 one of the Kings of Arms also supervised the whole of Ireland but in that year the Irish government established its own state Herald who still works in close co-operation with Norroy King of Arms who now supervises Ulster.

Conjoined – Joined together.

Colomb – An alternative Heraldic name for the dove.

Column – The architectural column appearing occasionally as a charge and of which the type must be stated in blazon.

Combatant – Describes two animals rampant facing each other on a shield as if in battle.

Combed – An expression referring to the crest of a cock.

Compartment – The space below the shield on which the supporters stand. Until the reign of George V the compartment was variously a small strip of ground, pedestals, pelmets and even a decorative form of motto scroll. In present day Heraldry, however, it generally consists of a shallow mound representing grass or sand sometimes decorated with flowers and stones to give the achievement a more solid appearance.

Complement – Applied to the moon when full.

Componé, compony, gobony – Refers to a single line of squares of two tinctures which may be found in connection with an ordinary or subordinary. e.g. The bordure company.

Componé counter componé – A double line of squares of two tinctures used in a similar manner to componé.

Compony

Concave – Arched.

Coney – The Heraldic name for the rabbit.

Confirmation of Arms – A document issued by the College of Arms or Lyon Office confirming a man's right to armorial bearings. Issue of such confirmation generally follows research into his ancestry and definite proof of lineal male descent.

Constellations – A general term applying to heavenly bodies which may be found as charges used in Heraldry. An example being the Southern cross which is frequently to be found in armorial bearings applicable to Australia.

Contoise – A scarf bound round the helm.

Contourné – Turned (contrary to the normal rule) to face the sinister.

Occasionally used as a synonym for regardant.

Corbie – Crow or raven.

Corded – An expression used when a cross or any other ordinary is bound with cords.

Cormorant – The bird of that name which is generally blazoned as liverbird.

Cornish Chough – A bird of the crow kind which is very common in Cornwall. It is black with red or orange coloured beak and legs. When found as a charge generally has to be emblazoned in its proper colours.

Cornucopia – The horn of plenty. A horn-like basket generally filled with fruit.

Cornucopia

Coronet – Coronets of the Peerage.
Coronets do not appear to have been worn in anything like their present form until the reign of Edward III. From about that time coronets of various forms were worn by Princes, Dukes, Earls and even Knights but apparently rather by way of ornamentation than distinction or possibly as a mark of gentility.

Coronets acquired some approxi-

mation to their present form in the reign of Henry IV. They were first granted to Viscounts by James I and to Barons for the coronation of Charles II.

CORONETS

1. Baron

2. Viscount

3. Earl

4. Marquess

5. Duke

42

6. Heir Apparent

The pattern of all coronets has now been laid down as follows:

Dukes. A silver gilt circlet decorated as if jewelled, but without actual gems, surmounted with eight gold stylised strawberry leaves of which five are seen by the viewer. The coronet of a duke must not in any way be confused with the so called ducal coronet (q.v.).

Marquesses. A silver gilt circlet as above surmounted by four gold strawberry leaves alternating with four silver balls which are slightly elevated on points above the rim, three leaves and two balls are seen by the viewer.

Earls. A silver gilt circlet as above with eight elevated rays of which five may be seen by the viewer, each ray being topped with a silver ball and between each pair of rays is a gold strawberry leaf.

Viscounts. A silver gilt circlet as above surmounted by sixteen silver balls adjacent to one another, nine being seen by the viewer.

Barons. A plain silver gilt circlet surmounted by six large silver balls of which four may be seen by the viewer.

All these coronets are normally worn over a crimson cap with gold tassle which is turned up ermine the ermine lining appearing below the rim of the coronet. The cap is generally omitted in representations.

The silver balls used on coronets are known as pearls and in Heraldry they are thus represented but the use of imitation pearls and in fact the setting of any jewel or precious stone in peers' coronets is banned.

In an achievement the peer's coronet is normally shown (with or without its cap) resting on the shield with the helm and crest rising above it. It is sometimes depicted as if encircling the base of the helm with complete disregard to their related size.

Royal Coronets. The Coronet of the Heir Apparent differs from the Royal crown by virtue of the fact that it has only one arch. It appears both as part of the crest and surmounting the inescutcheon of Wales in his armorial bearings and is also worn by the lion on the crest and the dexter supporter.

Coronets of the other sons and daughters, also the brothers and sisters of the Sovereign consist of a silver gilt circlet surmounted by crosses patté and fleurs-de-lis alternately, but without arches. The circlet is chased as though jewelled but bears no actual gems.

Other more distant direct relatives of the Sovereign who use coronets have them with varying numbers of strawberry leaves, crosses patté and fleurs-de-lis.

Corporate Heraldry – This is the name which covers Heraldry dealing with civic bodies, institutions, hospitals, schools, and in fact all bodies which bear arms as an enterprise rather than as a private individual.

Cotise – A very narrow diminutive of the fess, bend or bend sinister. In modern Heraldry the cotise is never borne singly but in pairs. In English Heraldry, however, a single cotise was sometimes used as a mark of difference.

Couchant – Lying down. Beasts thus blazoned should be drawn with their heads upright to distinguish their position from dormant. In this particular position the tail is normally drawn as folded under the body and appearing between the dexter hind leg and the stomach and from there elevated over the back.

Coulter – A plough share.

Counter – This term may be employed with several variations of meaning. When applied to two animals it signifies that they are turned in a direction opposite to normal; for example, two foxes counter salient. If only one animal is spoken of it means that it faces to the sinister.

Counter changed – This expression appears very frequently in Heraldry and it signifies that a field consists

Per Pale, a Chevron
counter changed

of metal and colour separated by one of the lines of partition named from the ordinaries the charges or parts of charges placed upon the metal are of the colour and vice versa.

Counter flory – Used particularly in connection with a double tressure

signifying that it is decorated with fleurs-de-lis on both sides.

Counter Passant – Passant to the sinister.

Counter Potent – A fur (q.v.).

Counter Vair – A fur (q.v.).

Cooped – Cut off in straight line as for the head or a limb. It is generally of importance to give details as to where the limb has been severed.

Couple close – A diminutive of the chevron of which it is one quarter the width. They are always borne in pairs, frequently in conjunction with the chevron which is then said to be between couple-closes. Some Heralds use the expression of a chevron cotised, however.

Courant – Running at full speed as the white horse of Hanover.

Courtesy Titles – In many cases the second title of a peer may be conceded by Royal Grace to be borne by his eldest son during his lifetime. Courtesy Titles do not carry any right to use coronet, supporters or peer's helm.

Court of Chivalry – This was formed during the 13th and 14th centuries for the purpose of adjudicating in cases arising from deeds of arms outside the Kingdom and those within it that could not be settled by common law.

The Court of Chivalry is seldom active in modern times and in 1954 it sat after an interval of 223 years for the purpose of trying a case between the Manchester City Corporation and a private company operating a fun fair which set up the Manchester City arms over the entrance of their establishment.

In early days the Constable and the Marshal held sway over the Court of Chivalry but in modern times it is the responsibility of the Earl Marshal who at its last sitting delegated his authority to the Lord Chief Justice acting as his deputy.

Covered Cup – Similar to a chalice (q.v.) but provided with a dome shaped cover.

Coward – A lion or other beast whose tail is hanging between his hind legs is said to be coward.

Crane – The bird of that name which must not be confused with the stork or heron.

A Fess Embattled
(Crenelated)

Crenelated – Embattled. The apertures of an embattled wall are known as the crenels or embrasures and the walls standing between them as the merlons.

Crescent – A figure resembling a half moon with the horns uppermost. When placed in other positions it is called increscent or decrescent (q.v.).

The crescent is the ensign of the Turks and was introduced into Heraldry by the crusaders.

It is the mark of cadency assigned to the second house.

Cressit – A fire basket.

Crest – A figure anciently affixed to the helm of every commander for purposes of identification in the confusion of battle and certainly in use long before the hereditary bearing of coat armour. It is frequently confused with the badge which is a totally different thing and in many cases modern writers refer loosely to the expression crest when in fact they mean Coat of Arms or even Achievement.

Crests were not considered as being a part of the family arms until the commencement of the 14th century. They were originally confined to a few and given by Royal grant and even to this day there are several old families who have never used them; conversely, there are families bearing two and even three crests.

Ancient crests were for the most part the heads of animals or plumes of feathers. Such inappropriate figures as buildings, rocks, clouds and thunder bolts were never used for crests when Heraldry was used as a means of identification.

Unless the contrary be explicitly mentioned a crest is always placed upon a wreath and it was not until the reign of Elizabeth when the ducal coronet and chapeau came to be granted on occasions as an alternative.

Crests may not be used by clergymen or ladies as of course neither is considered capable of wielding a sword.

Crest Coronet – Generally blazoned as a ducal coronet but it has no relationship to ducal rank and no resemblance to the coronet worn by the Duke.

It was originally used on occasions as an alternative to the torse and they were seldom borne together.

The crest coronet is seldom

45

granted today but is frequently found in earlier grants of arms. It is represented by a silver gilt circlet chased as if gemmed, but with no actual jewels, surmounted by four strawberry leaves, of which one and two halves are visible to the viewer and between each pair of leaves stands a small silver gilt protuberance fully surrounded by nine small circlets.

Crest Wreath – An alternative name for the wreath or torse (q.v.).

Crested – An expression used when the crest of a bird is referred to.

Crined – An expression used with reference to the hair of a human being or the mane of a horse or unicorn when of a different tincture from their bodies.

Crosier, Crozier – Refers to the crook of a bishop which may appear as a charge or in connection with the arms of a See.

Cross – A cross may be used in Heraldry both as an ordinary in which case it is a plain cross (which may be subject to the lines of decoration but which always reaches the sides of the shield) or it may appear as a charge in one of its many forms.

Over 500 distinctive types of cross have appeared in Heraldry and there has been great confusion amongst the various writers on the specific types which bear little difference one from another.

It is not proposed to set out all the types of cross but a few of the more important should be readily recognisable to the student of Heraldry.

1. Tau cross. This is probably the oldest cross on record as it appeared in many countries as a symbol during the stone age. It is shaped like a T but with the two ends of the transverse arm slightly raised.

Tau Cross

2. Cross botonné or treflé. An ordinary cooped cross with three rounded knobs at the end of each arm.

Cross as an Ordinary

Cross Botonné

3. Cross Calvary. A passion cross elevated upon three steps.

4. Cross Crosslet. An ordinary cross cooped with a small additional bar placed across each arm towards its end thus making four passion crosses conjoined in the centre.

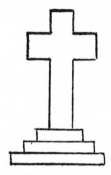

Passion Cross

Crosslet

5. Cross Flory. Plain cross cooped having the upper part of a fleur-de-lis attached to each extremity. It must not be confused with cross patonce.

8. Cross Patonce. An ordinary cross cooped of which the end of each arm continues into three leaf like structures.

Cross Patonce

Cross Flory

6. Cross moline. Same as for the milrind from which it is derived.

7. Passion cross. This resembles the true cross in form but is seldom seen as a charge, however, it occurs more often as a calvary cross.

9. Cross patté. A cross cooped with the end of each arm splayed outwards with curved lines.

10. Cross formé. As above but with straight lines.

11. Cross patriarchal. A double cross similar to the cross of Lorraine.

12. Cross potent. So called because its arms terminate in potents.

Crossbow – The weapon of that name firing bolts rather than arrows.

Crosslet – See Cross Crosslet.

Crow, Cornish – When given in blazon generally refers to the Cornish chough.

Crown – There have been a number of different types of crown used in Heraldry through the ages some of which were in use prior to the Norman conquest. The most generally used seems to have been the simple circlet with four uprights, one and two halves of which were visible to the viewer.

King Stephen used a crown surmounted by four fleurs-de-lis of which once again one and two halves were visible. These were connected by ornamental arches which disappeared after his reign until the time of Henry V.

For the remainder of the Plantagenets and in fact until the time of Henry V the Royal crown consisted of a richly jewelled circlet surmounted generally by leaves resembling the strawberry leaf.

During the reign of Henry V the crown consisted of a jewelled circlet surmounted by four crosses alternated with eight fleurs-de-lis in pairs and two arches rising from behind the crosses, supporting at the top a mound and cross. From this time until the present day the Royal

Heraldic Crown

crown has continued in the same form but with minor differences in almost every reign.

Representations of the Royal crown in one of its forms appears in several cases in armorial bearings but in modern times it is very jealously guarded and may not be used without Royal license.

Other types of crown found as charges and which have been used in crests include the following (a) Mural crown. This is the most common as it frequently appears in civic Heraldry. It is masoned and embattled and is occasionally found granted as part of an augmentation to military personnel. (b) Naval crown. A circlet on the rim of which are mounted representations of the

Mural Crown

Naval Crown

Astral Crown

sterns, and sails of ships alternately. This form has been granted both as a crest coronet and as part of an augmentation to distinguished Naval personnel. It is also used to ensign ships badges of the Royal Navy and it forms part of the badge of the

48

merchant navy. (c) Astral crown. This consists of a circlet rising to eight points on its circumference, on four of which are mounted stars each star being placed between a pair of elevated wings. (d) Crown Vallary and Palisade Crown are both derived from defensive works. They are very similar to look at and are often used interchangeably. Each consists of a circlet surmounted by a number of projections. In the case of the Crown Vallary they are similar to the figures used in the representation of the fur vair and in the Palisade Crown they resemble the top half of a spear point. (e) Eastern crown. A circlet surmounted by eight inverted ' v ' shaped projections five of

Crown Vallary

Eastern Crown

Edward II's Crown

which can be seen by the viewer. (f) Celestial Crown. This is similar to the Eastern Crown but has a star at the point of each ray.

Crusades – These were the expeditions aimed to free the Holy Land from the influence of Islam. All but the first, in which Jerusalem was captured and after which the Kingdom of Jerusalem and a number of principalities were set up, were abortive.

They are largely of interest to students of Heraldry because they were instrumental in providing the reason for the introduction of the surcoat and the mantling and they helped considerably in the rapid spread of Heraldry.

Crucilly – Semé of cross crosslets.

Cubit Arm – An arm cooped at the elbow.

Cuff – In cases where the cuff is to be of a different tincture from the remainder of the sleeve the fact must be so stated in blazon.

Cup – There are several different types of cup occurring in Heraldry but that most commonly found resembles a plain chalice with stem and foot. If it is to have handles the fact must be so stated. If it has a lid it is termed a covered cup (q.v.).

Cushion – A square or lozenge shaped pillow, generally with a tassel at each corner.

Cyclas – A form of surcoat considerably longer at the back than at the front.

Cypher – A monogram sometimes found as part of a charge in Heraldry but more generally as a badge e.g. The present Royal cypher E.II.R. ensigned with a crown.

Clarenceux – One of the senior Officers of Arms. (q.v.).

D

Dagger – A shortened form of sword used principally for stabbing. It appears as a charge in Heraldry when it is given a much more pointed blade than the sword.

Damasked – See diapered.

Dancetté – One of the lines of decoration differing from indented (with which the old Heralds often confused it) in that the indentations are considerably wider at the base and between the points.

Dancetté floretty – Similar to dancetté but each point is decorated with the upper half of a fleur-de-lis.

Dannebrog – A Danish order of chivalry. The cross patté argent fimbriated gules in the arms of Denmark is known as the cross of Dannebrog and appears in the arms of George of Denmark and Queen Alexandra consorts of Queen Anne and King Edward VII respectively.

Debruised – An expression used where a charge has an ordinary laid over it.

Dechaussé – Dismembered.

Decked – An expression used in the case of feathers trimmed at their edges with a different colour.

Declinant – Applied to the tail of a serpent when hanging down.

Decollated – Having the head cut off at the neck.

Decorations – Awards including the Victoria Cross, George Cross, Albert Cross, Distinguished Service Cross, Military Cross, Distinguished Flying Cross, etc., awarded by the Sovereign, may be suspended by their appropriate ribbon below the shield in armorial bearings in their correct order of precedence, the senior being to the dexter.

Decrescent – A half moon where the horns are turned to the sinister.

Deer – An animal of the stag type sometimes found as a charge.

Defamed – An expression applied to an animal who has lost his tail.

Degraded – A charge placed upon degrees, grieces or steps is said to be degraded.

Degrees – Steps generally three in number, representing the three graces; Faith, Hope and Charity.

Dejected – Hanging down. Used of the head or tail of an animal.

Demi – When an animal is referred to, its upper or fore half is always intended. When anything inanimate, it is generally the dexter half per pale.

Dexter – The right hand side of the shield from the point of view of the man behind it, that is the left hand side to the viewer.

Diaper – An old-fashioned method of relieving the plain tinctures of fields and charges by artistic enrichment of the surfaces.

Difference – A method used to assist the identification of other branches of a family for illegitimacy or cadency (q.v.).

Dimidiation – Chiefly used with reference to a method of joining the arms of a husband and wife which was used before the introduction of impaling. It consists of taking the dexter half of the dexter shield and the sinister half of the sinister shield and joining them. It was an unsatisfactory method and was soon discontinued.

Diminutive – A lesser form of ordinary which is never charged.

Disarmed – An expression used in connection with a beast of prey borne without teeth or claws, or of a bird of prey without beak and talons.

Dismembered – An expression used to denote that the head and limbs have been cut off but retained in their correct positions.

Lion Dismembered

Displayed – Expanded, principally used to express the position of the eagle and other birds.

Distinguished Service Order – An order introduced in 1885 for bestowal on commissioned officers of the fighting services who have appropriately distinguished themselves.

Dolphin – A fish which, though in reality straight, is almost always borne embowed. If the blazon merely used the word ' dolphin ', the position naiant is implied; other positions must be stated specifically.

Dolphin naiant

Dormant – Sleeping with the head resting on the fore paws. If the expression is used in conjunction with a title it implies that it has been unclaimed.

Double – Used in conjunction with a charge it implies that there are two of the particular charge stated.

Doubling – The lining of a robe or mantle which should in all ordinary cases be of the fur or metal of the arms. If Or or argent it is supposed to be of cloth of gold or white fur, thus it is blazoned as gold or white, as the case may be.

Dove – A bird found occasionally as a charge, sometimes blazoned as colomb.

Dove tailed – A line of decoration.

Dragon – The dragon is one of the monsters (q.v.) which is fairly frequently found as a charge in Heraldry. It is also the badge of Wales.

Drops – See Gouttée.

Ducal Coronet – See Crest Coronet.

51

Duchess – The title and rank of the wife of a Duke.

Duke – The highest title in the British Peerage. The first Dukedom created in England was that of Cornwall which Edward III conferred upon the Black Prince, his son, in 1337 since which time the eldest son of every Sovereign has been styled Duke of Cornwall from his birth.

There are two types of Dukes, those of Royal blood generally uncles, brothers or younger sons of the Sovereign and those not of Royal blood.

Dunghill Cock – The farmyard cock (q.v.).

Eagle displayed

E

Eagle – The eagle is the principal charge amongst birds. It is of very early origin and was emblazoned upon the standards carried by the Romans in battle. It was the emblem of the Roman empire and has been used extensively in Germany and by the Czars of Russia. It was also used under Napoleon Buonaparte as the standard of the empire of France.

The most commonly found position for the eagle is 'displayed', when the body is affronté, with the wings and legs spread out on either side, the wing tips upwards and the head turned to the dexter.

An alternative to displayed is with wings inverted, it is otherwise the same position with the tips of the wings downwards.

Other positions occur in connection with the eagle such as preying, close, rising and with the wings in different positions. It may also be crowned, gorged with a collar or coronet or charged on the body or wings and it may grasp any object in its talons and even some in its beak.

Eagle rising, wings elevated and adorsed

52

Eagle close

Eaglet – The diminutive of eagle. When two or more eagles occur in the same coat and are not separated by an ordinary they are frequently blazoned as eaglets.

Earl – The third order of the British Peerage. The word is of Saxon origin and the Saxon equivalent was the governor of a shire. The first hereditary Earl in England was Hugh D'Avranches who was created by William the Conqueror.

Earl Marshal – Until 1386 he was called Lord Marshal. This office was anciently granted by the Sovereign at pleasure, sometimes for life and sometimes *durante bene placito*. It was more than once made hereditary but never continued long in one line until in 1672 King Charles II annexed it to the Dukedom of Norfolk.

The insignia of office of the Earl Marshal are two gold batons the ends enamelled black having the Royal arms at the upper end and those of the Earl Marshal at the lower end. The batons are borne in saltire behind the arms of the Earl Marshal

Ear of Corn – Generally refers to wheat unless otherwise stated.

Eastern Crown – An early type of crown (q.v.).

Ecclesiastical Heraldry – Emblems of a religious nature were employed in the seals of the bishops before they began to use armorial bearings. In many cases these emblems were repeated and the arms subsequently granted.

The See of Worcester

Archbishops and diocesan bishops may impale their personal arms on the sinister side with those of their See. Other bishops use only their personal arms. Bishops are not granted a crest and may not use a helm, instead however, they ensign their shield with a mitre and they may also place two pastoral staves in saltire behind their shield.

The use of armorial bearings by dignitaries of the Roman Catholic Church have evolved along somewhat different lines, primarily by the use of a variety of different ecclesiastical hats to signify their appropriate rank and differing

53

Cardinal Godfrey

numbers of tassels borne either side of the shield. See attached Chart.

Eel – Has no specific Heraldic characteristics but may be blazoned as conger eel.

Eight foil – A floral figure with eight petals which is sometimes blazoned as double quatre-foil.

Electoral Bonnet – See bonnet.

Elephant – May be found alone but more frequently with a castle on his back. Elephant heads also occur as charges.

Elephant and Castle

Elevated – An expression used in

connection with the wings of birds when they are raised.

Elk – The animal of that name which is but infrequently found as a charge.

Embattled – Crenellated (q.v.).

Emblazon – The act of translating a blazon to paper or other material in full colour.

Embrasure – The open space between two merlons. See Crenellated.

En Soleil – An expression used in respect of a charge irradiated with rays of the sun.

Enarched – Arched or raised in the middle.

Endorse – A diminutive of the pale of which it is $\frac{1}{4}$ in width. It bears exactly the same relation to the pale as the cotise to the fess or bend.

Enfield – A type of monster (q.v.).

Enfiled – Encircled as by a coronet, etc.

Engoulé – Pierced through the heart.

Engrailed – A line of decoration consisting of small arcs of a circle between points, thus giving a kind of scalloped edge. When engrailed the ordinary has the points outwards. The points inwards give ' invected '.

Enhanced – Raised above the normal position.

Entire – An expression used in connection with certain ordinaries when they are extended to the edges of the shield.

54

INSIGNIA WHICH SHOULD ACCOMPANY SHIELDS OF ARMS IN THE R.C. CHURCH:

Degree	Colour of Ecclesiastical Hat	No. and Colour of Tassels each side	Other Insignia	Remarks
1. Cardinal	Red	15 Red	According to rank i.e. archbishop, bishop	Cardinals may not wear any other insignia or accessories except the crosses of the Orders of Malta and of the Holy Sepulchre
2. Patriarch and Primate	Green	15	A cross with two bars in pale behind the shield. Residential patriarchs and primates may surround their shield with the pallium	No insignia of temporal dignity or nobility are now allowed, even any which may belong to the See. The rules are now the same as for Cardinals
3. Archbishop (not a Primate)	Green	10 Green	As for Patriarchs	As for Patriarchs
4. Bishop	Green	Green 6	A cross with a single bar in pale behind the shield: If the pallium is possessed by special concession it may be used as above	As for Patriarchs
5. Abbot and Prelate	Green	6 Green	A mitre above the shield and a crozier in pale behind the shield with a veil attached to it.	There is no specific order preventing the use of temporal insignia by these and lesser dignitaries but they should abide by the rules as the higher prelature.
6(a) Abbot and Priest who receive ablatial benediction	Black	6 Black	As above	
6(b) Superiors and general provincial of most religious Orders and Congregations their vicars and some others	Black	6 Black	As above	
6(c) Titular Apostolic Protonotaries				
6(d) Vicars-general and others possessing similar privileges				
6(e) Canons and certain chapters				

Degree	Colour of Ecclesiastical Hat	No. and Colour of Tassels each side	Other Insignia	Remarks
7. Prelate 'di Fiorchetto'. (The Vice-chamberlingue of the Holy Roman Church, The Auditor General. The Treasurer General of the Apostolic Chamber and the Majordomo of His Holiness	Violet	10 Red		Some of these prelates are often archbishops, in which case they use archipiscopal insignia
8. Apostolic Protonotary (except titular)	Violet	6 Red	No other	
(a) Apostolic Protonotaries 'de numero Partici Partium'				
(b) Assessors and Secretaries of the Sacred Roman Congregations				
(c) The Master of His Holiness' Chamber				
(d) The Secretary of the Apostolic Signature				
(e) The Dean of the Roman Rota				
(f) The Deputy of the Secretary of State				
(g) The Vicars Prefects and Administrators Apostolic during their term of office	Violet	6 Red	No other	
(h) Supernumary Apostolic Protonotaries				
(i) Apostolic Protonotaries 'ad instar Participartium'				
9. Domestic Prelate	Violet	6 Violet	No other	
(a) The Auditors of the Sacred Roman Rota				
(b) The Clerks of the Apostolic Chamber				
(c) The Voters of the Apostolic Signature				
(d) The Confirmed Members of the three colleges of Prelature				
(e) The Referenders of the Apostolic Signature				
(f) All Apostolic Prelates nominated by apostolic brief				
10. Privy Chamberlain and Privy Chaplain to His Holiness	Black	6 Violet	No other	These insignia not yet firm.

56

Degree	Colour of Ecclesiastical Hat	No. and Colour of Tassels each side	Other Insignia	Remarks
11. Canons				
(a) Canons Ordinary	Black	3 Black	No other	
(b) Canons of Chapters having privilege of protonotary Apostolic	Violet	6 Red	No other	
(c) Canons of Chapters having privilege of Domestic Prelates	Violet	6 Violet	No other	
(d) Canons of Chapters having Privilege of Privy Chamberlains	Black	6 Violet	No other	Not yet firm
(e) Canons of Chapters Privileged to use Mitre	Black	3 Black	A mitre above shield	
(f) Canons of Chapters possessing the collective title of Counter Baron	Black	3 Black	The coronet of a counter baron above the shield	
12. Dean, Minor Superior Archpriest, Diocesan Functionary	Black	2 Black	No other	Matter of Custom only
13. Priest	Black	1 Black	No other	
14. Abbess	None	None	A Crozier with a veil attached in pale behind shield. A rosary encircling shield	Crozier only used with entitlement to carry it on official occasion. All may use rosary.

Bendlets enhanced

Equipped – Fully armed or caparisoned.

Eradicated – Uprooted. An expression used of a tree when it is to be emblazoned with the roots showing.

Tree Eradicated

Erect – Upright.

Ermine – A type of fur (q.v.).

Ermines – A type of fur (q.v.).

Ermine Spots – The spots as used on the fur ermine which are occasionally found singly or in multiples

used as a charge. There are a number of different methods of depicting ermine spots.

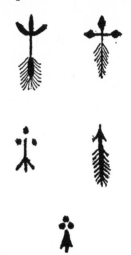

Types of Ermine Spots

Erminois – A type of fur (q.v.).

Erne – An alternative, but seldom used, name for the eagle.

Escallop – The scallop shell. A charge which is frequently found in connection with families from whom an ancestor went to the crusades.

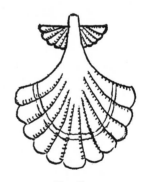

Escallop

Escarbuncle – A precious stone of such brilliance that in early days it

58

was believed to be capable of shining in darkness. It is represented in Heraldry by a series of rays (generally eight in number) each terminating in the head of a fleur-de-lis.

Escarbuncle

Escartelly – A line of decoration with a small oblong portion raised in the centre.

Escroll or scroll – A strip of parchment bearing a motto.
   At one time these escrolls were considerably elongated and decorated and used as a base for the supporters.

Escutcheon – A shield which may also be used as a charge.

Escutcheon of Pretence – A shield containing the arms of an heiress placed in the centre of her husband's arms instead of being impaled with them.

Esquire – A gentleman of the rank immediately below a knight. It was originally a military office, an esquire being a knight's attendant and shield bearer. In present times it has come to be used quite incorrectly as a means of address on envelopes to almost anybody above the artisan classes.

Estate, Cap of – See Cap of Maintenance.

Estoile – A star of five or six points wavy. Estoiles sometimes occur with a greater number of points such as eight or sixteen in which case the points should be wavy and straight alternately, the straight points being reserved for those palewise, fess wise and, if applicable, bendwise.

Estoile

Eyrant – Applied to eagles and other birds in their nests.

Eyrie – The nest of a bird of prey.

F

Falchion – A kind of scimitar having a straight blade on one side broadened out on the other.

Falcon – A bird of the hawk family which is almost invariably represented with bells and jesses.

False – Voided. An orle has, on occasions, been described as a false escutcheon and an annulet as a false roundle.

Fan – Fans of various types are occasionally found but details must be given in blazon.

Fasces – The lictor's axe in its bundle of rods. This emblem taken from the Roman era may occasionally be found in the arms of judges.

59

Falcon

Feathered or **flighted** – Refers to the feathers of an arrow when of a different tincture from the shaft.

Fer-de-moline – The alternative name for the millrind (q.v.).

Fermail – A buckle (q.v.)

Ferr – A horse shoe.

Ferrated – Semé of horse shoes.

Fess – An ordinary containing between $\frac{1}{5}$ and $\frac{1}{3}$ the height of the shield but its proportion depends largely upon artist's license and the number and nature of charges to be placed on the fess or on the remainder of the field.

Fess Point – The centre point of the shield.

Fesswise – Said of two or more charges placed horizontally.

Fetterlock – The old-fashioned type of shackle and padlock.

Field – The ground or surface of the shield upon which all charges are placed. When several coats are marshalled on one escutcheon each has its different field. Fields may be of one tincture or more than one as when party per pale, per chevron, etc., or when checky, lozengy, etc.

Fetterlock

Figured – Charged with a representation of the human face. This expression may be used both with the sun and with the moon.

Fillet – An early Heraldic diminutive of the chief being $\frac{1}{4}$ of that ordinary. Its position is across the honour point.

Fimbriated – Having a narrow edging of a different tincture from the rest of the charge.

Cross argent fimbriated sable

Finned – An expression used with reference to the fins of fish.

60

Fire Ball – A round bomb or grenade with fire issuing from a hole in the top or sometimes from two or more holes.

Firme – Extended to the extremities of the shield.

Fish – Many different kinds of fish are used as charges. Occasionally the blazon will state 'fish' without specifying the variety. A fish may be bla⁻oned as naiant – swimming fesswise, urinant – palewise with the head in base, i.e. diving, or hauriant – palewise with the head upwards i.e. rising.

The following fish may be blazoned specifically: the dolphin, pike, luce, salmon, herring, roach, trout, eel and barbel.

Fish Hook – A seldom seen charge.

Fitché – Pointed, generally at the lower part. This expression is applied chiefly to crosses when the lower arm will be pointed as if for sticking in the ground. Sometimes the expression used will be 'Fitché at the foot'.

Cross formée fitchée at the foot

Fitzalan Pursuivant Extraordinary – One of the supernumerary officers of arms (q.v.) available for use in connection with special state occasions.

Flags – The earliest reference to emblems of any sort with a Heraldic flavour is given in the Bible where, in the book of Numbers, it states that the children of Israel placed their standards before the tents of their leaders as rallying points.

Throughout the ages flags of various types have been used by countries, states, institutions, etc.

Flags are frequently incorrectly so named when the term banner should be applied.

Flambeau – A torch.

Flanche – Flanches are always borne in pairs and are formed by a curved line extending from the dexter chief to the dexter base and the sinister chief to the sinister base. It may be charged.

Flanches

Fleam – An ancient instrument shaped somewhat like an open razor and borne in the arms of the company of Barbers and Surgeons.

Fleece – A charge representing the skin of a sheep. It is depicted hanging by a broad belt under the stomach which terminates at a ring above the body.

Flesh Hook – A fork used for the purpose of removing meat from the cauldron.

Flesh Pot – A cauldron usually seen

standing on three legs and provided with handles.

Fleece

Fleur-de-lis – There has been considerable controversy with regard to the origin of this bearing some believing it to represent the lily, others the iris and some even the iron head of a warlike weapon.

It featured distinctively in the bearings of the Kingdom of France and it has also appeared quartered with the arms of England.

The Fleur-de-lis has been used in many cases to decorate ordinaries, sub-ordinaries and charges. It appears on the Royal Crown and various coronets and in numerous other positions, including, of course, the Royal Tressure of Scotland.

Fleury, Flory – An expression used to denote that a charge is adorned with fleurs-de-lis.

Flexed – Bent or bowed.

Flighted – Refers to the feathers of an arrow.

Flory – Alternative for fleury (q.v.).

Flotant – Floating.

Flowers – A number of different flowers appear as Heraldic charges other than the fleur-de-lis (q.v.).

Chief among them are the lily which may be found in the arms of Eton College; the rose which is represented by a stylised form of the wild dog rose, normally with five petals but occasionally superimposed by another smaller one also of five petals; the thistle which is the well known floral emblem of Scotland; and the various foils from trefoil to eight foil.

Other less well known flowers may be found including the lotus, teasel, gilly flower, blue bottle, columbine, sunflower and gentian, but the blazon must give full details.

Flukes – These refer to the points of an anchor which may be blazoned of a different tincture.

Foliated – Having leaf-like cusps.

Forcené – A word used in connection with a horse when standing on his hind legs representing rage.

Formé – Describes a cross the arms of which are splayed out by straight lines.

Fountain – The fountain most generally used in Heraldry is a roundle barry wavy of six, argent and azure, representing water. There are, however, occasions where the natural fountain has appeared as a charge.

Fountain

Fourché – Forked.

Fox – The animal of that name.

Fret – A bendlet and a bendlet sinister interlaced with a mascle.

Fretty – Describes a field or a charge covered by bandlets and bendlets sinister interlaced with the field or the background of the charge showing through.

Sable fretty argent

Fructed – Bearing fruit.

Fruits – Various kinds are used as charges, their usual position is erect but they may also be seen pendent or fesswise.

In the case of a tree described as fructed it implies that the appropriate fruit may be seen amongst the leaves.

Funeral Hatchments – It was the custom up to the end of the 19th century on the death of an armiger to prepare a funeral hatchment which would be hung on the front door of his residence and another in his Church.

This generally consisted of an extremely decorative achievement on a diamond shape on which the armiger's arms appeared impaled with those of his wife.

If it was the armiger himself who had died then the dexter half of the hatchment would be given a black background and if the wife was still alive the sinister half would have a white background. If it was the wife who had died the armiger was still living the colours of the background would be reversed and if both partners were dead the whole background would be black.

In cases where the armiger had had two wives and the first wife was dead, then the upper quarter of the sinister half would be black and the lower quarter white thus denoting that the first wife was dead and the second wife was still alive.

Ermine

Ermines

Vair

63

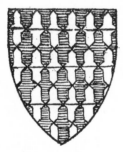

Counter Vair

Potent

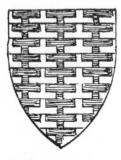

Counter Potent

5. Vair – consisting of alternative white and blue bell shaped pieces with the white bells having the open end upwards.

Note: If vair is required to be emblazoned the other way it must be blazoned 'vair azure and argent'.

6. Counter vair – also argent and azure but where the open end of one white bell meets the open end of that in the next line and so on, thus giving a continuous perpendicular line of white bells, one upward, the next downwards, and so on, similarly with the blue bells.

7. Vairy – as for vair but specifying other tinctures.

8. Potent – alternate white and blue pieces shaped like half a capital letter 'H' lying on its side. Other tinctures may be used but details must be given.

9. Counter potent – With both blue and white pieces joined to each other vertically, as described for counter vair above.

Fusil – A charge resembling the lozenge but longer and narrower.

Fusil

Furs – There are a number of different furs used in Heraldry which were originally derived from the skins of fur bearing animals. These are as follows:

1. Ermine – black spots on white
2. Ermines – White spots on black.
3. Erminois – black spots on gold.
4. Pean – gold spots on black.

Fusilly – An expression used to denote that the field is completely covered with fusils of alternate tinctures somewhat similar to checky.

Fylfot – Another name used for the gamadion or swastika.

64

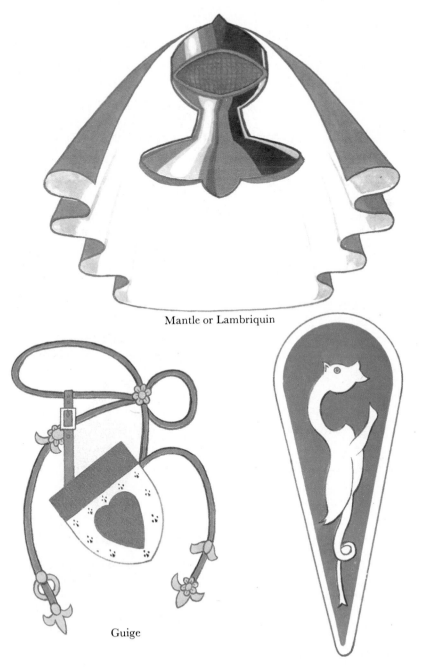

Mantle or Lambriquin

Guige

Long or Kite-Shaped shield

G

Gadfly – The Heraldic name for the horse fly which has been used on occasions as a charge.

Galley – See lymphad.

Gamadion –The swastika or fylfot (q.v.).

Gamb – The leg of a beast.

Gamecock – Similar to the farm yard rooster but has his comb cut and his spurs strengthened for fighting.

Garb – A sheaf of corn.

Garb

Gardant – An expression used to denote that an animal has his face turned towards the viewer.

Garland – See Chaplet.

Garnished – Appropriately ornamented.

Garter – A strap of ribbon secured with a buckle arranged so as to form a circle with the end pendent. Occasionally used as a charge but more

generally known by that of the Order of the Garter surrounding the Royal Arms since the time of Henry VI.

Garter, Order of – The Senior British Order of Chivalry instituted by King Edward III.

Garter, Principal King of Arms – The Senior Officer of Arms (q.v.).

Gate, Gateway – A towered and embattled portway similar to a castle but in order to emphasise the nature of the charge the gate itself is depicted considerably larger in size than is the case with a castle.

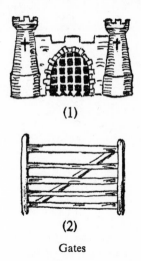

(1)

(2)

Gates

Gauntlet – A glove of mail or plate frequently used as part of a charge or crest. An arm said to be vambraced does not automatically include the gauntlet unless specifically stated.

Gem Ring – A gold circlet set with a single jewel.

Gemelles – An expression used in conjunction with the bar to denote a pair of narrow barrulets or closets.

Genet – An animal rather similar to a fox but considerably smaller in size and usually grey spotted with black. It is included amongst the badges of the House of Plantagenet.

Gentleman – A person of noble descent however high his rank. In modern Heraldry, however, it has come to mean the lowest rank of armigerous persons.

Geoffrey of Anjou – The first recorded bearer of coat armour in England. In 1127 Henry I knighted his son-in-law, Count Geoffrey of Anjou and in doing so hung a blue shield charged with golden lions round Count Geoffrey's neck. A similar coat was used by the Earl of Salisbury, Count Geoffrey's grandson, in the Third Crusade.

Giraffe – A charge sometimes used in Heraldry but blazoned as camelopard and classified amongst the monsters.

Glissant – Gliding.

Glove – When glove is specifically blazoned as opposed to gauntlet it refers to the falconer's glove and should be shown with tassels pendant.

Goat – Appears occasionally as a Heraldic charge but emblazed with horns more curved than normal and ears similar to those of a talbot.

Gobony – See Compony.

Gold – Or, one of the metals in Heraldry.

Gore – A charge which may be either dexter or sinister. The former is always an honourable charge but the latter tinctured tenné is said to be an abatement for cowardice in battle.

Gorged – Collared. When the word is used alone a plain collar is implied, however, it is frequently found, particularly with animals, as ' ducally gorged ' and then a ducal coronet is used.

Goutté, Gutté – Strew with an indefinite number of drops. A distinctive term is used in English Heraldry to denote the tinctures employed:

goutté d'eau, white drops representing water.

goutté de larmes, blue drops representing tears.

goutté de poix, black drops of pitch.

goutté de sang, red drops of blood.

goutté d'huile, green drops of oil.

goutté d'or, drops of gold.

Gradient – Walking slowly in a manner similar to the tortoise.

Grand Quarters – Where a shield is divided into four quarters and one or more of the quarters is further sub-divided into quarters the original divisions are known as grand quarters.

Grant of Arms – Official permission granted by the College of Arms, London, or Lyon Office, Edinburgh and signed by the appropriate King or Kings of Arms allowing the grantee to bear and display armorial bearings.

Grappling Iron – An instrument used in naval engagements. It is represented in Heraldry as an anchor with four flukes. If any other number is required it should be stated in blazon.

Grasshopper – Occasionally found in Heraldry and emblazoned as such.

66

Grenade – Similar to the fire ball (q.v.).

Grieces – Steps or degrees (q.v.).

Griffin, Gryphon – One of the monsters (q.v.).

Gringolé – An expression used with the arm of a cross is depicted as decorated with snakes heads.

Grosvenor – One of the parties in the Grosvenor - Scrope - Carminow controversy. Three knights arrived at a tournament all bearing similar arms, namely *azure a bend Or*. One of these, Carminow, was an elderly man having no issue and living in the South Western extremity of England, he was permitted to retain the arms for the remainder of his life.

With regard to the other two, considerable argument ensued lasting over a number of years eventually coming before the King, Richard II, for settlement. The King settled in favour of Scrope and Grosvenor was ordered to assume alternative arms namely *azure a garb Or*. The proceedings lasted from 17th August 1385 to 27th May 1390.

Gules – Red.

Gyron – A charge, possibly of Spanish origin, as the word in that language signifies a gusset or triangular piece of cloth sewn into a garment. Seldom if ever found singly in English Heraldry.

Gyronny – One of the sub-ordinaries produced by dividing the shield per pale per fess, per bend and per bend sinister into eight triangular portions.

If any number other than eight is required the blazon must state details.

Gyronny

H

Habited – Clothed or vested.

Hackle. An alternative name for the hemp brake (q.v.).

Halo – Sometimes known as a 'glory'.

Hammer – Various types of hammers occur in Heraldry including the plasterer's hammer, the claw hammer and the square hammer. The type must be stated in blazon.

Hand – The human hand is often borne as a charge or as part of a crest. When no particular position is mentioned it is understood to be apaumé as in the Baronet's badge. The blazon should state whether it is the dexter or sinister hand and the tincture if other than 'proper' is required.

Harboured – An expression applied to animals of the chase when at rest. Sometimes described as 'lodged'.

Hare – The animal of that name; seldom seen in modern Heraldry, and in early Heraldry is generally associated with the bag-pipes (q.v.).

Harp – This is not a common charge but frequently found in connection with Ireland. Generally the harp is plain but on occasions, particularly in later Heraldry, it is decorated with the head and wings of an angel. It is generally stringed of another tincture than the frame.

Harpy – An imaginary creature not classified as a monster represented as a vulture with the head and breast of a woman.

Harpy

Harrow – Two forms of harrow may be found in charges; one is square the other triangular. The shape must be stated in blazon.

Hart – Found both as a charge and as one of the early Royal Supporters.

Hatching – Frequently, particularly in old-fashioned books on Heraldry, in order to give some realism to illustrations a form of decoration was given to each of the Heraldic colours. These were as follows:

Argent – left plain,
Or – rows of black spots,
Azure – horizontal lines placed close together,
Gules – perpendicular lines placed close together,
Sable – horizontal and perpendicular lines drawn close together,

Vert – diagonal lines bend wise drawn close together,
Purpure – diagonal lines bend-sinister wise drawn close together.
Sanguine – diagonal lines bend-wise and bend-sinister wise drawn close together.
Tenné – diagonal lines bend-wise and vertical lines drawn close together.
Unfortunately no method has ever been discovered whereby charges, etc., emblazoned in their proper colours could be treated in this way.

Hatching is not used in tricking arms.

Hatchment – See Funeral Hatchments.

Hauriant – An expression used to describe a fish palewise with the head upwards.

Hausé – Enhanced.

Hawk – A bird similar in type to the falcon frequently also found belled and jessed.

Hawk's Bell – A small circular bell which is attached to the hawk's leg by means of a jesse or thong of leather. Sometimes found as a charge by itself.

Hawk's Lure – A decoy used in

Hawk's Lure

68

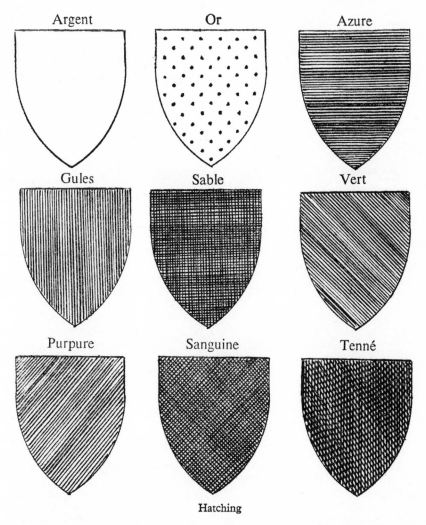

Hatching

falconry to entice the bird to return to the falconer. It consists of two wings joined with a line, to the end of which is attached a ring.

Hayfork – An alternative name for the Shakefork.

Heads – Are quite often found as charges in Heraldry including Blackamore, Boy, Cherub, Children's, Englishman, Fiend, Maiden, Moses, Saracen, St. John, Saxon, etc.

The type and position must be carefully stated in the blazon.

Heart – Generally blazoned as body heart (q.v.).

Heathcock – A bird having the head and body of the farm yard cock but tail feathers of a pheasant.

Hedgehog – Depicted similar to the natural animal but frequently blazoned as urchin.

Helm – The shortened form of the word helmet which applied generally to the tilting helmet and is so described in the armorial bearings.

Helmet – There are five types of helmet used in Heraldry to denote the rank of the bearer. These are as follows:

(a) For Sovereigns and Princes of the blood, full faced helm of demasked gold with six bars.

(b) For Dukes, not of Royal blood and Marquesses a full faced helm of steel demasked with gold and with five gold bars.

(c) For Earls, Viscounts and Barons, a sidelong steel helm with five gold bars, three of which are shown in profile.

(d) For Baronets and Knights, a full faced helm of steel with the visor open.

(e) For Esquires and private Gentlemen a sidelong helm of plain steel with the visor closed. This helm is always used in the arms of corporate bodies.

In cases where the son of a member of the peerage bears his father's Courtesy Title he is not entitled to use a helm of the Courtesy rank.

In certain instances a helm may be replaced by a cap of maintenance but this substitution is not found in modern Heraldry.

Helve – The shaft of an axe or similar instrument.

Hemp-brake – An instrument used for bruising hemp which is occasionally found as a charge.

Heraldic Antelope – Classified as one of the monsters (q.v.).

Heraldic Tyger – Classified as one of the monsters (q.v.).

Heraldry – An expression used originally to describe all the duties of a Herald as opposed to armory which was used to describe the study of armorial bearings. In modern times, however, many of the old-fashioned duties of a Herald having ceased to exist, the term Heraldry is used generally when referring to the study of any work in connection with armorial bearings.

Heraldry Societies – The original Heraldry Society was started in England shortly after the second World War, with the headquarters in a cottage in Wiltshire and it has grown into a very thriving Society. Its address now is 59 Gordon Square, London, W.C.1.

Branches of the Heraldry Society were opened in three of the dominions namely Australia, Canada and New Zealand. At the present time, however, both Australia and Canada have formed their own Heraldry Societies, that in New Zealand still remaining as a branch of the London Society.

There is also a Heraldry Society in the United States of America.

Heralds – Originally employed by Noblemen to carry messages in times of peace and war particularly with reference to tournaments at which they acted as masters of ceremony and in various other capacities.

In the early days they were of very low social standing being classified with minstrels and the like. Through the years, however, as their offices grew in importance so their social status rose until they became experts in all matters pertaining to Heraldry. They are now some of the principal Officers of Arms (q.v.).

Heron – A bird sometimes found as a charge not to be confused with the stork.

Herring – One of the fish found in Heraldry (q.v.).

Heurt – A type of roundle (q.v.).

Hind – An animal of the stag type sometimes used as a charge.

Hippocampus – A sea-horse.

Hippogriff – A hybrid of the griffin and horse.

Hoist – The apparatus used to raise a flag.

Holy Lamb – A seldom used name for Paschal Lamb (q.v.).

Honour Point – A point on the shield which appears approximately in the centre of the base of a chief.

Hoofed – An expression used when applying a different tincture to the hooves of animals.

Horn – See bugle horn.

Horn of Plenty – An expression sometimes used for the Cornucopia.

Horned – An expression used when referring to the horns of animals.

Hornet – An insect occasionally found as a charge.

Horns – Refers to the horns of all animals except those of the stag type for which the term 'attire' is used.

Horse – The horse may be found in one of several positions in coat armour and occasionally the horse's head.

Horse Shoe – A charge frequently found held in the mouth of the ostrich. May be blazoned as ferr.

Hounds – The most common types found in Heraldry consist of the talbot, which is an animal rather resembling the golden labrador, and the greyhound.

Hull – Refers to the hull of a ship or lymphad.

Human Beings – When human beings are used as charges or as supporters the blazon must carefully state their attitude, costume and action and the type of man or woman to be depicted, e.g. Sailor, Crusader, Wildman. Parts of the human body are of far more frequent appearance.

Humetté – Cooped. An expression applicable to ordinaries only.

Hurst – A small group of trees generally borne upon a mount in base.

Hydra – A seven-headed dragon.

I

Ibex – The Heraldic animal called by this name is not the ibex of nature but it resembles the Heraldic antelope, with the exception of the horns which are straight and serrated.

Illegitimacy and Adoption –
Illegitimacy
It is customary in modern Heraldry to use certain marks to denote illegitimacy but in early days Heralds had no regular system to distinguish persons of illegitimate birth or their descendants and generally speaking the form of difference used was that most suit-

able for the particular occasion.

Persons of illegitimate birth are not entitled to assume arms of their putative father at will even with an appropriate difference. First they must prove their paternity and then petition for the arms to be granted. The alternative is of course to apply for an entirely new grant of arms, and this is the course normally adopted.

Adoption

Family arms can only in the most exceptional circumstances and by re-grant be transferred to ' strangers in blood '. Adopted children with no blood connection cannot inherit or receive matriculation of arms, nor can they be entered in any pedigree.

Impaled – Two coats joined together on the one shield, for example, the arms of husband and wife, a Bishop and his See, the Kings of Arms.

Imperial Crown – One of the most important crowns in English Royal Regalia. It has a platinum frame which is set with more than 3,000 precious stones of which the majority are diamonds and pearls. The most important stone is known as the Black Prince's Ruby which is set in the cross in the front of the crown.

Increment – An expression describing the moon when in a similar position to an increscent.

Increscent

Increscent – Describes a crescent when the horns and points are to the dexter.

Indented – A line of partition or a method of decorating an Ordinary which is notched in a similar manner to dancetté but the spaces between the points are considerably smaller.

Inescutcheon – A small shield used as a charge and placed in the centre of another shield.

Inflamed – Burning with fire.

Infulae – The ribbons hanging from a mitre.

Insects – A number of insects appear as charges in Heraldry chief amongst them being the bee which is a symbol of industry. Occasionally a single bee appears and sometimes a number is shown surrounding a hive. Other insects include the grasshopper, stagbeetle, butterfly, scorpion, cricket, hornet, ant, spider, and gadfly.

Interchanged – An expression which has sometimes been used instead of counterchanged.

Invected – A line of partition or decoration the exact reverse of engrailed, namely, with the points inwards.

Inverted – Reversed. For example it is used to describe wings where the points are downwards.

Irradiated – Illuminated by rays or beams of light.

Issuant – Arising from the bottom line of a field or chief, from the upper line of a fess, or from a crown or coronet.

J

Jack – The common or slang name for the Union Flag of England.

Javelin – A short spear or dart with a barbed head.

Jelloped – An expression used to describe the comb and wattle of a cock when of a tincture different from its body.

Jessant – Sprouting as for plants from the earth.

Jessant-de-lis – An expression used generally in connection with a leopard who has the lower half of a fleur-de-lis protruding from his

Leopard's face jessant-de-lis

mouth like a tongue and the upper part issuing from the top of his head.

Jesses – The thongs by which bells are fastened to the legs of a hawk or falcon. They may be borne flotant or vervelled.

Jupon – A shortened form of surcoat, approximately thigh length, which replaced the original form which hung below the knees.

K

Key – A very common charge in the bearings of Sees and Religious Institutions.

Kings of Arms – The Senior Officers of Arms (q.v.).

Kintyre Pursuivant – One of the Scottish Officers of Arms (q.v.).

Kite – A bird used as a charge, sometimes blazoned as buzzard.

Knight – A title of honour derived from the Anglo-Saxon age. Originally referred to those who attended Kings upon horse-back as can be seen by their name in many other languages

A boy who was destined to become a Knight was generally placed in the household of some Nobleman at the age of about six years. He spent the early part of his life with the women folk learning simple household duties. Soon he was given a pony on which he learnt to ride and generally how to look after it. Later he became a Page and waited upon his Lord at table, looked after his armour and weapons and generally learnt to be useful. At this time too, much of his time was spent in learning how to use his various weapons and in familiarising himself with the laws of chivalry.

The next step was to make him

an Esquire when he would ride forth with his master acting as a mixture between body servant and aide-de-camp.

When he was about eighteen, providing his master thought he was fit in every respect he was Knighted as a Knight Bachelor, the lowest form of Knighthood. From then onwards he would ride into battle with a pennon on his lance, in command of a number of men.

There are various orders of Knighthood including the Order of the Garter, the Order of the Thistle, Order of St. Patrick, Order of the Bath, Order of St. Michael and St. George, Order of the British Empire.

Knife – Various types of knives may be found as charges but the blazon must state the type and give full details with regard to the tinctures of both blade and handle.

Knots – Knots were fairly frequently seen as charges in early Heraldry but they are less common today, the principal being Bouchier's Knot which is similar to the ordinary reef knot; Bowen's Knot, a continuous loop of cord laid in a square with a loop at each corner and the Staffordshire Knot which can best be described as the first half of a reef knot.

Knowed – See Nowed.

L

Label – A charge which has come to be used exclusively as a mark of cadency. In the case of the Royal family a label of either three or five points argent suitably adorned is used by all members of the Royal family other than the Sovereign.

For other than Royalty, a label of three points of a suitable tincture is used by the eldest son during his father's lifetime, and of five points by the eldest son's eldest son during his grand-father's lifetime. On the death of the armiger, his eldest son removes the label and reverts to his father's arms, the grandson changing his label to one of three points.

Lamb – Used on its own the Lamb is seldom found as a charge but more frequently as the Holy or Paschal lamb (q.v.).

Lambrequin – The mantling (q.v.).

Laminated – An expression used in connection with a monster or animal in connection with its scales.

Lancaster Herald – One of the Officers of Arms.

Language of Heraldry – One of the fascinations of the study of Heraldry is its language and its form of expression. The language is a mixture of Norman French, old English and modern English, and its form of expression is designed so that the many and varied blazons can be succinctly set out and understood by any Heraldic artist who has never seen the bearings emblazoned.

Langued – An expression used when referring to the tongue of an animal.

Lantern – May refer to a ship's lantern or a globular lamp. The blazon must give full details.

Latin Cross – A cross of which the upright arm is longer than the transverse arm.

Leaves – Various kinds are used in

Heraldry but care must be given in describing the type and position.

Leg – The legs of men are not infrequent bearings. They are generally, but not necessarily, arrayed in armour and the knee is always embowed.

Legged – An expression used if the leg is to be tinctured differently from the remainder of the body. Applies generally to birds but occasionally to animals.

Leopard – In early days the lions of England were depicted as leopards, however, they do occasionally appear as charges in modern Heraldry and also may be found as supporters.

Leopard's Face – When this expression is used in blazon no part of the neck must be showing. It is not infrequently found as jessant-de-lis (q.v.).

Letters – Certain letters of the alphabet, generally in the form of capitals, have been used as charges either as single letters or as part of an inscription. The blazon must state the type of lettering viz Roman, Gothic, etc.

Lily – The flower of that name generally emblazoned to look rather like a lotus.

Lily as in the Arms of Eton College

Lily pot – An early type vase, with handles, which is normally emblazoned with five lilies, three upright in bend, in pale, and in bend sinister and one drooping on either side.

On occasions the blazon may say 'a pot of lilies'.

Engrailed		Angled	
Invected		Bevilled	
Undy		Escartelly	
Wavy		Nowy	
Nebuly			
Indented		Battled Embattled	
Dancetty		Enarched	
Embattled		Double Enarched	
Raguly			
Dovetailed		Urdy	
Potenty			
		Rayonny	

Lines of Partition

75

Lined – An expression which may be used with two meanings:

1. When referring to the lining or doubling of the mantling.

2. In connection with an animal for example a greyhound gorged and lined would state that he had a collar with a lead or line attached.

Lines of Partition, Lines of Decoration – Lines which may be plain or ornamental which are used when dividing the shield into separate sections or for outlining some of the figures placed upon it. The line of partition is always plain unless the contrary is stated in the blazon.

In modern Heraldry there are considerably more decorative lines than was the case with the early Heralds. The following shows a complete list of the decorative forms some of which are seldom found in present day grants of arms.

Line of Roses – An infrequently found expression referring, more particularly in connection with a crest, to a continuous line of roses joined together and probably attached to a collar.

Lion – The principal animal charge in Engilsh Heraldry. He may be found in a number of positions including the following: Rampant, erect with his sinister hind paw on the ground and the dexter hind paw slightly raised forward, the dexter front paw is raised level with the top of his head and his sinister front paw stretched forward slightly below the shoulder, he has a ferocious expression on his face, which is looking to the dexter, with his mouth open and his tongue extended.

Variations of rampant include rampant gardant, where his head is turned to the viewer, and rampant

Rampant

regardant, where his head is turned over his left shoulder.

Other variations of rampant include queue fourché, with two tails; coward, with his tail drawn forward between his legs; double headed, with two heads; man lion, where he has the face of an old man and combatant, where he is turned facing the sinister and fighting another lion facing in the normal way. Statant, where he is standing with

Statant

Passant gardant

all four paws on the ground looking either to the sinister or to the
viewer, when it will be statant gardant. Passant, where he is walking
to the dexter with the dexter fore
paw raised and the other three on
the ground. In this position he may
also be gardant and regardant.
Saliant, with both hind paws on the

Couchant

Saliant

ground and the two fore paws raised
level with his head. Sejant, which
may be either gardant or regardant

Dormant

Sejant regardant

or erect when he is shown sitting on
his haunches; couchant or dormant,
when he is either lying down with
his head erect or sleeping with his
head between his paws. In tri-corporate he has three bodies; winged,
he has a pair of wings; sea lion, his
front feet are webbed and he dis-
cards his hind quarters in favour of
a fishes tail.

One may also find a demi-lion
and a lion's head.

In all cases with a lion rampant,
unless the blazon states differently
or the field is gules, irrespective of
the tincture of his body he is considered to be armed and langued
gules.

Lioncel – Where more than one lion
appears on a shield they will be
blazoned as lioncels in which case
their position is normally rampant.

Liver Bird – The Cormorant.

Livery – In early days when servants
were arrayed in livery it was customary to choose the principal colour
and metal of their Lord's arms.

Some of the better known liveries
were as follows: The later Plantagenets, white and red; the House of

77

York, murrey and blue; the House of Lancaster, white and blue; the House of Tudor, white and green; the House of Stuart, yellow and red; the House of Hanover, scarlet and blue.

Lizard – In early days the Heraldic lizard resembled a wild cat with brown fur and darker spots. In modern Heraldry the lizard is normally blazoned as a scaly lizard and unless otherwise stated the tincture used is vert.

Lodged – A word equivalent to 'couchant' when applied to beasts of the chase.

Long Bow – When the expression bow is used in blazon it refers to the normal bow and it is customary to use a different tincture for the strings.
　The other type of bow is the cross bow and for this, full details must be given in the blazon.

Lozenge – A figure resembling the diamond on a playing card.

Lozenge

Lozengy – Describes a field or charge which is divided by lines per bend and per bend sinister into equal sized diamonds of two different tinctures.

Luce – An alternative name for the pike.

Lure – Sometimes blazoned as hawks lure (q.v.). When the expression conjoined in lure is found it implies two wings joined in the centre with the tips inverted.

Lymphad – An ancient galley which may be blazoned with sails furled or in full sail. It may have oars in

Lymphad

position in which case they are in the water or there may be two oars placed in saltire against the mast.
　It is a commonly found charge in Scottish Heraldry and full details must be given.

Lynx – An animal found frequently in connection with ophthalmic institutions.

Lyon King of Arms – Lord Lyon King of Arms is the Senior Scottish Officer of Arms (q.v.).

M

Mace – In early days a mace was a club-like weapon which was used throughout a number of centuries. There were various different shapes and most of them acquired such fanciful names as 'Morning Star',

'Good Day', etc. For some reason the mace was particularly popular with Soldier-churchmen such as Odo, Bishop of Bayeux and brother of Richard the Conqueror, the reason being that the Mace, though a brutal weapon, was a bruising weapon whereas a sword spilt blood, which was forbidden to churchmen.

In modern times the mace is merely a symbol of judicial or civic authority.

Madonna – A charge which appears in a number of ecclesiastical arms.

Maiden's head – One of the head series of charges (q.v.).) It may be found in the arms of Reading.

Maintenance, Cap of – See Cap of Estate.

Majesty, In his – An expression used for an eagle crowned and holding a sceptre.

Mallet – A square ended hammer and generally associated with particular trades. It appears in Heraldry as a charge but details must be given in the blazon.

Maltese Cross – The cross of eight points.

Maltese Cross

Maned – Refers to the mane of a lion and occasionally used in connection with a horse, though in the case of the latter the expression crined (q.v.) is more generally used.

Man lion – A lion rampant with the head and face of an old man which is facing the viewer.

Man-lion

Mantle – Refers to the cloak worn by members of the Peerage on state occasions. They are crimson velvet edged with miniver and the cape furred with pure miniver with bars of ermine varying in number according to the rank of the wearer. e.g. A Duke, 4 bars; a Marquess, $3\frac{1}{2}$ bars; an Earl, 3 bars; a Viscount $2\frac{1}{2}$ bars; and a Baron, 2 bars.

Mantling or Lambriquin – This was a shoulder length cape hanging from the top of the helm and was designed originally to keep the heat of the sun from the head and neck of the wearer. Subsequently it was found to be an added protection in battle owing to the difficulty of cutting through loose material with a sword, though naturally it sustained a number of cuts and tears.

The mantling which is now used as a decorative measure in an achievement is derived from the old-fashioned lambriquin and its scalloped edges represent the cuts received in battle.

Marchmont Herald – One of the Scottish Officers of Arms (q.v.).

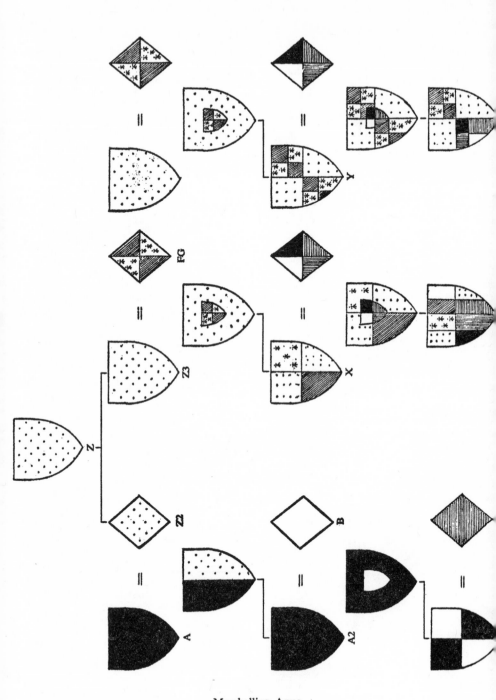

Marshalling Arms

Decrescent

Maltese Cross

Molet

Lion Rampant

Fusil

Gyronny

Fountain

Marined – An expression used of an animal having the lower parts of a fish.

Marquess – The second rank in the peerage of England being below a Duke but above an Earl. The first marquess was created by King Richard II in 1386.

Married Women – A married woman, through the right of courtesy, may bear on a shield her paternal arms impaled with those of her husband. If her husband is non-armigerous she continues to use her paternal arms only borne upon a lozenge as was her right before marriage.

Should she happen to be an heiress she bears her arms impaled with those of her husband during the lifetime of her father and, on her father's death, her paternal arms are borne on an inescutcheon of pretence which is placed in the centre of her husband's bearings.

Should her husband pre-decease her she will then, as a widow, bear her paternal arms on a lozenge.

Marshalling – Is the art of arranging several coats of arms on one shield generally for the purpose of denoting the alliances of a family. The system is divided into two parts.

1. Temporary and non-hereditary combinations such as the impalement of arms of husband and wife and the impalement of personal arms with those of an office.

2. The permanent and hereditary combination of arms as in the case where a man marries an heiress and his issue who succeed to the arms of their mother as well as their father.

The system can best be shown by means of a simple diagram as follows:

The diagram shows the principle of Marshalling the Arms of husband

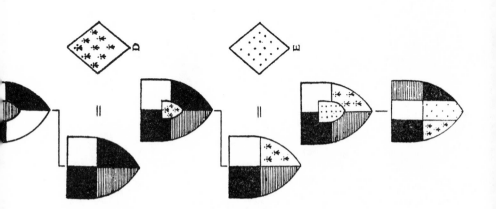

Marshalling Arms

and wife and the transmission of the Arms of an Heiress to her descendants.

A married Z2 who is not an heiress because she has a brother. The Arms of A and Z are therefore impaled and their sons inherit only the Arms of A.

Their son A2 married B, an heiress. He therefore places the Arms of B on an Escutcheon of Pretence in the centre of the shield because he pretends to the representation of the family B. When the wife dies A2 removes the Escutcheon from his shield because the representation of the family B passes to the children of the marriage. At the mother's death the children of this marriage place their father's arms in the 1 and 4 quarters and their mother's Arms in the 2 and 3 quarters. This process continues as before with every marriage to an heiress as is illustrated in the diagram. Thus the quarters are continually increased.

In the case of Z3 who marries heiress FG who possesses a quartered Coat, the same process continues, but the normal practice is to divide the wife's Coat as shown at X. If however for any reason the Coat is of long standing or quartered by Royal Licence etc., the quartering will be carried out as in Y.

The English System of breaking up quartered Coats and redistributing them is for the sake of simplicity. The Scottish system tends to retain them. It is not necessary for a man to use all the quarterings to which he is entitled, but he may make a selection from them. If however he includes a particular quartering brought in by an heiress he must include the one which brought it in. Thus Z5 can only quarter G if he includes F.

Martlet – One of the birds borne as a charge, particularly in the attributed arms of Edward the Confessor, and also associated with the County of Sussex.

Martlet

Mascle – A lozenge voided.

Mascle

Masculy – Covered with mascles either conjoined at the angles or on all their sides. The former may be distinguished as being a pattern formed of lozenges and mascles alternately, the latter should be described as masculy of the two appropriate tinctures counter changed.

Masoned – A term used to describe the lines formed by the junction of stones or bricks in a building. The term is used in conjunction with a tincture when it is different from that of the wall or building.

Wall embattled, masoned

Matriculation of Arms – In Scotland the right to bear arms does not extend to younger sons until the arms have been matriculated with such marks of cadency as the Lord Lyon may determine. The bearings thus differenced again descend to the heir male whose younger brothers must again matriculate to receive further differences.

Maunch – An ancient sleeve worn by a lady.

Maunch

Malusine – A mermaid with two heads.

Membered – Refers to the legs of birds when of a different tincture from the body.

Mermaid and Merman – Classified as monsters (q.v.).

Merlon – The raised portion between two embrasures in an embattled wall.

Metals – Two of the colours used in Heraldry are described as metals, namely gold and silver. Under the laws of Heraldry a metal may not be placed upon another metal but only upon a fur or tincture.

Millrind – Sometimes called fer-de-moline. The iron fixed to the centre of a mill stone on which it rotates.

Mirror – A small circular or oval looking-glass with a handle, which is always carried by a mermaid.

Mitre – One of the principal insignia of the episcopal office. It occasionally takes the form of a charge on the shield but is more generally found surmounting the shield instead of the helm torse and crest as used by non-ecclesiastical armigers.

Moldiwarp – A mole.

Mole – Generally blazoned as moldiwarp.

Molet, Mullet – Generally represents the rowel of a spur. It has five points unless the blazon states otherwise and is frequently pierced When associated with a crescent it represents a star.

Moline Cross – May refer to the millrind but is generally emblazoned as a cooped cross with the end of each arm splayed out to two points.

Molet

Monsters – A number of monsters and hybrids are found in British Heraldry. They originated from classical and mediaeval mythology combined largely with the imagination of early Heralds. The principal among them are the following:

The Dragon, a monster with a horny head and forked tongue, a scaly back and rib-like armour on his chest and belly, bat-like wings, four legs ending in talons and a pointed barbed tail. It may be found rampant (generally termed segreant) passant and statant and very rarely displayed.

Dragon passant

The Wyvern (wivern) is a kind of dragon but with only two legs and a knowed tail, on which he sits, in place of his hinds legs. When blazoned proper he has a green head, back and legs and a red chest, belly and insides to his wings.

Wyvern

The Cockatrice is similar to a wyvern but with a cocks head, comb and wattles.

Cockatrice

The Griffin (gryphon) has the head, breast, fore-feet and wings of an eagle, the only difference being that it has ears, and the hind quarters and tail of a lion. When rampant it is normally termed segreant and it may also be found in other positions. If it is blazoned as a male griffin he is shown without wings and sometimes with horns and a spiked tail.

Griffin segreant

The Opinicus has a griffin's head, neck and wings, a lion's body and a bear's tail.

Opinicus

The Unicorn resembles a horse in head and body but has one long projecting horn from the forehead, cloven hoofs and a lion's tail and tufted locks and a beard.

Unicorn

85

The Pegasus, though occasionally found used as a supporter in modern Heraldry, is seldom seen elsewhere. He appears as an emblem of air transport, emblazoned in the traditional manner.

Pegasus

The Enfield has a fox's head and ears, a wolf's body, hind legs and tail, an eagle's shanks and talons for his fore legs.

Enfield

The Heraldic Antelope has a head and body similar to the Heraldic Tyger but with serrated horns and the legs of a deer.

Heraldic Antelope

86

The Heraldic Panther resembles the natural panther but has flames issuing from his mouth and ears.

The Heraldic Sea-Lion is a lion terminating in a fishes tail. It must not be confused with the natural sea-lion which also appears as a charge.

The Camelopard, believed by early Heralds to have been a cross between the camel and leopard, is in fact a normal giraffe and is emblazoned thus.

Tyger

The Salamander is emblazoned as a lizard from which flames are issuing in all directions.

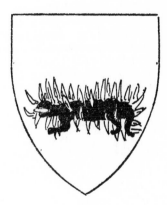

Salamander

The Mermaid and Merman have the appropriate human figure above the waist terminating in a fish's tail. The Mermaid is nearly always emblazoned with the traditional comb and glass.

Mermaid

87

Moon – Occasionally borne in her complement i.e. full, and occasionally figured i.e. with a human face. It may also be illuminated i.e. surrounded by short rays.

Otherwise the moon is treated in a similar manner to the crescent.

Moorcock – Similar to the heathcock.

Moore's Head – Sometimes blazoned as blackamore's head.

Morse – A clasp frequently ornamented. Used for fastening a robe.

Motto – A word or sentence upon a scroll generally placed below the shield but sometimes, especially in Scotland, above it. It should never be inscribed upon a Garter or circlet and is never found in the arms of a woman other than the Sovereign.

In English Heraldry the motto is not part of the grant and it can thus be changed at will by the bearer. In Scotland, however, it is part of the grant and can only be changed on application to Lord Lyon.

Mound – An orb surmounted by a cross. It is an emblem of Sovereignty and forms the highest ornament on the Royal Crown.

Mount – A piece of ground generally slightly raised and covered with grass which may occupy the base of a shield and on which stands another charge; for example, a tree or a cock.

Mounted – Applied to a horse when carrying a rider.

Mullet – There are two types of mullet:
1. The molet (q.v.).
2. The fish so called.

Muraillé – Maisoned.

Mural Crown – An embattled crown (q.v.).

Murrey – An alternative name for sanguine. The old-fashioned redish purple tincture which is rarely seen today.

Musimon – The hybrid of a ram and goat but with four horns, two of which resemble a goat's horns and the other two those of a ram.

Mutilé – Dismembered.

N

Naiant – Swimming.

Naissant – An expression applied to a charge rising from the upper line of a fess or other ordinary or the lower line of a chief.

Naval Crown – See Crown.

Navel Point – Is a point halfway between the fess point and the base.

Nebuly – A line of partition which being intended to represent clouds is rarely used otherwise than horizontally.

Nerved – An expression referring to the fibres of leaves.

Nimbus – A halo.

Noble – In Heraldry any person entitled to bear a coat of arms and whatever his rank is *Nobilis* which actually means 'Known'. In Scotland any armigerous person is looked upon as being Noble but this distinction does not apply in English Heraldry.

Nobility – In its widest sense this term includes the greater nobility viz. the Sovereign and Royal family, the Dukes, Marquesses, Earls, Viscounts and Barons and the 'Lesser Nobility' refers to Baronets, Knights, Esquires and untitled Gentlemen.

Nombril Point – Similar to Navel Point.

Norfolk, Duke of – The Premier Duke and Hereditary Earl Marshal of England. He is the titular head of the College of Arms and responsible for all state ceremonial functions.

Norroy, King of Arms – One of the Senior Officers of Arms (q.v.).

Nova Scotia, Baronet of – See Baronets.

Nowed – Knotted.

Nowy – A line of partition two-thirds of which is horizontal and the remaining one-third in the centre arched to form a semi-circle.

O

Oak – A tree frequently found as a charge; very often described as acorned or fructed.

Oars – Occasionally found as a charge, as for example 'two oars in saltire', and in connection with a lymphad when the oars may be in action from the sides of the ship or placed in saltire against the mast.

Obsidional Crown – A garland of twigs and grasses.

Of the Field, of the First – An expression frequently used in blazon where a tincture of the field is repeated, to save repetition of its name.

Officers of Arms – Since the incorporation of the College of Arms there have been many different Officers of Arms, some for specific occasions, some who have changed their position from King of Arms to Herald and vice-versa and many who have risen from Pursuivant up through Herald to King of Arms.

At the present time there are thirteen Officers of Arms consisting of three Kings of Arms, Garter, principal King of Arms, who is in charge of the College of Arms under the Earl Marshal and who is Officer of the Order of the Garter; Clarenceux King of Arms, who is responsible for that part of England south of the River Trent and Norroy and Ulster King of Arms who is responsible for that part of England north of the River Trent and for the six counties comprising Ulster.

There are six Heralds namely Chester, Lancaster, Richmond, Somerset, Windsor, and York and four Pursuivants who work under the fascinating names of Blue Mantle, Portcullis, Rouge Croix and Rouge Dragon.

From time to time certain supernumary Officers of Arms are created to assist in particular functions such as coronations, investitures etc., including such titles as Norfolk Herald Extraordinary and Fitzalan Pursuivant Extraordinary.

The Officers of Arms in Scotland consist of Lord Lyon King of Arms who as a Great Officer of the State, has complete control of all Heraldic matters in that country. He has working under him three Heralds, Marchmant, Rothsay and Albany and three Pursuivants, Dingwall, Unicorn and Carrick.

The Scottish Heraldic Authority is a department of state and as such, Officers of Arms are paid considerably higher salaries than in England where they are part of the Royal Household.

Ogress – A roundle sable.

Opinicus – A type of monster (q.v.).

Oppressed – An expression meaning debruised.

Or – Gold.

Orange – A name originally given to a roundle tenné which is seldom seen today. It may also be found as a charge both as a fruit and in connection with an orange tree that has been fructed.

Ordinaries – The honourable ordinaries were derived from the simple charges which arose from the early habit of painting the supporting metal bands of the shield.

There are nine of them and they are used extensively today and the student of Heraldry must therefore be conversant with them.

1. The chief. This is formed by a horizontal line containing the uppermost part of the shield, generally $\frac{1}{3}$ to $\frac{1}{5}$ of its depth depending largely on the charges to be displayed both on the field and on the chief.

Chief

2. The fess. A section approximately $\frac{1}{3}$ to $\frac{1}{5}$ the depth of the shield drawn horizontally through the fess point.

Fess

There are a number of diminutives to the fess as follows.

(a) Bars. Two such sections drawn horizontally approximately half the width of a fess so placed to divide the remainder of the shield into sections approximately the same depth. If more than two bars are to be used the number must be stated, only the remarks with regard to their positioning remain the same.

Bars

(b) Barrulets. These are similar to bars but smaller in width and they are generally placed in couples, in which case they are generally termed 'bars gemelles'.

Barrulets (Bars gemelles)

(c) Fess cotissed. Here a normal fess is employed with a barrulet on either side leaving a small section of the field showing between.

Fess cotissed

(d) Fess double cotissed. Similar to fess cotissed but with two barrulets on either side.

3. The pale. A vertical section drawn through the fess point containing from $\frac{1}{3}$ to $\frac{1}{5}$ the width of the shield in the centre of the shield.

Pale

Diminutives of the pale consist of:

(a) Pallets. These are a number of smaller segments each approximately $\frac{1}{2}$ the width of the pale, spaced so that the remainder of the field is divided roughly into equal sections.

Pallets

(b) Pale endorsed. The expression implies the same as cotissed with the fess but the term endorse is used for the pale and it implies a small section on either side of the pale with the field showing between.

Pale endorsed

4. The Bend and the Bend Sinister. The bend is a part of the shield contained by two diagonal lines from dexter chief to sinister base.

Diminutives of the bend consist of:

91

Bend

(a) Bendlets. When there are two or more sections similar to the bend but of half its width or less according to the number used.

Bendlets

(b) Bend cotissed. In this case a cotisse appears on each side of the bend in a similar manner to the fess cotissed.

(c) Baton. This applies to a cotisse cooped i.e. cut short at the ends and not reaching to the edge of the shield. This may also apply equally as for the bend sinister.

Baton

5. The Chevron. The chevron, as its name implies, is a segment contained by two parallel lines drawn from the dexter base and the sinister base meeting in the centre of the shield with the point uppermost. Two chevrons may be used on one shield but if more are required the diminutive is used.

Chevron

(a) Chevronel. Three or more chevrons of a width suitable to divide up the field and allow the field to be seen between them.

(b) Chevronels interlaced. In this case the chevronels, generally three in number, are placed side by side with the arms interlaced.

Chevronels interlaced

(c) Chevron cotissed. The chevron may be cotissed or double cotissed in a similar manner to the fess and bend.

92

6. The Pile. A wedge-shaped figure normally issuing from the chief but occasionally from the side or base of the shield. More than one pile may appear on the same shield.

Pile

7. The Pall. This is a figure resembling the capital letter 'Y' with its arms extending to the dexter chief, sinister chief and base of the shield.

Diminutive; the shakefork which is similar to the pall but the ends do not reach the edge of the shield and they are generally trimmed to be parallel with the sides of the shield to which they point.

Pall

8. The Saltire. This figure, which is similar to the cross of St. Andrew is formed from a single bendlet crossing a bendlet sinister.

Saltire

9. The Cross. The cross of which there are over 500 different varieties used in Heraldry (see Cross) may also be found as an Ordinary in which case it is formed from a narrow fess and a narrow pale crossing each other.

Cross

In some cases, particularly in early coats of arms, one may find two Ordinaries in use on the same shield, for example 'Or a chief and a saltire gules' (Bruce). 'Argent a pile sable and a chevron counter changed' (Alwell) and 'Or a fess between two chevrons gules' (Fitzwalter).

Ordinary of Arms – An Heraldic index containing armorial bearings classified according to their principal charges.

Oriflamme – Originally the banner belonging to the Abbey of St. Denis near Paris but it is a name which has been given to other flags probably of a similar colour and form.

The Oriflamme borne at Agincourt is said to have been an oblong red flag terminating in five points.

Orle – A small bordure around the field but instead of running round the edge of the shield a small strip of the field of similar width is left outside the orle. The orle may be a continuous strip or it may consist of a number of the same charges placed in orle.

Ostrich – The bird of that name occasionally used as a charge and almost invariably carrying some metal object in its mouth.

Ostrich Feathers – May appear as a charge or a part of a crest, for example the Black Prince's shield of peace was *sable three ostrich feathers argent*.

Otter – The animal of that name appearing as a charge or as a crest. Sometimes blazoned with a fish in its mouth.

Over All – An expression used with reference to a charge when it is borne over all the others.

Overt – Open, particularly applied to wings.

Owl – A bird which is always depicted full face either as a charge or in a crest.

P

Padlock – In early Heraldry the form of this charge varied but at the present time the form used is the fetterlock (q.v.).

Pairlie, Tierced in – This expression describes a shield which is divided in three parts, a line per pale from the centre chief to the fess point and thence per chevron.

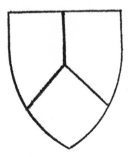

Tierced in Pairlie

Pale – One of the principal ordinaries (q.v.).

Pale Wise – Describes a number of charges which are placed vertically one upon the other or the position of a single charge e.g. a sword, which is to stand erect.

Palisado Crown – Similar in type to the Crown Vallery (q.v.).

Pall – The Heraldic figure of this name may be described as the upper half of a saltire conjoined to the lower half of a pale and it is found frequently as an ecclesiastical charge. It originated from the stole hanging around a clergyman's neck.

Pallet – The diminutive of the pale. It is never borne singly.

Pallium – Alternative name for the Pall.

Palmer's Staff – A straight tapering staff with a nobbed top sometimes known as Burdon or Bourdon.

Paley – An expression used when a shield is divided into an equal number of vertical parts. The number and appropriate tinctures must be given.

Panache – An arrangement of feathers sometimes found forming a crest.

Panther – This animal is always borne gardant and generally incensed (q.v.).

Parrot – The bird of that name but blazoned as popinjay.

Parted, party – Divided. An expression used when a shield is divided as party per pale, party per fess. In modern Heraldry the word party is generally omitted from the blazon.

Partition, Lines of – See elsewhere under 'Lines of Partition'.

Paschal Lamb, or Holy Lamb – Which is always emblazoned facing the dexter and holding aloft a flag bearing the cross of St. George.

Passant – A word used to express the position of a beast walking to the dexter. His dexter paw is raised but the other three are firmly on the ground. He is looking to his front unless blazoned gardant or regardant.

Passion Cross – An alternative name for the Latin Cross (q.v.).

Pastoral Staff – The Crosier.

Patté – A term applied to the cooped cross with each arm splayed outwards with curved lines.

Patonce – Describes a frequently used cross, the arms of which terminate in three points.

Pawne – Sometimes used as a name for the peacock.

Peacock in his Pride – The term generally used when blazoning the peacock who is then depicted affronté with his tail extended.

Pean – One of the furs (q.v.).

Pear – This, like other fruit, may be pendant, erect or fesswise.

Pearls – An expression sometimes used to describe the silver balls on certain coronets but never actually represented as pearls.

Peer – A general name given to the Nobility of Great Britain, thus indicating their equality of rank as a class irrespective of their differences in degree within the peerage.

Peeress, In her own Right – A lady who succeeds to her father's peerage in default of heirs male.

Pegasus – A winged horse classified as a monster (q.v.).

Pelican in her Piety – The pelican is normally blazoned in her piety when feeding her young with drops of blood drawn from her breast. The wings are always shown adorsed.

Pellet – An alternative name for the roundle sable. In early Heraldry the pellet might be a roundle of any colour.

Pendant – Hanging down as a leaf or fruit with the stalk upwards.

Pennant, Pennon – The small two tailed flag carried by a Knight. Pennons were not charged with arms but only with crests, Heraldic and

Ornamental devices and mottoes.

Penned – An expression used when referring to the shaft or quill of a feather.

Per – By means of. Used in conjunction with a dividing line e.g. per fess, per pale, denotes that the shield is divided into sections as given.

Pheon – The head of a dart or arrow which is barbed and engrailed on the inner sides. It is invariably shown with the point downward unless otherwise blazoned.

Pheon

Phoenix – Represented as an eagle issuing from flames.

Pierced – Applied to any bearing which is perforated. The colour of the field or charge on which it is placed being seen through the aperture. Alternatively it may be blazoned as pierced of a different tincture.

The pierce hole should be circular unless otherwise stated.

Pike – The fish.

Pile – A wedge shaped sub-ordinary generally pendent from the top of the shield or from the lower line of the chief but it may be from either side or even from the base. Its size

will depend upon the number and whether or not it is charged.

Pillow – Treated in the same way as cushion (q.v.)

Pily – Is a division of the field into an even number of parts by piles placed perpendicularly and counter posed, the number must be given.

Pily Bendy – A field divided into a number of pile shaped pieces bend wise.

Pincers – Emblazoned as the ordinary working tool.

Pinioned – An expression rarely found, which means having wings.

Pinson – Chaffinch.

Pipe Banner – A method of displaying arms used extensively in Scottish regiments, where each company commander (who is expected to matriculate in Lyon Register) displays his own arms. In some regiments the whole achievement is emblazoned on the banner which is made in the colour of the regimental facings. In others, the shield charge only is emblazoned.

Planta Genista – The broome plant which was one of the well known badges of the House of Plantagenet.

Plate – A roundle argent.

Plenitude – An alternative expression denoting fullness of the moon.

Plume – Generally refers to a number of feathers grouped together in a crest.

Plummet – The leaden weight, sometimes found as a charge.

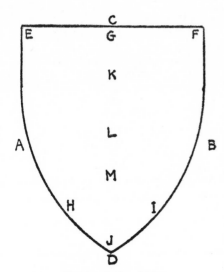

Points of the shield:

Points of the shield – The various points of a shield are:

A. Dexter side
B. Sinister side
C. Chief
D. Base
E. Dexter chief
F. Sinister chief
G. Centre chief
H. Dexter base
I. Sinister base
J. Centre base
K. Honour point
L. Fess point
M. Nombril point

Pomegranate – The fruit of that

Pomegranate

name. May be used as a charge to denote fruitfulness. One of the badges of Mary I.

Pomme – Apple. Also used as the name for a roundle vert.

Pommel – The rounded section at the end of the hilt of a sword.

Popinjay – The Parrot. When blazoned proper he should be vert, beaked and membered gules.

Port – The gateway of a castle.

Portcullis – A frame of wood strengthened and spiked on the lower arms with metal, used for the defence of the gate of a castle. It is invariably emblazoned with chains hanging down on either side. It was used as one of the badges of the Tudors.

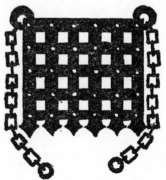

Portcullis

Portcullis Pursuivant – One of the Officers of Arms (q.v.).

Potent – One of the furs. It is depicted by a number of pieces similar in shape to half a Capital ' H ' lying on its side. It is invariably tinctured argent and azure.

The potent figure can be used in several ways, namely, to terminate the arms of a cross and as a decoration for a line of partition in which case it is blazoned as potenté.

Poudré – An expression occasionally used for semé (q.v.).

Presta John – The figure of a man vested and hooded sitting upon a plain seat (generally termed a tomb stone), his right hand extended in the attitude of benediction and the left holding an open book. In his mouth a sword fesswise, the point to the dexter.

Proboscis – The trunk of an elephant.

Pronominal – An expression used when referring to the paternal coat in a quartered shield which generally forms the first quarter.

Proper – An expression used in blazon to denote that the charges affected are to be shown in their proper colours.

Punning Arms – Arms which allude in punning form to the name of the bearer.

Purfled – Garnished. The term applied largely to the ornamentation of armour.

Purpure – The tincture commonly called purple.

Pursuivant – Virtually a junior Officer of Arms under instruction prior to promotion to the position of Herald.

Q

Quadrate – Sometimes found in connection with a cross which if termed quadrate denotes a square as part of the cross in the centre.

Quarter – In early Heraldry a quarter was used instead of the present canton (q.v.).

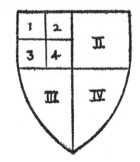

1 to 4 = Quarters
II to IV = Grand Quarters

Quarters

Where a number of coats of arms, more than two, are marshalled on one shield each is known as a quarter. If any of the resulting quarters are again subdivided into quarters the original divisions are known as grand quarters.

Quarterly – A line of partition produced by dividing the shield per fess, and per pale.

Quatrefoil – A four petalled figure similar in type to the other foils.

Queen Consort – The wife of the reigning sovereign. Until the time of George II the Queen Consort was accustomed to bear the arms of the King her husband impaled with her own with the King's dexter supporter and the sinister supporter of her father's arms but since that period the Queen consorts have used Royal supporters.

Queen Regnant – The Queen ruling in her own right who, as such, is the only female privileged to bear her arms on a shield. She is also entitled to a helmet, mantling, crest and motto and may surround her shield with the garter and collars or ribbons of all other orders of Knighthood of which she is sovereign.

Queue = The tail of an animal.

Queue fourché – A forked tail.

Quill, quilled – Expressions referring to the feather of a pen.

Quintfoil – The early expression used occasionally instead of cinquefoil for the five-petalled member of the foil family.

R

Rabbit – See Coney.

Radiant or Rayonné – One of the lesser used lines of partition. May also be applied to an ordinary or subordinary encircled with or formed of rays.

Ragged Staff – A ragged staff is sometimes seen in conjunction with a bear. It implies that the staff which is cooped to about the height of the bear's neck has a number of branches which are also cooped.

Raguly – An expression applied to an ordinary having pieces like cooped branches from it in a slanting direction.

Railway Locomotive – This has appeared as a charge in modern Heraldry.

Ram – Both the ram and the ram's head may be seen as charges recognisable by their horns.

Rampant – This expression is only applicable to beasts of prey. It implies rage, when the beast is shown standing on his sinister hind foot, his dexter hind foot raised slightly and the fore paws outstretched with the dexter higher than the sinister. He is facing the dexter with his mouth open and tongue extended, but there are alternatives to rampant which include gardant, regardant, queue fourché etc.

Raven – Generally emblazoned in a manner similar to the Corby.

Rays – These are always used when emblazoning the sun or an estoile.

Rebated – Having the points cut off.

Reflexed – Bent or curved. It especially applies to a line or chain affixed to the collar of a beast and thrown over his back.

Regardant – Having the head turned backward to face the sinister.

Regimental Insignia – Regimental badges, formation signs and flashes are, of course, a form of Heraldry which, in fact, date back to the Roman era when such formation and unit signs were inscribed upon the shield.

Regimental Colours – Control of regimental colours is under the auspices of Garter, Principal King of Arms.

Reindeer – Occasionally found in Heraldry and distinguished from the stag by double attires one erect the other pendent.

Removed – An expression used in connection with an ordinary that has fallen from its usual and proper place.

Reptiles – Serpents or snakes may be found, particularly in the arms of medical institutes. Other reptiles include lizards (q.v.).

Resignant – Concealed. Applies particularly to a beast whose tail is concealed.

Reremouse – The bat (q.v.).

Respectant, Respecting – Terms used to describe two animals borne face to face, rampant beasts of prey so borne are said to be combatant.

Reversed – Turned upside down.

Richmond Herald – One of the Officers of Arms (q.v.).

Rising – An expression used in connection with a bird opening his wings as if preparing to take flight.

Roach – A fresh water fish.

Rook – The bird blazoned as corby. The chess piece of that name is termed chessrook.

Rose – Frequently found in English Heraldry and never to be drawn with a stalk unless such an addition is expressly directed in the blazon. It should never be described as proper for there are roses of many colours. The word ' proper ' applies to the barbs or calix and seeds meaning that the former are green and the latter gold. A rose is the difference for the seventh house.

Rothsay Herald – One of the Scottish Officers of Arms (q.v.).

Rouge Croix Pursuivant – One of the Officers of Arms (q.v.).

Rouge Dragon Pursuivant – One of the Officers of Arms (q.v.).

Roundle, roundel – A circular charge distinguished by different names according to their tinctures. for example, gold roundles are named bezants, from the gold coin of Byzantium; argent-plates; azure-heurts; gules-torteaux; purpure-golpes (seldom used today); and sable-ogresses, pellets or gunstones.
Roundles barry wavy of six argent and azure are known as fountains.
When roundles are parted, counter changed, or of any of the furs they retain the name of roundles with the appropriate tinctures.

Rowel – The spur rowel (q.v.).

Royal Heraldry – There is no definite proof that any English King prior to Richard I used armorial bearings, though arms have been attributed to the various rulers as far back as Egbert A.D. 802–839. Furthermore it is known that Henry I presented his son-in-law, Count Geoffrey of Anjou with a shield emblazoned with arms which continued to be used by his descendants. It is therefore likely that both Henry I and Henry II used some sort of bearings though whether or not Stephen did so is problematical.
Richard I, according to his first great seal, is believed to have used two lions rampant combatant when going to the crusade, but on his return his second great seal definitely shows three lions passant gardant.
These arms were used by Kings of England until the reign of Edward III.
On laying claim to the throne of France, King Edward III quartered

with the arms of England those of France (ancient) namely azure semé-de-lis. Originally he is said to have put the French arms in the second and third quarters, but subsequently, after a complaint by the King of France, he changed them to the first and fourth quarters.

Richard II bore the same arms but by a personal whim preferred to impale them with the arms attributed to Edward the Confessor, namely '*azure a cross patonce between five martlets, Or*'.

Henry IV reverted to the same arms as borne by Edward III, but he reduced the number of fleurs-de-lis to five in the French quarterings.

Henry V reduced the number of fleurs-de-lis once again to three in the French quarterings and in this form the arms on the French quarters have been known ever since as '*France (modern)*'. It is believed that he took this step to follow the example of his father-in-law Charles VI of France who had also reduced the fleurs-de-lis to three, possibly with a view to making the arms different from those quartered by the English Kings.

Henry VI, Edward IV, Richard III, Henry VII, Henry VIII, and Edward VI continued to bear the same arms.

On the accession of Mary I to the throne she chose to bear the arms upon a lozenge. She also substituted the lions of England in the third quarter for the arms of her mother Katherine of Aragon.

Elizabeth I returned to the bearings as used by her father.

On the accession of James I (James VI of Scotland), to the throne of England there was a great change and the new bearings were as follows – quarterly I and IV, 1 and 4 France (modern), 2 and 3 England, II Scotland and III Ireland. These arms continued to be borne down to and including the time of William and Mary, the only difference lying in the arms of the latter sovereigns. Due to the fact that they ruled jointly, in this instance we see the same coats impaled with each other upon the one shield but William's coat, on the dexter side, has the addition of an escutcheon of Nassau, '*Azure billetté a lion rampant Or*'.

Queen Anne used the same arms as were borne by James I until 1706 when the Act of Union was passed and the Royal Arms were remarshalled thus quarterly 1 and 4 England impaling Scotland, 2 France modern, 3 Ireland. Note: In spite of the fact that the arms in 1 and 2 quarter are impaled the left or dexter half of the Scottish tressure was removed.

George I used the same arms as Anne had after the Act of Union but substituted for the fourth quarter a new coat as follows: '*per pale and per chevron, 1 gules two lions passant gardant in pale Or* (Brunswick). *2. Or semé of hearts proper a lion rampant azure armed and langued gules* (Luneburg). *3. Gules a horse courant argent* (Saxony) *Surtout on an escutcheon of pretence gules the crown of Charlemagne gold*.

These arms were also borne by George II and at the commencement of George III's reign. In 1801, however, the French arms were finally removed and the arms of England and Scotland occupied the first and second quarters respectively. The arms of England were replaced in the fourth quarter and the coat originally borne by George I in the fourth quarter was placed on an escutcheon of pretence ensigned by the Electoral Bonnet. In 1816, in consequence of the Electorate of Hanover being elevated to a kingdom the Electoral Bonnet was changed to the Hanoverian Royal Crown.

These arms were borne by George IV and William IV.

In 1837 when Queen Victoria came to the throne it was obviously ludicrous for her to lay claim to the Kingdom of Hanover and therefore the escutcheon of pretence and the Hanoverian crown were finally removed from the arms of Great Britain and they were thus marshalled as quarterly 1 and 4 England, 2 and 3 Ireland, and have remained thus to the present day.

The only difference lies in the arms as borne by the monarch when in Scotland, which are marshalled as 1 and 4 Scotland, 2 England and 3 Ireland.

Since the reign of Henry VIII the Royal arms have been encircled by the Garter.

S

Sable – Black.

Sagittary – The centaur, half man and half horse holding an arrow upon a bent bow.

Sail – The sail figures largely in ship charges which may be blazoned in full sail or with sails furled.

Saint Andrew – The patron saint of Scotland. It is upon the cross of St. Andrew (a saltire) upon which St. Andrew is said to have been crucified.

Saint George – The patron Saint of England who figures largely in the regalia of the Knights of the Garter.

Saint Patrick – The patron Saint of

Ireland after whom the order of St. Patrick (now extinct), was named.

Saliant – Applied to a beast when depicted as if leaping at its prey i.e. with both hind feet on the ground and both fore feet raised.

Saliant appears to be an accidental variation from rampant which may have arisen in early Heraldry.

Salmon – The fish of that name.

Saltire – The cross of St. Andrew which may be found used as an ordinary or as a charge, or the shield may be divided per saltire. As an ordinary its edges may be subject to decoration.

Sanglant – Blood stained.

Sanglier – An alternative name for the wild boar.

Sanguine or Murrey – One of the old Heraldic tinctures seldom found today. It is redish purple in colour.

Saracen's Head – One of the heads which may be found as a charge dating from the early crusades. It is depicted as the head of an old man with a savage countenance.

Sarcellé – Cut through the middle.

Saxon Crown – One of the crowns found in old Heraldry.

Scallop – A shell used as a charge which had its origin in the crusades.

Schools, Arms and Badges – Many British schools possess armorial bearings and the tendency is for those who only possess badges or other non-armorial insignia to acquire arms also. In some cases the bearings used are taken from those of the founder of the school.

102

Scimitar – A curved sword with a blade wider towards the end.

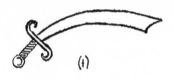

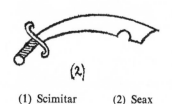

(1) Scimitar   (2) Seax

Scintillant – Sparkling or throwing off sparks.

Scottish Heraldry – In Scotland the Heraldic system is somewhat different from that in England. The Scottish Heraldic authority is Lord Lyon King of Arms who as a High Officer of State, has complete control over all matters pertaining to Heraldry. Under Lord Lyon there are six Officers of Arms (q.v.).

In Scotland armorial bearings only pass by right from father to eldest son; all younger sons being required to matriculate at Lyon Office to receive appropriate differences.

Scottish System of Differencing – When a younger son in Scotland establishes an independent position or marries he must matriculate the parental arms with an appropriate difference usually based on what is known as the 'Stodart System', and he then abandons any temporary differences he had used previously. The temporary differences are similar to those used in English Heraldry which may be seen under

'Cadency'. The Stodart System is is based on the chart on page 104.

Scrog – The branch of a tree.

Scrope – Grosvenor Controversy – See Grosvenor.

Sea-dog – A talbot-like dog with a dorsal fin and webbed feet.

Sea-horse – Has the fore part of a horse conjoined to a fish's tail.

Sea-lion – Found in both natural and Heraldic forms.

Seals – A great deal of information with regard to early Heraldry has been obtained from the old seals. In early days few Knights and Noblemen were able to write and it therefore became the custom to seal documents instead of signing them. As soon as Heraldry became popular seals generally consisted of the Knight concerned on horse back, armed cap-à-pie and displaying his shield on which were his armorial bearings.

It is also thought by some that the origin of the supporters dates back to the early seal makers who may have found it necessary to fill a blank space on the reverse side of the shield with something realistic to support the shield.

Seax – A scimitar-like weapon dating back to the Saxon era distinguishable by a notch cut in the back of the blade.

Segreant – An expression meaning rampant when applied to the gryphon or dragon.

Sejant – Seated. The position of a lion sejant differs from that of a squirrel sejant. The fore paws of the latter being raised and the lion

Stodart System of Differencing

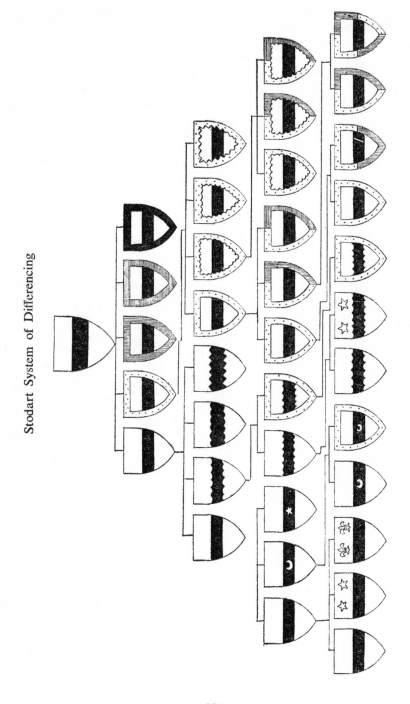

borne thus would be described as sejant rampant.

Semé – Scattered with small charges; for example semé-de-lis (scattered with fleurs-de-lis), semé of roses, etc. In some cases an alternative word entirely is used, for example 'Crusilly', meaning semé of cross crosslets.

Serpent – See reptiles.

Shack Bolt, Shackle – See fetterlock.

Shafted – Applied to the quill of a feather and to the shaft of an arrow.

Shake fork – A pall with the limbs cut and pointed.

Shamrock – The three-leaved clover or trefoil.

Sheaf of Arrows – Generally refers to three arrows, two in saltire and one in pale, with the points downwards unless otherwise stated.

Sheaf of Arrows

Sheaf of Corn – Garb (q.v.).

Sheep – Appear in Heraldry in several forms principally the ram, lamb and fleece.

Sheldrake – A water fowl closely resembling a duck.

Shield – There have been many changes in the shield throughout the ages, they have been long, round, square, kite-shaped and of other peculiar shapes some decorated and some not.

The shield has always been of prime importance in Heraldry as it is upon the shield that armorial bearings are borne.

In modern times the standard shield is approximately four units in width and five units in depth.

Ship – Various ships appear as charges including the lymphad or galley, the clipper and even modern steamships. The blazon must always give full particulars as to direction, sails, oars and tinctures.

Ships badges – As the result of the unofficial adoption of Badges by many ships during the first World War a commission was set up to consider and assign approved badges to ships. These are now considered as Heraldic.

Signs, Army, Corps and Divisional – See Regimental insignia.

Sinister – The left hand side of the shield from the point of view of the bearer i.e. the right side to the viewer.

Siren – Mermaid.

Sixfoil – One of the members of the foil family containing six petals.

Slip – A twig with two or three leaves.

Slipped – An expression referring to a flower which has a stem with two or three leaves attached to it.

Snake – See Reptile.

Soaring – Flying aloft.

Somerset Herald – One of the Officers of Arms (q.v.).

Spancelled – An expression used for a horse when two of its legs are fettered to a log of wood.

Spear – May appear as a charge in various forms. Unless otherwise stated it takes the form of a tilting spear. It may also be described as a shivered lance or a broken spear in which case the upper half has normally been broken off or severed.

Sphere – See globe.

Spider – Sometimes found as a charge.

Spread Eagle – An eagle displayed.

Spur – When used as a charge is generally borne with the straps pendent and the rowel downwards.

Spur rowel – The pointed wheel at the back of the spur similar to a mullet but generally borne pierced.

Squirrel – The animal of that name.

S.S. Collar of – See Collar.

Stafford Knot – See Knot.

Stag – An animal much used in Scottish Heraldry bearing antlers or attires.

Stall plate – A square or oblong plate emblazoned with the arms of Knights of the Garter, the Thistle and the Bath and fixed to the stalls in their respective chapels. Those of the Garter Knights at St. George's

Chapel, Windsor are generally referred to as 'Garter Plates'.

Standard – Used particularly in early days, was a narrow and tapering flag (sometimes with swallow tails) always of considerable length, the higher the rank of its owner the longer the standard. It was used solely for purposes of pageantry and particularly for the display of badges and livery colours.

Star – See Estoile.

Statant – An expression applied to an animal standing on all four feet.

Steam Ship – See Ship.

Steps – See Degrees.

Stock – The stump of a tree and sometimes applied to the shaft of an anchor.

Stork – A bird seldom distinguishable from the heron and the crane.

Stringed – Having strings or ribbons attached such as those on the bugle horn. May also refer to the strings of a harp when of a different tincture from the frame.

Sub-ordinaries – Considered as lesser charges from the ordinaries (q.v.) but of very frequent appear-

Bordure

106

ance in Heraldry. They consist of:

1. The Bordure. This is the Heraldic name given to a border and merely consists of a different colour placed right round the shield, or if the blazon includes a chief, the Bordure merely refers to the remainder of the field.

2. The Escutcheon. This may be borne singly or in multiples and it merely consists of a shield placed upon or within the field. If it is borne singly it must obviously be drawn appreciably smaller than the field would be if merely within a bordure.

Escutcheon

3. The Orle. This is a small bordure around the field but instead of running round the edge of the field a small strip of the field of similar width is left round the outside of the Orle. The Orle may be a continuous strip or it may consist of a number of the same charges placed 'in orle'.

Orle

4. Double Tressure. This is virtually an orle voided. In other words it consists of a double strip half the width of an orle placed in a similar position. A good example of a double tressure is that appearing in the arms of Scotland. A tressure is generally flory or flory counter flory, i.e. garnished with fleurs-de-lis.

Tressure

5. The Canton. This is virtually a miniature quarter which always appears in the dexter chief. It almost invariably carries a charge and in some cases an augmentation of honour.

Canton

6. The Gyron. One section taken from the Ordinary 'gyronny' which is placed in the dexter chief, adjacent to the dexter edge of the shield and with the hypotenuse of the triangle on its upper edge.

107

Gyron

7. Flaunches. These are always borne in pairs and consist of two arcs of a circle drawn from the dexter and sinister chief and terminating approximately ⅔ down the appropriate side of the shield.

8. The Lozenge. A diamond shape placed centrally on the shield but not reaching to its edges and with the longest part in pale.

9. The Fusil. Similar to, and treated in the same way as, the lozenge but it is longer and narrower.

10. The Mascle. A lozenge which has been voided and which leaves a small diamond shape the same colour as the field in the centre, or the void may be tinctured differently.

11. Fretty. The term fretty is normally used to describe the field, thus *gules fretty Or,* and could for this reason almost be added to the lines of partition as one finds checky, etc. It consists of bendlets and bendlets sinister interlaced. A diminutive of fretty is 'the fret' which consists of one bendlet and one bendlet sinister interlaced with a mascle.

12. The Billet. Is an oblong figure placed upright in the centre of the shield. It is seldom found on its own but more often in its diminutive form billetté, or semé of billets.

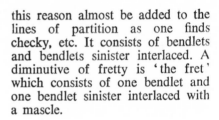

Billet

13. The Label. This consists of a strip placed horizontally across the honour point with three or five small strips pendent from it. It may be drawn to reach the sides of the shield or its ends may be cooped. The pendent strips may be oblong or splayed out at the bottom.

In early Heraldry it was sometimes used as a charge but in modern times it is always the difference mark for the eldest son (three

Fret

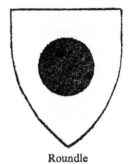

Roundle

points) or the eldest grand-son (five points) and used thus during the lifetime of the armiger.

14. The Roundle (q.v.).

15. Annulet. Is simply a ring and may be used singly, in multiples and on occasions interlaced.

Sun – Generally borne in his splendour but may be rising, setting or issuing from clouds.

Sunburst – The name given to several rays of the sun issuing from a cloud.

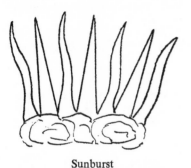

Sunburst

Supporters – The origin of supporters is obscure. One idea is that they were derived from the early practice of a knight sending two of his retainers dressed in costumes resembling animals or mythological beasts, etc. to the tournament field and there to support his shield, prepared to receive challenges, from other knights. This practice must have added greatly to the general gala atmosphere of a tournament and it was possible for a knight who did not distinguish himself in the actual fighting to become the talk of the tournament by the wit he displayed in dressing his supporters.

The other and less romantic possibility is ascribed to the seal makers who, finding two empty spaces on either side of the armorial bearings on the seal filled it with two animals or mythological beasts.

Supporters are said to have been introduced during the reign of Edward III but there is no actual certainty of their use prior to the time of Henry VI.

Supporters are now restricted to the following classes of armiger:

1. Peers of the realm. The supporters descend with the peerage. This does not, of course, apply to life peers. Spiritual peers do not use supporters.

2. Knights of the Garter, the Thistle and St. Patrick and Knights Grand Cross or Knights Grand Commanders of other orders.

3. County, City and Borough Councils and certain Corporations. Though a grant of supporters to these bodies is not compulsory. It depends entirely whether or not they are prepared to pay for them.

4. A few baronets and private individuals who have for some reason been granted supporters in the past.

There have been many different supporters used in the Royal arms until the arrival of the lion and the unicorn which were first used during the time of the Stuarts.

Henry VI –
　　Two antelopes argent
　　A lion and an antelope.
Edward IV –
　　A lion and a hart both argent.
　　A lion Or and a bull sable.
　　Two lions argent.
Edward V –
　　A lion and a hart both argent
　　the latter gorged and chained
　　Or.

Richard III –
A lion Or and a boar argent.
Two boars argent.

Henry VII –
A dragon gules and a greyhound argent.
Two greyhounds argent.
A lion Or and a dragon gules.

Henry VIII –
A lion Or and a dragon gules.
A dragon gules and a bull sable.
A lion Or and a greyhound argent.

Edward VI –
A lion Or and a dragon gules.

Mary I –
A lion Or and a dragon gules.
A lion Or and a greyhound argent.

Note: During the time that the Royal arms were impaled with those of Philip of Spain Mary used for supporters an eagle and a lion.

Elizabeth I –
A lion and a dragon both Or.
A lion Or and a greyhound argent.

James I –
A lion rampant gardant Or regally crowned proper (for England) and a unicorn argent armed unguled and crined Or gorged with a coronet composed of crosses patté and a chain affixed thereto passing between the fore legs and reflexed over the back Or (for Scotland). Since when they have remained the same.

When the Royal arms are used in Scotland the supporters are transposed.

Sur tout – Over all (q.v.).

Surcoat – The light cotton coat first used during the crusades when of knee length and later cut short to thigh length on which was emblazoned the arms of the wearer. Sometimes called jupon.

Surmounted – Applied to a charge over which another charge is laid.

Swallow – Similar in every respect to the Martlet (q.v.).

Swan – Generally borne with extended wings but it is essential that the blazon should give full details.
The swan gorged with a ducal coronet to which is affixed a chain reflexed is often blazoned as a Cygnet Royal.

Swastika – A gamadion or fylfot.

Sword – The usual form of this weapon is a long straight blade with a cross handle. Any variations of this form must be given in blazon.

T

Tabbard – The name was originally given to the frock commonly worn by peasants. Eventually, however, it became essentially a Heraldic garment on the lines of a jupon worn by all Heralds and emblazoned with their Master's armorial bearings. It allowed the early Heralds to travel throughout the country and overseas with diplomatic immunity.
It is now worn by Officers of Arms on all ceremonial occasions.

Talbot – A kind of dog of the labrador type but with longer ears and generally emblazoned with his tail curved over his back.

Talent – An alternative name for the bezant.

Tau Cross – One of the early symbols found in many places throughout the world dating from prior to the Stone Age. Taken as a Heraldic charge it is found on occasions in early Heraldry but is seldom used today.

Teazel – A species of thistle used in the process of dressing cloth. It is found occasionally as a charge.

Tenné – One of the early tinctures, orange in colour, which is said to have been associated with abatements.

Thistle – Usually depicted slipped and leaved, appears on numerous occasions in Scottish Heraldry.

Thistle

Thistle, Order of – One of the senior orders of chivalry.

Thunderbolt – A bearing derived from classic mythology in which it belongs to Jupiter. It is represented by a twisted column of flame between two wings and two darts of lightning in saltire barbed at both ends.

Tierced – Divided into three parts.

Tiger – May be used in Heraldry in its natural form in which case the blazon will state Bengal Tiger or in its Heraldic form when it is treated as a monster.

Tinctures – A term loosely covering all the colours used in Heraldry including metals, colours and furs, however, in its correct application it refers only to the colours as opposed to metals and furs.

There are five tinctures used in modern Heraldry and two which may appear from time to time if reference is made to early Heraldry.

The ones in general use consist of gules-red, for which most Heraldic artists use a plain vermilion; azure-blue, the most popular tint for this colour is cobalt-blue; sable-black the best type of lamp black should be employed and not Indian ink which fades to a brown tinge; vert – green, the colour most writers recommend is emerald but as this is a very brilliant green it is probably better if mixed with an equal portion of Hooker's green; purpure – purple, purple lake is the tint employed.

Students of Heraldry setting out to become Heraldic artists should purchase Designers' colours for Heraldic work as these provide the very best quality and the effect will be slightly opaque.

Torteau – A roundle gules.

Torse – Wreath (q.v.).

Torse or Wreath

Tower – A tower is commonly represented as a single masoned

111

crenellated structure with a doorway and three windows. When the blazon states a 'tower triple towered' the three small additional towers will be issuant from the turret.

Transfixed – Pierced through.

Tower

Transposed – Reversed or otherwise placed contrary to the usual position.

Trees – Appear frequently in Heraldry, sometimes rising from a mount in base, sometimes eradicated in which case a decorative form of root system must be emblazoned and if the tree is blazoned as fructed, the appropriate fruits must be shown, generally out of proportion for emphasis.

Trefoil – Sometimes considered to be the clover leaf and sometimes the shamrock. It is the member of the foil family with three blades and the only one which is slipped.

Trefoil

Tressure – Sometimes described as a diminutive of the orle, the tressure is always double and is almost invariably flory counter flory in which case it is decorated with fleur-de-lis on the outer and inner edges.

Trick – A rough sketch of armorial bearings usually in pencil in which the tinctures are marked by abbreviations.

Tri-corporate – An expression describing a beast having three bodies conjoined to one head which is always placed on the fess point and generally shown affronté.

Trident – A fork with three barbed prongs.

Trippant – A term analogous to passant applied to animals of the chase.

Trout – The fish of that name.

Trumpet – If trumpet is stated specifically in the blazon it is to be shown as a long straight tube expanding towards its end.

Truncheon – A short cylindrical staff. A truncheon is the official badge of the Earl Marshal of England. It consists of a golden rod tipped at each end with black enamel and having the Royal arms emblazoned at one end and the Earl Marshal's at the other.

Tudor Rose – Represents the joining of the Houses of York and Lancaster. It is represented by one rose superimposed upon another either argent upon gules or vice versa and occasionally emblazoned per pale.

Turned Up – Refers to the brim of the Cap of Estate or similar type

Thomas de Berkeley 1243 in wall of South Aisle in choir of Bristol Cathedral.

of hat or bonnet when tinctured of another colour than the crown.

Tyger – Refers to the Heraldic tyger (q.v.).

Tynes – The points of a stag's attires or antlers.

U

Ulster, Badge of – Sometimes known as the bloody hand of Ulster, blazoned as argent a sinister hand cooped at the wrist apaumé gules.

Ulster, King of Arms – Originally Ulster was the name given to the King of Arms who supervised the whole of Ireland and his position continued even after the formation of the Irish free state, until in 1943 when the Republic of Ireland set up its own Chief Herald. From this date the duties of Ulster King of Arms, which were combined with Norroy, were restricted, in so far as Ireland was concerned, to the six counties of Ulster. Under the present system he works in close contact with the Chief Herald of Ireland and each recognises grants of arms made by the other.

Undé – A deeper form of wavy when applied to a line of partition.

Unguled – An expression referring to the hooves of animals when they are to be tinctured of a different colour than the body.

Unicorn – Classified as a monster (q.v.). One of the supporters of the British Royal Arms.

Unicorn Pursuivant – One of the Scottish Officers of Arms (q.v.).

Union Flag, Union Jack – The flag of Great Britain. It combines the cross of St. George, the cross of St. Andrew (saltire) and the cross of St. Patrick (saltire).

Urchin – Hedgehog (q.v.).

Urdé – A line of division which is drawn similar to the way in which the fur vair is depicted but without its horizontal line.

Urinant – Diving. An expression to denote a fish palewise with head downward.

V

Vair – One of the furs used in Heraldry (q.v.).

Vairey – Similar in shape to vair but so named when tinctures other than argent and azure are employed.

Vert – The tincture green.

Vested – Clothed.

Virolles – The bands encircling the bugle or hunting horn.

Viscount – The fourth rank in the British Peerage.

Visitations – Due to the difficulty of communication during the Middle Ages a great many people assumed arms to which they had no entitlement. In some cases these arms were similar to those already used by somebody else, and it was therefore deemed advisable to exercise greater control. For this reason by a warrant of Henry VIII dated April 6th, 1530 Thomas Benolt,

113

Clarenceux King of Arms was confirmed in his powers to travel throughout his province and summon to appear before him all persons described as Esquires or Gentlemen who were to give him adequate proof of their right to be so styled and to make use of armorial bearings. He was further empowered to enter all castles, houses, churches or other buildings and there to survey all arms and other Heraldic devices and to pull down or deface those unlawfully assumed whether they be on plate, jewels, paper, parchment or glass.

This may be described as the first of the visitations and periodically during the next two centuries further visits were made to different parts of the country by other Officers of Arms.

Detailed records were maintained of all the visitations which provide a considerable amount of valuable information in connection with Heraldic research.

Voided – The expression used where a charge has its centre removed leaving little more than the outline. Unless a specific tincture is mentioned it will be the colour of the field which shows in the gap.

Volant – Flying.

Vulned – Wounded so that the blood drips.

W

Water – Is generally shown in Heraldry by barry wavy argent and azure. If it is blazoned as waves of the sea it is normally depicted in its natural form.

Water Bouget – A charge which is based on the old-fashioned yoke on which two waterskins were hung. It is the charge which is associated with a number of crusading families.

Wattled – Used with reference to the cock's comb and wattles.

Waves of the Sea – See water.

Wavy – A line of division of narrower contour than undé (q.v.) and used particularly with barry to denote water.

Weather Vane – A charge used occasionally in old Heraldry but seldom depicted in the traditional style.

Well – Usually shown in circular form and masoned.

Wheat – Sometimes blazoned as an ear of wheat but more generally as the garb (q.v.).

Wheel – Two principal types of wheel appear as charges. If no further details are given the traditional wagon wheel should be drawn with eight spokes; if catherine wheel is mentioned the rim should be continuous and on its outer edge a small curved point protrudes from each spoke.

Whelk – Refers to the conical type whelk shell.

Whirlpool – Is depicted as a target type figure extending throughout to the edge of the shield.

Wild man – Sometimes blazoned as a savage and found frequently as supporters in Scottish arms. He is generally shown with long hair and beard, habited in a skin, bare footed and carrying a club.

Windsor Herald – One of the Officers of Arms (q.v.).

Wings – Unless otherwise stated the wings of an eagle are generally understood. A pair of wings with tips downwards are said to be conjoined in lure, if the tips are upwards they are conjoined and elevated.

Wolf – The wolf and wolf's head are seen as charges in several different positions.

Women, Bearing of arms by – Unmarried daughters by right of courtesy may bear their paternal arms including quarterings and any marks of cadency their father may use but they add no mark of difference of their own. They bear these arms on a lozenge without crest or accessories but sometimes a knot or ribbon may be draped over the top for reasons of decoration.
An unmarried woman holding office, as, for example, the principal of a college, may impale the arms of the college with her own on a lozenge during the time she holds that office. A married woman impales her paternal arms with those of her husband upon a shield.

Woodman – An alternative name for wildman.

Woolpack – A pack of wool tied on each corner.

Wreath – See torse. The six fold band placed on top of a helm in an achievement upon which the crest stands or out of which it issues. It is said to represent the ' lady's favour ' with which the old-fashioned knights went into battle.

Wyvern – One of the monsters (q.v.).

Y

Yale – An animal resembling the stag but with mouth open and tongue extended and bearing the horns of a bull.

Yellow ochre – The colour generally used to depict the gold in Heraldic painting.

York Herald – One of the Officers of Arms (q.v.).

PART TWO

GENEALOGY

INTRODUCTION

THE REASON for adding a section on Genealogical Research to a book primarily dealing with heraldry is because heraldry and genealogy are so completely bound up in each other. Without genealogy and its relevant family histories true heraldry cannot exist and without some knowledge of heraldry no genealogist can proceed very far, as armorial bearings are bound to crop up in much of the research that he will carry out.

Genealogy can be a most fascinating subject if it is handled properly, conversely it can be extremely dry and dull if one does not take the necessary 'one step further' and follow, in some measure, the personal histories of the people who crop up in the various pedigrees.

A matter of vital importance that the genealogist must always bear in mind is accuracy. Each step that he undertakes must be proven and if possible a second proof should be found confirming the first. Human error will always creep in and even such documents as birth, marriage and death certificates provided by the appropriate authorities are occasionally at fault. For example, an old man may die, who has been living on his own, with his relatives many miles away. His death has to be registered and the information given, possibly by his landlady or his Doctor or one of his friends is given in all good faith, but it may be very wide of the mark. His age maye be registered as 65 when in fact he is over 70. His wife's name may be put down on the death certificate as 'Bessie', which was the name the old man referred to her by, when in fact her real name was Margaret. It is in ways like this that errors arise and which makes matters more complicated for the genealogist.

This dictionary of genealogy does not aspire to tell the searcher how to proceed but rather to tell him where information can be obtained and the sort of things that he can look for.

A final word of warning to the would-be Genealogist. Information comes from the most unlikely sources, and I have found from experience that most bodies whether they be institutions, or even industrial companies, if appealed to, will always send a courteous and frequently helpful reply, and as an example I have obtained information from the following: The Post Office Museum, British Railways, Lloyds, Institute of Merchant Seamen, and many others, far too numerous to list in full.

A

Abbreviations – There are a number of abbreviations used in the preparation of a chart which are generally understood by all genealogists. The following list consists of the principal ones.

apptd.	– appointed.
b.	– born.
bapt.	– baptised.
Bt.	– Baronet.
bur.	– buried.
ca.	– circa (about)
co.	– county.
d.	– died.
dau.	– daughter.
diss.	– dissolved.
div.	– divorced.
d.s.p.	– **decessit sine prole.** (died without issue).
d.s.p.l.	– **decessit sine prole legitima.** (died without legitimate issue).
d.s.p.m.	– **decessit sine prole mascula.** (died without male issue).
d.s.p.m.s.	– **decessit sine prole mascula superstite.** (died without surviving male issue).
d.s.p.s.	– **decessit sine prole superstite.** (died without surviving issue).
d. unm.	– died unmarried.
d.v.p.	– **decessit vita patris.** (died within the lifetime of the father).
d.v.m.	– **decessit vita matris.** (died within the lifetime of the mother).
educ.	– educated at.

Exor.	– Executor.
Gov.	– Governor.
J.P.	– Justice of the Peace.
k.	– killed.
Kt.	– Knight.
m.	– married.
pr.	– proved.
s.	– succeeded.
yr.	– younger.
yst.	– youngest.

In addition to the above abbreviations one will find those more generally used referring to honours and awards, ranks and positions in the Services and Government and letters awarded for such appointments as Fellowship of the Royal College of Surgeons (F.R.C.S.) etc.

Abeyance – An expression used to describe a Peerage when it is vested in two or more coheirs both or all of whom have an equal claim. When there are several equal claimants e.g. descendants of the daughters and coheiresses of a deceased Peer, none can maintain a claim against the others and the Peerage remains in abeyance and cannot be held by any of them until, by the death of the other claimants, one only remains and he has the right to claim the title.

Achievements Limited – The business name for the centre of Heraldic and Genealogical Research and Art Work. A non-profit making organisation which is establishing a complete record of all Parish registers. This undertaking will take many years to complete but it is frequently worth while putting a Parish register enquiry direct to them in the first instance. Their address is:

82 Northgate,
Canterbury,
Kent.

Armigerous Families – A great many details with regard to armigerous families can be obtained from such publications as *Burkes Peerage*, *Burkes Landed Gentry*, and Fox Davies' *Armorial Families*.

Attainder – Absolute deprivation of every civil right and privilege involving a transmission of the same penalty, and a consequent forfeiture even of pure blood and descent, as well as of all hereditary claims. This was used particuarly in connection with charges of treason. It needed a special Act of Legislature and had to remain in force until it was revoked by a similar process.

Australian Research – Enquiries for birth, marriage and death certificates should be made in the first instance to the appropriate authority in the relevant state. These are as follows:

Australian Capital Territory:
The Registrar,
Birth, Death and Marriage Registry,
Canberra,
A.C.T. 2607
(For records after 1930 only)

New South Wales:
The Registrar General,
Births, Deaths and Marriages Branch,
Prince Albert Road,
Sydney,
N.S.W. 2000

Northern Territory:
The Registrar General,
P.O. Box 367,
Darwin,
N.T. 5794

Queensland:
The Registrar General,
Treasury Buildings,
Brisbane, B7,
Queensland 4000

South Australia:
The Principal Registrar,
G.P.O. Box 1351 H,
Adelaide,
South Australia 5000

Tasmania:
The Registrar General,
G.P.O. Box 875 J,
Hobart,
Tas. 7000

Victoria:
Government Statist,
295 Queen Street,
Melbourne,
Vic. 3000

Western Australia:
Registrar General,
Oakleigh Building,
22 St. Georges Terrace,
Perth,
W.A. 6000

Fees for these certificates vary with each state but it is safe to send the equivalent of $2 Australian and the balance, if any, can then be returned.

Records are available in these offices from the year 1856 but prior to this time a great many additional records were kept for the whole of Australia in Sydney, as it should of course be appreciated that before 1850 most of the arrivals to Australia were to Sydney and then immigrants travelled overland to the other states.

A great deal of information can be obtained from the shipping records which give details of the arrival of immigrants, their occupation, names of children and in many cases from where the originated.

These records are not kept at the same office that births and deaths are registered at but enquiries should be sent initially to one of the following addresses according to the appropriate state:

New South Wales:
The Honorary Secretary,
Society of Australian Genealogists,
History House,
8 Young Street,
Sydney,
N.S.W. 2000

Queensland:
The Archivist,
Commonwealth Archives Office,
Canon Hill,
Brisbane,
Queensland 4000

South Australia:
The Principal Librarian,
Public Library of South Australia,
Archives Department,
North Terrace,
Adelaide,
S.A. 5000

Tasmania:
State Librarian,
State Library of Tasmania,
Archives Section,
91 Murray Street,
Hobert,
Tas. 7000

Victoria:
The State Librarian,
State Library of Victoria,
Archives Division,
304-324 Swanston Street,
Melbourne,
Vic. 3000

Western Australia:
The State Librarian,
The J. S. Battye Library,
State Library of Western Australia,
3 Francis Street,
Perth,
W.A. 6000

In some cases it may be found that all trace is lost after the arrival of a passenger to Australia. The reason for this is that, particularly in the early days, many families shipped a disappointing son to Australia, also many people who could not make good at home decided to try their luck in a new country and in many cases immigrants wished to cut themselves completely adrift from their old ties. For this reason many changed their names on landing in Australia.

Registrations in the various Parishes in the early days left a lot to be desired and many details are missing. Early graveyards have been neglected and though headstones exist many are completely illegible.

For those wishing to obtain amateur assistance or advice a letter to the:

Honorary Secretary,
Society of Australian Genealogists,
History House,
8 Young Street,
Sydney,
N.S.W. 2000

will always produce a helpful and informative reply.

Those who wish to retain the services of a professional genealogist in Australia, application should be made to:

Heraldry Enterprises,
Suite 2, 513 Toorak Road,
Toorak,
Vic. 3142

B

Bahamas – Records date back to 1851 for births, 1850 for deaths and to 1799 in the case of marriages. Application should be made to the Registrar General, Nassau, Bahamas.

Barbados – Records of births commenced in 1890, deaths in 1924. In some cases registration is carried out by the rectors of parishes or police magistrates, the remainder by the Registrar. Registers of baptism, marriage and burial go back to as early as 1631 but prior to 1826 the information is limited to the person baptised, married or buried.

Barristers – Of those who achieve 'silk' in England all are admitted through one of the four Inns of Court, namely Lincolns Inn, The Middle Temple, The Inner Temple and Grays Inn. All the Inns except Inner Temple have published admission registers. In the case of the Inner Temple it is necessary to write to the librarian for information.

Bermuda – The Registrar General, Hamilton, has the completed registers back to 1866. Before civil registration began, church records of baptisms, weddings and burials were kept, some dating back to the 17th Century.

Bishop's Transcripts – In 1597 the Province of Canterbury decreed that copies of Parish Registers should be sent to the Registrar of each diocese at Easter time. These returns are particularly valuable where the original registers have disappeared or when seeking information with regard to birth, marriage or death in any one of a number of Parishes within the same locality.

Botswana – No information is available with regard to the supervision of records in this State.

Boyd's Marriage Index – An index available at the Society of Genealogists which lists the various marriages which have taken place in England during the period of Parish Registers. It is not fully complete but when one realises that by 1937 it was estimated that the index contained over three and a half million names, omissions are not surprising.

British Guiana – Completed registers of births and deaths from 1869 and marriages from 1903 are available from the Registrar General, Georgetown.

British Honduras – Registers of births and deaths from 1885 and marriages from 1881 are with the Registrar General, Belize.

British Military Records –
INTRODUCTION. Before the Civil War, 1642-49, there was no Regular Standing Army in England. Regiments were raised to meet special occasions and requirements and were usually known by the names of the Colonel who raised them. Of systematic records of such regiments there are none. References to military operations, and sometimes to individual officers and soldiers, may be found in 'State Papers, Domestic and Foreign', in the 'Exchequer and Audit Office Accounts', and in the Privy Council Registers. It would, however, be exceptional to find any reference in these sources to the birth-place, wife or family of any individual. 'State Papers, Domestic' include a few widows' petitions.

For the period of the Civil War and Commonweath the officers of both armies, with their regiments, are listed in *The Army Lists of Roundheads and Cavaliers*, by Edward Peacock (1865), and for Parliamentary troops much detailed information will be found in *The Regimental History of Cromwell's Army* by Sir Charles Firth and Godfrey Davies (1940). If further information is required various series of *Calendars for State Papers* during the Interregnum will probably be found to be the best starting point. Unpublished material of importance is among the Commonwealth Exchequer Papers (S.P.28).

After the Restoration of the Monarchy (1660) the sources became far more abundant. They are most conveniently approached in the first instance through the four main Lists of War Office Records. These are the printed Lists and Indexes LIII and XXVIII, and the two typescript War Office Supplementary Lists. The classes listed here cover a wide range of subjects, including military operations and administration, finance, supplies, courtsmartial etc. Some of these are not normally of much use for biographical purposes; but almost any of them may sometimes supply valuable details. Lists and Indexes LIII is an Alphabetical Guide and includes a list of the numbers and names of regiments. There are also card indexes to various classes.

Records from the War Office selected for preservation, in common with records from other Government Departments, are in general open to public inspection when they are 30 years old, though certain records, such as Embarkation Returns, are available after 5 years. There are gaps in most series due to loss or destruction; but defects in one series can often be made good by the aid of another.

RECORDS OF OFFICERS. The service records of Commissioned Officers of the British Army can be traced with approximate completeness from the year 1660. Family details and birth-places of officers were seldom recorded until the end of the 18th century. Occasionally they can be found in the applications for Commissions among

Commander-in-Chief's Memoranda (W.O.31), Certificates VOS & OS (W.O.42) from about the same time. The principal records of officers' are:

Records of Officers' Services.

Systematic records of Officers' Services were introduced only in 1829. Similar records were compiled at intervals throughout the nineteenth century. They are arranged by regiments. Some regiment's records have not been transferred to the Public Record Office and are feared lost. These records are most useful and the main series are:

(i) Returns of Officers' Services (Military Service only 1808–1810) Registers Class W.O.25. These contain no personal details.

(ii) Services of Officers returned on Full and Half-Pay, compiled in 1828, Registers Class W.O.25. These give age on being commissioned, dates of marriage and births of children.

(iii) Services of Officers on the Active List, 1829–1919, Registers Classes W.O.25 and W.O.76. These include date and place of birth, particulars of marriage and children.

The date of an officer's death, if it cannot be ascertained from any other source, can usually be found in the Paymaster General's Records of Full and Half-Pay (P.M.G. 3 & 4).

RECORDS OF OTHER RANKS. Records of Soldiers are arranged for the most part, by regiments, so that it is almost essential to know the name of their regiment in which a soldier served in order to trace his record. If it is known where he was serving on a given date, it may be

124

possible to discover his regiment from the Station Returns (W.O.17), which show where particular regiments were stationed during any particular year. Once his regiment is known, the best sources for tracing a soldier's record are as follows:

Regular Soldiers' Documents (W.O.97). These date back to 1756. Among other service records they contain the 'Discharge Certificates'. Up to the year 1883 the Certificates of soldiers 'discharged to pension' were kept separately from those discharged for other reasons, such as 'limited engagements' or 'discharges by purchase'. After 1883 all discharge certificates are preserved in one group. The records of soldiers who died whilst serving, and thus never received discharge certificates, together with those who were not pensioned, were accidentally destroyed by fire many years ago.

All discharge certificates, except for a few of the earliest, record the place of the soldier's birth and his age on the date of enlistment. After 1883, details of the next-of-kin, wife and children are sometimes given.

Pay Lists and Muster Rolls. These form an extremely comprehensive series dating from 1760 and are very useful for establishing the dates of a soldier's enlistment, and his movements throughout the world, and of his discharge or death. They are arranged by regiments in volumes, each covering a period of 12 months. There are separate classes dealing with Royal Artillery (W.O.10), Royal Engineers (W.O.11) Cavalry, Guards and Line Regiments (W.O.12), and Yeomanry, Militia and Volunteers (W.O.13).

In many of these volumes a form showing 'Men becoming Non-Effective' will be found at the end of each quarter. Where this exists, it should show the birth-place of the men discharged or dead, his trade, and his date of enlistment. Before 1883 this sometimes provides the only means of discovering the birthplace of a man not discharged to pension. By tracing him back through the *Muster Books* it may be possible to find his age shown on the day of enlistment as a recruit.

N.B.: Few W.O. classes quoted above are in themselves complete. The periods of time to which they refer can only be ascertained by reference to the lists and indexes of War Office classes.

Birth-places of soldiers may be found in the following series in War Office classes.

Description Books (W.O.25/266-688)
  Royal Artillery, Royal Engineers (W.O.54/260-316); (W.O.69/74–80)
  Royal Irish Artillery 1756-1774 (W.O.69/620)
Depot Description Books (W.O.67/1-34)
Casualty Returns (W.O.25/1359–2410. 3251–3472. Ind: 7880–8223)
  Royal Artillery, Royal Engineers (W.O.54/317–337)
Chelsea Hospital Pension Registers From 1715 (W.O.116/1 – 151; W.O.117/1 – 70; W.O.121/136)
  Foreign Regiments (W.O.122/1-14)
Royal Hospital, Kilmainham, Dublin – Pension Registers (W.O.118/1–43; W.O.119/1-70)
Regular Soldiers Documents, from about 1760 to 1900 (W.O.97/1-4231)
  Before 1883 the documents refer to pensioners only. Others which were kept separately – were eventually destroyed by fire.

Royal Artillery Records of Ser-

125

vice (W.O.69/1–16, 74–177; 626–641)

These terminate about 1877.

Marriage and children of soldiers may be found in: Lists, except for Regiments in India where they generally appear at the beginning. They only exist from about 1868. Certain *Regimental Registers of their children* are preserved at the General Register Office, Somerset House, Strand, W.C.2.

Recruits: The entry of a recruit in the Musters generally states his age and where he joined, but does not give his birthplace.

Monthly Returns

When the unit in which a man served is not known, but a place and date are given, the Regiments stationed at that place can be found from monthly Returns (W.O.17 and, from 1859 W.O.73)

(–1872 Up to about 1872 these are generally bound in with the other Musters of the Regiments at home. If they are not there look at the end of Vol. 2 of the (W.O.12) List (W.O.12/12122–13184).   The depot of the Regiment can be found from Hart's Army Lists. (1873-1880) *Musters of Brigade Depots* (W.O.12/10216–10335. W.O.16/2177–2283)   covering the period 1873–1880 are only for infantry.

N.B.: The number of the Brigade Depot does not correspond with the number of the Regiment. The number of a Regiment's Brigade Depot should be found, in the Army Lists. (1880–1888) Brigade Depots were succeeded in 1880 by Regimental Districts as at the time the Regiments were re-designed by their district rather than their number, a practice that had been out out of use for the previous sixty years (about 1820–1880). In 1880 the Regiments numbered 1-25 consisted of two battalions, those bearing numbers higher than 25 consisted of one battalion. At this time, when the territorial names were re-introduced, many of the regiments consisting of one battalion were amalgamated to form Regiments of two battalions. Thus the 84th Foot became the 2nd battalion of the York and Lancaster Regiment (formerly the 65th Foot). The numbers of the Regiment's Districts correspond with the former numbers of the Regiments; but where Regiments were amalgamated, the number which the new second battalion formerly bore is dropped. Thus there is a 65th Regimental District but no 84th Regimental District. The Regiments with which Regiments were amalgamated are given in the list of Musters (W.O.16).

Militia Records

A few Militia soldiers qualified for pensions during the French Revolutionary and Napoleonic Wars. Discharge Certificates showing place of birth and age on enlistment will be found in the class *Soldiers Documents* (W.O.97/1091–1108).

Militia Attestation Papers from 1860–1914 (W.O.96/1–1522) show place and date of birth, employer etc.

South African War 1899–1902

British Auxiliary Forces (i) City Imperial Volunteers. Certain

126

Records held at Guildhall. These show the volunteer's original unit. Enlistment papers in original unit will be found in (W.O.108/4–6).

(ii) Imperial Yeomanry – *Soldiers Documents* (W.O.128/ 165) South African Local Armed Forces (i) *Enrollment Forms;* showing place of birth, age, next of kin (W.O.126/1) (ii) *Nominal Rolls* (W.O.127/ 1–23).

N.B. The Service documents of British Regular Soldiers who served in the South African War were, for the greater part, destroyed by enemy bombing in World War II. Those which survived are held (1967) at the:

> Army Record Centre,
> Bourne Avenue,
> Hayes,
> Middlesex.

The class of Medal Rolls from 1793–1904 (W.O.100/1–371) sometimes contain a few details relating to the soldier.

RECORDS OF THE AMERICAN WAR OF INDEPENDENCE (1776–83) Muster Books and Pay Lists of many Regiments that took part in this war may be found; but the Discharge Certificates of men discharged in North America, showing place of birth and age, can very seldom be traced. A man's name, rank and date of discharge may appear, but it is very unlikely that anything else will be found.

For Hessian Troops, certain Regimental Pay Lists have been preserved, besides Account Books, etc. Here again a man's name may be found in a Pay List, but with personal details only in a few cases.

Loyalist Regiment Muster Rolls 1777–1783 (Provincial troops) are preserved at the Public Archives of Canada, Ottawa.

RECORDS OF SERVICE IN INDIA. Service records of the Regular Army in India will be found in many of the sources mentioned. The record of a man's discharge appearing in the Muster of a regiment in India gives no particulars about the man. Casualty Returns often mention the wife's name as next of kin i.e. when the soldier has actually died. Musters of regiments in India 1883–1889 are to be found in (W.O. 16/2751–2887). There are no Musters here of Artillery or Engineers in India. A soldier discharged on his return from India will be found either in the Depot Musters of his Regiment or 1863–1878 in the Musters of the Victoria Hospital, Netley (W.O.12/13077–13105), 1875–1889 in the Musters of the Discharge Depot, Gosport (W.O.16/ 2284, 2888–2916). Those of European Officers and soldiers of the Honourable East India Company's Service and of the Indian (Imperial) Army are preserved at the:

> India Office Records,
> 194 Blackfriars Road,
> S.E.1.

BOOKS OF REFERENCE.
The following may be found useful, in addition to those already mentioned:
Army Lists (Printed from 1760).
Hart's Army Lists, from 1840.
C. Dalton: *English Army Lists and Commission Registers* 1661–1714.
Col. Kingsley-Foster: *Military General Service Medal* 1793–1814. Lists by Regiments of all officers and men who received the medals when issued in 1846–47:
C. Dalton: *Waterloo Roll.* List of regiments and officers who took

part in the Battle of Waterloo, with biographical notes.

E. Dwelly: *Waterloo Muster Rolls – Cavalry Lists* of N.C.O's and men who took part. Dwelly did not live long enough to complete the Infantry Muster Rolls.

J. Kane: *List of Officers, Royal Artillery*, 1716–1899.

T. W. T. Condly: *List of Officers Royal Engineers*, 1660–1898.

Johnston: *Roll of Army Medical Services* 1727–1898.

Lt.-Col. M. E. S. Laws: *Battery Records of the Royal Artillery*, 1716–1857.

There are also various Histories of Individual Regiments. References to Military operations and personnel will be found in Admiralty, Colonial Office, Foreign Office and Home Office Records.

British Solomon Islands – No records exist before 1893, but information regarding Births, Marriages and Deaths may be obtained from the Registrar, Births, Deaths and Marriages, Suva, Fiji.

Brunei – The Registrar of Births and Deaths and the Registrar of Marriages hold completed registers. These go back in the case of births and deaths to 1922 and for Moslem marriages to 1913. There was no registration for other denominations prior to 1948.

C

Canadian Research – The Vital Statistics Act of each particular province is generally the authority governing the registration of births, marriages and deaths of that pro-

vince. Full details of the procedure can be found in ' Abstract of Arrangements respecting Registration of Births, Marriages and Deaths in the United Kingdom and other countries of the British Commonwealth of Nations and in the Irish Republic ' (published by H.M. Stationery Office), however, the following should be noted:

Alberta. The Registers dating from 1885 are with the Deputy Registrar General, Bureau of Vital Statistics, Edmonton.

British Columbia. Is divided into seventy-three registration areas and all records emanating from these areas are sent to the Director of Vital Statistics, Parliament Buildings, Victoria, British Columbia. Compulsory registration commenced in 1872 but there are many churches which have their own records dating from 1836. Indians are not subject to the normal registration but are covered by eighteen Indian Agents.

Manitoba. Completed registers dating from 1882 are deposited with the Division of Vital Statistics, Department of Health and Public Welfare, 327 Legislative Building, Winnipeg, Manitoba. A few records are held in many churches dating back some sixty years earlier.

New Brunswick. Early records prior to 1920 are held by the Secretaries of the County Boards of Health. Since 1920 when compulsory registration commenced records are deposited with the Registrar General of Vital Statistics, Province of New Brunswick, Department of Health, Fredericton, N.B.

Newfoundland. Civil registration commenced in 1891. Prior to that

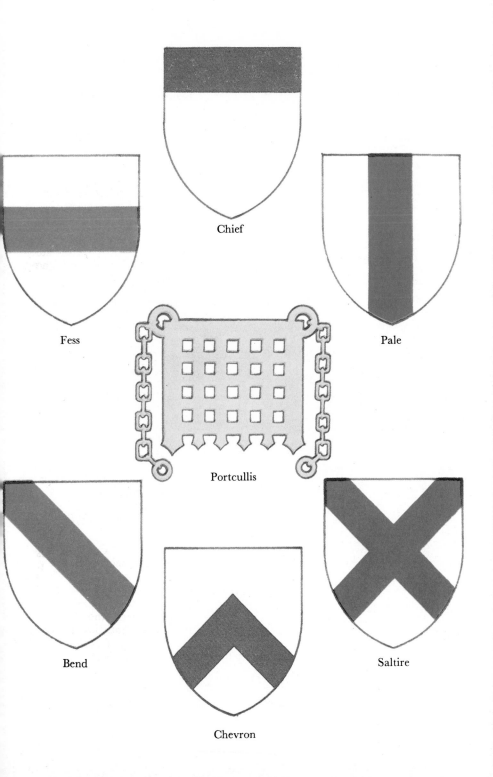

Chief

Fess

Pale

Portcullis

Bend

Chevron

Saltire

time records were held by individual registering officers. All records since 1891 are with the Registrar General, Department of Health and Welfare, St. Johns, Newfoundland.

Nova Scotia. It is not known when civil registration became compulsory but all inquiries should be addressed to the Registrar General of Nova Scotia.

Ontario. Many church records go back to 1812. The civil records date from 1869 and are available from The Registrar General of Ontario, Montreal.

Prince Edward Island. Records date from 1906 and are available from The Registrar General, Vital Statistics Branch, Department of Health and Welfare Charlottetown, Prince Edward Island.

Quebec. Duplicate registers are maintained by each of the principal denominational churches. One copy must be sent to the prothonotary of the Superior Court of the District in which the registers are kept. Registers go back to as early as 1617.

Saskatchewan. Civil registration began in 1879 prior to which there are no records of any sort. Inquiries may be sent to the Division of Vital Statistics, Department of Public Health, Regina, Saskatchewan.

Yukon. Registers dating from 1898 are maintained by the Registrar of Vital Statistics, Administration Building, Dawson, Y.T.

Northwest Territories. The registers, which date from 1870, are kept by the Registrar General of Vital Statistics Bureau of Northwest Territories and Yukon Affairs, Ottawa.

Indians. Registration for Indians is carried out on a similar basis in each province. The Indian Agents are Civil Servants and act as District Registrars of births, marriages and deaths and forward their original registrations to the Director of Vital Statistics in each province where they are retained separately from other records.

Cayman Islands. No records are available prior to 1886 when civil registration began. Inquiries should be made to the Registrar General (Commissioner).

Census – A complete record of the population taken as at a specific date. The census is held every ten years except during the War years of 1941, commencing in 1801.

The first census of value to the Genealogist is that of 1841 which is available for research purposes at the Public Record Office (q.v.).

The Returns of the Census taken on 30th March, 1851, which are also (so far as concerns England and Wales) among the Home Office Records in the Public Record Office (H.O.107), give full names, exact ages, the relationship of each member of a household to its head, and the sex, occupation and Parish and County of Birth of each person enumerated. The same information is also given in the Returns of the Census taken on 7th April, 1861 which are (so far as concerns England and Wales) among the Records of the General Register Office in the Public Record Office (R.G.9).

Census Returns of 1841, 1851 and 1861 – The Census Returns of 1841, 1851 and 1861 for addresses in England and Wales are preserved in the Public Record Office, where they may be inspected without charge by the holders of Readers' Tickets.

Temporary Readers' Tickets, valid for 7 days, may be obtained on personal application at the Enquiries Desk. Application forms for three-yearly Readers' Tickets and copies of 'Information for Readers' will be sent on request.

For persons unable to make a personal search, the Public Record Office can provide the names and addresses of two independent record agents who might be prepared to undertake a search in these Returns. The Public Record Office accepts no responsibility for arrangements made between such agents and their clients, nor can it supply information as to the scales of charges of such agents or offer any opinion of the probable cost of any particular search undertaken by them.

Alternatively, the Public Record Office is prepared to search for the entry relating to a particular household at a particular address in any one of these Returns at a fee of £3 0s. 0d. (£3 5s. 0d. for correspondents overseas) *for each such search,* and, if the search is successful, to supply a copy of the entry or particulars of the information therein contained.

Returns are arranged by enumeration districts and no search can be undertaken unless the village, or, in the case of towns, the district and street, where the household was living at the time of the Census, can be supplied. There are no street indexes to some towns, some Returns are missing or defective and some households were not at home on the Census days. *There can, therefore, be no guarantee that the required entry will be located,* and the Public Record Office will retain the fee when a search has been made even though it has produced no positive results. The Public Record Office reserves the right to decline searches where insuffi-cient preliminary information has been provided; in such cases the fee will be refunded and the names and addresses of two independent record agents supplied.

Applications for searches should be made on the appropriate form. Payments should be made in sterling, and for the exact amount specified, either by postal order or by cheque drawn on an English account or by International Money Order, payable to the Public Record Office. Applications for up to three searches may be made on any one form; further forms will be sent on request.

There may be a delay of some weeks before searches can be undertaken and the results notified to the enquirer.

Census Returns Ireland – From 1861 to 1891 these were not preserved and most earlier returns were lost in the destruction of the Four Courts during the civil wars. The few surviving Returns are kept at the Public Record Office of Ireland, Four Courts, Dublin.

Census Returns Scotland – Are kept at the General Register Office, New Register House, Edinburgh 2.

Ceylon – The original registers of general and Moslem births, marriages and deaths, and both original and duplicate registers of Kandyan marriages are deposited, when complete, in the custody of the Provincial Registers. The duplicate registers of general and Moslem births, marriages and deaths are filed with the Registrar General. Kandyan registrations date from 1859, others from 1867. Some additional records prior to civil registration are also available in the Registrar General's Office, Colombo. These are:

130

(i) Ola Thombus written up by schoolmasters 1704–1822.
(ii) Ola Thombus 1822–1851.
(iii) Records (on paper) 1852–1867.
(iv) Wesleyan records, 1822–1867.
(v) Roman Catholic records 1822–1867.
(vi) Baptist records 1822–1867.

Chancery Proceedings – Chancery proceedings can be of great importance in early research as it has been said on many occasions that very few of the land owning families have gone through history without some dispute resulting in a Chancery case. Such a case, if one is discovered, may well reveal a host of information regarding relationships and the papers of the case may include chart, pedigrees, certificates of baptisms, abstracts of deeds and wills and many other documents.

One of the many difficulties in using Chancery Proceedings is the discovery of their existence. Apart from some very early proceedings there are no printed calendars, and the M.S. calendars in the P.R.O. are divided between the six clerks in Chancery or Prothonotaries as they were called. Thus it is necessary to search each year's proceedings in six different places. Occasionally one may be fortunate enough to find the mention of a Chancery suit in a Will and once you know that the suit existed, it is not so difficult to ascertain at least the approximate date of it. Many of the deeds relating to lease and release which do have to be registered centrally, but were merely held by the two parties concerned, are at last finding their way into the various County Record Offices and gradually some record of land holdings is being built up in these offices.

Christian Names – There is a great tendency in many families for christian names to continue in some form of pattern, for example, in some families the eldest sons will always be named after their father, in others it is the custom for the eldest son to be given his mother's maiden surname as a second Christian name. Researchers will very quickly notice regular sequences of this nature and it can frequently help them in their task.

Clan Associations – Most of the larger Scottish Clans have a Clan Association which can assist very considerably in helping with genealogical enquiries. The address of the various associations can be obtained from the

Office of Lord Lyon,
King of Arms,
New Register House,
Edinburgh 2.

Class Distinction – Though one realises that in modern days all men are equal, in mediaeval times this was far from being the case and there were virtually three classes amongst the population, the Nobility, the Freemen, and the Serfs.

Records of the Nobility are not hard to come by as, generally speaking, they have been fairly well preserved by the family or for their historical value. Records of the Freemen really only come into prominence in cases where they were landowners and information can be obtained from such lists as the Manor Court Rolls, Wills etc. Information with regard to Serfs is however practically non-existent though there is one case at least on record where a serf obtained his freedom and was eventually able to purchase the land on which he worked. His descendants still occupy the estate and bear a title.

College of Arms – The Headquarters of English Heraldic authority. Here though the work carried out is principally in connection with heraldry the Heralds and Pursuivants carry out a considerable amount of genealogical research. Though the fees are high, their opportunity for research is vast as they have the records preserved at the College available to them.

County Record Offices – County Record Offices are maintained by the County Council in each county and a great many of the earlier records are now gathered together under the one roof, though the actual extent of the records held vary somewhat in the different counties.

In many cases the Record Offices are extremely helpful and will carry out a limited amount of research in return for a comparatively small fee, in other cases these offices will merely reply offering the names of local researchers who can carry out the work for you.

Courtesy Titles – These are nominal degrees of rank conceded by Royal Grace to the children of certain Peers. It applies particularly where the father's second title is borne during his lifetime by his eldest son.

Cyprus – The completed registers are kept by the District Officers of the six Districts; Famagusta, Kyrenia, Larnaca, Limassol, Nicosia and Paphos. Dates of availability vary, being as follows:
  Famagusta – 1914 but incomplete records to 1830.
  Kyrenia – 1st April 1915–31st March 1920 and from 1st January 1926. Completed registers of Marriages are deposited with the Registration Officer, Nicosia from 1923.

Larnaca – 1914 but incomplete records from 1895.
Limassol – 1899, plus British births from 1896.
Nicosia – 1900, but incomplete records for years, 1890, 1893 and 1895.
Paphos – 1850.

D

Date Reform – There is one pitfall which one must avoid in searching for ancestors in Britain. Prior to 1752 the legal year ended on 24th March, thus records dated say, 20th February 1710 would in fact be 20th February 1711 according to the historical calendar. Thus, prior to 1752, January, February and up to 24th March must be considered as being the last three months in the year.

Domesday Book – See History Affecting Genealogical Records.

E

East India Company – A great company founded in 1601 which became one of the greatest administrative units in the world. The East India Company's records are amongst the finest there are and the material is available in the India Library, Commonwealth Office, King Charles Street, Whitehall, London S.W.1.

The records contain information about both civilians and of the officers and other ranks who served in the company's army, together with Embarkation Lists from 1753–1860, giving details of all ranks embarking for India and civilians, such as free merchants and their wives.

date from 1st January 1875. In addition he holds the consular records of births 1870–1874, marriages 1861–1874 and deaths 1870–1872.

F

Falkland Islands – Registers of Births from 1846, Marriages from 1854 and Deaths from 1849 are maintained by the Registrar General, Stanley, Falkland Islands.

Fees for Certificates – 1. Public Record Office. See 'Census Return of 1841 etc.'. 'Non-Parochial Registers and Records' and 'British Military Records'. 2. Somerset House. A short certificate merely recording the birth, marriage or death costs 3/-, a full certificate giving considerably more information, all of which is of value to the genealogist, costs 13/- plus postage in either case. 3. Parishes. The fee for a certificate where no specific research is involved is 5/-. The cost for searches amounts to 3/- for the first year of search plus 1/6 for each subsequent year, payable to the vicar.

Feet of Fines – A valuable record of land transfer of great importance because the vendor joined with his wife and children or other heirs in order to avoid or overcome entail order. The foot of the fine was enrolled in the Court, the other two pieces being held by the two parties concerned. These records are almost complete and date from the time of Richard I to 1834.

Fiji – The Registrar General, Suva holds the completed records which

G

Gambia – Civil registration commenced in 1845 for births, 1835 for marriages and 1834 for deaths and these records are held by the Colonial Registrar, Bathurst, Gambia. In addition, the local missions kept certain records prior to and since these dates:

Anglican Mission:
  Baptisms, 1834–1887.
  Marriages, 1832–1887.
  Deaths, 1855–1887.

Roman Catholic Mission:
  Baptisms, 1848–1887.
  Marriages, 1851–1887.
  Deaths, 1855–1887.

Ghana – The Principal Registrar of Births and Deaths and the Principal Registrar of Marriages, both located in Accra hold records from 1885.

Gibraltar – The Registrar, Registry of Births, Deaths and Marriages, Gibraltar holds completed registers dating from 1848 for births and 1869 for deaths and 1862 for marriages in the Registrar's Office and the Presbyterian and Wesleyan Churches; all other churches from 1902. The following records are also available prior to the years given above:

Church of England:
  Garrison Churches: Births 1769, Marriages 1771, Deaths 1786,

held in the custody of the Senior Chaplain.

Cathedral: Births, Marriages and Deaths, 1836, held by the Dean.

Roman Catholic:
Births 1704, Marriages 1705, Deaths, 1697, held by the Parish Priests.

Church of Scotland (Presbyterian): Births, 1840, Marriages 1842, Deaths 1855, held by the Minister.

Wesleyan Methodist: Births 1804, Marriages 1840, Deaths 1818, held by the Minister.

Jewish: Births 1807, Marriages 1823, Deaths 1828, held by the Registrar, Hebrew Community.

Gilbert and Ellice Islands – The registers which date from 1893 are retained in the custody of the High Commissioner, Tawara.

H

History Affecting Genealogical Records – The Romans occupied Britain in 55 B.C. and although they intermarried largely with the indigenous population, no records of any sort were kept and, though some people may like to believe that they are descended from these early times, any possible chance of proving it is quite out of the question.

When the Roman Empire had collapsed, Britain was invaded by the Saxon tribes from across the North Sea and 180 years later, when Britain once again made serious contact with Europe, there was nothing left which in any way resembled a Roman Province. Instead had risen a new country called Angleland which was divided into a number of small Kingdoms, known as the Kingdoms of Heptarchy, constantly at war with one another. Once again the few survivors of this invasion gradually became intermarried with the Saxons and once again no records were ever made of the population at this time. In fact the only possible link, which any family could claim today with the Saxon period, might be where a surname is similar to one of the old Saxon place names and this does arise in a few instances.

In 1066 Britain was once again invaded, this time by the Normans, and for the next two or three centuries they were completely under Norman influence.

With the coming of the Normans the system of record-keeping began. The Normans paid great respect to birth and nobility, probably because most of them possessed neither of these qualities until ennobled by William the Conqueror for the support they gave him during the invasion.

Everyone has heard of the Domesday Book which was the earliest form of record. However, this did not contain genealogical material, but was merely designed to set out how the land in England was held and the value placed upon it. Between 1066 and 1538 when Henry VIII ordered that all Parishes should maintain records of baptisms, marriages and burials, only a very few records of any sort were in existence, partly of course because so few members of the population could read or write.

Even in the families of the nobility and landed gentry, where a certain amount of recording was carried out, there is little which survives further back than the sixteenth century and where it does it is principally hearsay evidence which has survived being told by father to son up to the time when eventually committed to paper.

In spite of Henry VIII's order many parishes were very dilatory in complying with the instruction and for this reason only a few Parish records go back as far as 1538. However, by 1600 the story was rather different and in spite of the difficulties involved most parishes had some form of record in operation, though not always very accurate.

In 1837 an Act of Parliament decreed that records of births, marriages and deaths in both England and Wales should be registered at Somerset House.

Historical Events Affecting Genealogical Research – 16th century. Many agriculturally employed moved to different areas due to the break up of the mediaeval agricultural system and the dissolution of the monasteries. Entry of patch-cloth workers who settled in England.

1534 – Break between Church of England and Roman Catholics. Henry VIII assuming title of head of the Church of England.

1536 – First order issued with regard to the Keeping of Parish Registers.

1538 – Second order issued re keeping of Parish Registers. Approximately 600 English and Welsh Parishes comply.

1547 – Third order issued with regard to keeping of Parish Registers.

1549 – Approximately 1,250 English and Welsh Parishes have records dating back to this date.

1553–58 – Mary I makes every effort to force people to return to Roman Catholicism. This has considerable affect on registers of this date.

1559 – Elizabeth I issues edict repeating the order for keeping Parish Registers.

1563 – Papal recusants heavily fined for non-attendance at the Church. Records of these findings in the quarter sessions of the county courts and in the Queen's Exchequer Courts became valuable evidence in tracing Catholic pedigrees.

1567 – Flemish exiles settle in southern counties.

1571 – Introduction of Presbyterianism into England.

1578 – Earliest Quaker records (the Society of Friends).

1589 – Records of over 5,000 English Parishes exist back to this date or earlier. Many others have lost early records.

1592 – Congregational (Independent) Church formed in London. Earliest registers however commenced 1644.

1597 – Elizabeth I issues edict that Parish Registers should be kept on parchment, all earlier records at least back to 1558 to be recopied. The same edict ordered copies of Christening, Marriage and Burial entries to be sent yearly to the office of the Bishop of the diocese. These are known as Bishop's Transcripts.

1601 – Poor Law Acts of 1597–1601 order the appointment of two overseers of the poor in each Parish. These records are of Genealogical value.

1603 – Repetition of previous orders concerning keeping of Parish Registers.

1620 – Emigration of Congregationalists to America in Mayflower.

1642 – The commencement of civil war. This had considerable effect on the keeping of Registers until 1660. Many early records lost or destroyed.

1644 – Earliest Presbyterian and Independent (Congregational) Registers.

1647 – Earliest date for Baptist Registers.

1649 – Records of about 6,600 English Parishes existing back to this date or earlier.
Commencement of Commonwealth period, many Parish incumbents disappeared.

1653 – Introduction of civil commission to grant probates. These records absorbed into the Prerogative Court of Canterbury in London.

1654 – Solemnisation of marriages restricted to Justices of the Peace. Parish Registers appointed to record births, marriages and deaths, but many failed to comply.

1660 – Parish ministers, if still living returned to their Parishes but many registers prior to this date were lost or destroyed.
Provincial ecclesiastical probate courts reopened; all Parishes again record christenings, marriages and burials in the normal manner.

1662 – Poor Relief Act introduced and appropriate records provide genealogical information.

1663 – Earliest date of Roman Catholic Registers.

1665 – The Great Plague. Burial Register entries in London increased enormously.

1666 – The Great Fire of London. Many Churches and Parish Registers destroyed.

1684 – Huguenot French Protestant Registers commenced in London.

1688 – Separate burial grounds permitted for non-conformists, Roman Catholics and Jews. Thus Church of England Parishes would not record persons buried elsewhere.

1695 – Act of Parliament imposed a fine upon all who failed to inform the Parish Ministers of the birth of a child.

1714 – Land holders take oath of allegiance and renounce Roman Catholicism; quarter session records therefore provide information with regard to Protestant dissenters and Roman Catholic recusants.

1720 – Manufacturing towns increase in population. This indicated movement of population from country districts.

1741 – Earliest date in known Scotch Registers in London.

1749 – Records of over 10,000 English Parishes existing back to this date or earlier.

1752 – New style calendar inaugurated: year to commence on the 1st January instead of the 25th March.

1754 – Marriage Act. Introduction of the publication of banns in Parishes. Marriages must take place in one of the Parishes of residence unless a licence is obtained.

1757 – India becomes part of the British Empire, many families involved in the East India Company.

1759 – Introduction of Irish labour for use in construction of canals.

1760 – The commencement of the Industrial Revolution. This has the effect of increasing the importance of towns and the consequent migration of families from country districts to the north and the midlands. This process took place over approximately 100 years.

1780 – The earliest known Methodist Registers.

1783 – Parish Register Tax imposed. This had the effect of causing omissions in the Register of christenings, marriages and burials.

1788 – Commencement of the settlement of Australia.

1790 – Commencement of army records and registration of births, baptisms, marriages and deaths.

1793 – Considerable improvement in Military Records.

1796 – Commencement of Register-keeping by Army Chaplains.

1813 – Introduction of new type of Parish Register consisting of ruled and numbered pages.

1828 – Army Half-pay Return gives useful information with regard to military officers retained on half-pay.

1829 – Army Full-pay Return gives valauble information with regard to serving officers.

1830 – First passenger railroads resulting in many families having children in different areas.

1831 – The Government prepares lists of all Parish Registers dated prior to 1813. This is known as the 1813 Parish Register Abstract.

1837 – Introduction of Somerset House as from 1st July.
Over 6,000 volumes of Church Registers received by the Registrar General in London from non-conformists all over England. These are now at the Public Record Office.

1841 – First population census of value to genealogists.

1846 – Irish potato famine. Many Irish immigrants settled in North West, particularly Liverpool and Manchester.

1851 – Improved population census.

1858 – Probate Courts taken from ecclesiastical jurisdiction and placed on a district and national basis.

Hong Kong – Registers of Births and Deaths are held by the Director of Medical Services and date from 1873. A few of these were lost during the Japanese occupation. Records of marriages dating from 15th September 1945 are held by the Registrar.

Huguenots – There are three main groups of Huguenot Records available:

1. The Dutch Church of Austin Friars of which the records are now deposited in the Guildhall Library.

2. The Threadneedle Church Library, Threadneedle Street, London, E.C.

3. The French Hospital and the Huguenots' Society, University College, Gower Street, London.

I

India – Registration of Births, Marriages and Deaths of the Christian community was covered by the Christian Marriage Act of 1872. Records of all British personnel are available in the Commonwealth Relations Office, King Charles Street, London, S.W.1.

No compulsory registration exists for members of the numerous other religions in India.

Inquisitions Post Mortem – which were held on the tenants in chief relate only to the larger land owners but where they exist they are most valuable as they reveal the heir of the property concerned and his relationship to the previous owner. Indexes for these are available and some counties have printed abstracts in the County Record Office. They end with the close of Charles I's reign.

Ireland – Those people who wish to research into their family history in Ireland will in many cases find an extremely uphill task in front of them. This fact is due to the peculiar structure of Irish politics and the chain of events within the course of their history. Ireland, though known by the Romans was never colonised by them and their first real connection with the Christian world was during the 5th century when they were converted to Christianity by St. Patrick. At this time there were four provinces, Ulster, Munster, Leinster and Connaught. Each of these provinces had its own King and one of these was elected as 'Ardrig' which is the Irish name for High King, or if he was of sufficiently strong personality he generally took the position by conquest and did not wait to be elected.

In 1166 the King of Leinster was driven out of Ireland and he appealed to Henry II, King of England, for assistance, as a result of which Ireland was invaded by the English or, as they were then, the Anglo Normans.

The English rule over Ireland did not extend beyond Dublin and the immediate surrounding counties until during the time of the Tudor Sovereigns when the rest of Ireland was colonised.

When James I came to the English Throne there was a spate of Irish rebellions, as the result of which in 1609 the whole of the northern province of Ulster was cleared of its Irish inhabitants in favour of people from Scotland and England who were encouraged to settle there. Consequently the people of Ulster are mainly of Scottish and English stock and protestant in religion.

The population in the rest of Ireland is made up of three main factors. Firstly the Celtic families who are descended from the original Irish people. In many cases these families changed their names to the English equivalent in order to escape persecution during the early English rule.

The second group consists of the Anglo Norman families who settled in Ireland between 1485 and 1690. In some cases these families changed their names on settlement in Ireland to something that was more Irish in flavour.

Until the 6th December 1921 the whole of Ireland was united under the British Crown but on this date it was virtually divided into two separate countries. The six counties comprising Ulster came to be styled Northern Ireland which was united with Great Britain. The remaining twenty-six counties were formed into a republican state under the name Eire which is entirely independent of Great Britain. These counties of course comprise the old provinces of Munster, Leinster and Connaught.

On 13th April 1921 during a serious rebellion the Public Record Office in Dublin (the capital of Eire) was occupied by armed men and on the 30th June of the same year the block which contained all the Public Records was burned. These included a great many of the births, marriages and deaths and the wills.

Since that time a great deal of work has been carried out by the Irish to try and reconstitute the damaged records and though a very fine job has been done it is not unnatural to expect that there are still very serious gaps.

As most people know, Ireland is and always has been an agricultural country, dependent almost entirely on what they can grow for themselves. By 1845 the population of Ireland as a whole had risen to 8,000,000, but in 1851, as the result of the potato famine, this number had dropped to 6,500,000, while at the present time due to the constant great flow of immigrants from Eire, the population has dropped to very little over 3,000,000 in the three provinces.

These facts should be understood by the genealogist and bearing in mind that the majority of dwellers in Ulster are Protestant while almost exclusively those in the Republic of Ireland are Roman Catholics, the first question we must ask is what is the religion of the family for whom we are undertaking research. Let us now consider these two separate parts of Ireland in some detail.

Northern Ireland

Prior to 1921 the Registrar General in Dublin dealt with the registration of births, marriages and deaths in the whole of Ireland. However, since partition a Registrar General's Office has been created in Belfast, the address being as follows:

The Registrar General,
General Registry Office,
Fermanagh House,
Ormean Avenue,
Belfast.

It is here that the records of births, marriages and deaths in Ulster have been recorded since 1921. Here also will be found records of adoptions and the Census Returns of 1931, 1951 and 1961.

When applying for information to the Registrar General one should complete as much of the following information as possible.

Births:
    Full names of the child.
    Date of birth.
    Place of birth. (As much detail as possible).
    Father's name and rank or occupation.
    Mother's name and maiden surname.
Marriage:
    Full names of parties married.
    Date of marriage.
    Place of marriage. (Including address of church).
Death:
    Full names of deceased.
    Date of death.
    Place of death.
    Age.
    Rank or occupation.
    Marital status.

In addition to the above the Public Record Office was created in 1923. Here there is a permanent official, styled, The Deputy Keeper, from whom, particularly from overseas, one will always receive a courteous reply. The address is as follows:

The Deputy Keeper,
Public Record Office of Northern Ireland,
May Street,
Belfast.

Those people who are fortunate enough to be able to visit the Public Record Office may search there free of charge providing their research is Historical, Genealogical, Antiquarian or Academic.

Postal queries, providing they are for similar purposes, will generally be undertaken free of charge unless very extensive, but in this case the query must be addressed to:

The Secretary,
The Ulster Scott Historical Society,
Lawcourts Building,
Chichester Street,
Belfast.

Legal searches are not undertaken and for this purpose it is advisable first of all to contact a Belfast solicitor to undertake such a search on your behalf.

At the present time the Public Record Office contains all records of Court cases in Northern Ireland, official copies of district probate registries dated back to 1838. (Original wills only from 1900), Records of Government Departments back to the early 19th century and private archives of important families back to approximately 1600. In addition there are the usual documents to be found in a Public Record Office together with papers relating to families which in England would normally be found in a County Record Office.

Up to 1940, when Sir Neville Wilkinson, Ulster King of Arms died, the Office of Ulster was situated in Dublin Castle. However, in that year the Irish Government appointed its own Chief Herald and the Office of Ulster King of Arms became joined to that of Norroy, situated at the College of Arms, London and copies of all relevant documents are retained by each. Queries with regard to Ulster families should be sent to:

Norroy and Ulster King of Arms,
The College of Arms,
Queen Victoria Street,
London E.C.4.

There are a number of Presbyterian families in Northern Ireland and applications with regard to these families should be sent to:

The Secretary,
Church House,
Belfast.

All inquiries with regard to an ancestor who was resident in Ulster should contain as much information as possible, which for the sake of simplicity should be tabulated in roughly the following style:

(1) Surname.
(2) Christian Names in full. (It is much easier to trace John William Brown than it is to trace John Brown).
(3) Residence. (In as much detail as possible).
(4) Date and Place of birth. (If this is not available give similar details of baptism).
(5) Religion or Occupation.
(6) Date and Place of Marriage.
(7) Details of wife and of children.

Republic of Ireland – Eire

The first and most obvious place to apply for details of births, deaths, and marriages in Eire is the Registrar General's Office which opened on the 1st January 1864 when civil registration became compulsory. This office also contains the records of all Protestant marriages from 1845. The address to which to apply is:

The Registrar General's Office,
Custom House,
Dublin.

Applications for searches should in so far as is possible be sent in on the official form which will be supplied on application. The following details are asked:

Birth:
Full names of the person whose birth details are required.
Date of birth (or approximate age).
Place of birth. (Full details to be given).
Father's name and occupation.
Mother's Christian names and maiden surname.

Marriages:
Full names of the parties concerned.
Date of marriage. (If this is unknown give a period of five consecutive years in which marriage was likely to have taken place).

Deaths:
Full names of deceased.
Date of death (or period of five consecutive years within which death is believed to have occurred).

The Public Record Office for the Republic of Ireland was established in 1867. This came into being because the Public Records of Ireland were widely scattered and badly preserved. There is a permanent official in charge of this office to whom all applications should be sent.

The Deputy Keeper,
Public Record Office of Ireland,
The Four Courts,
Dublin.

As has been mentioned above, this office was largely destroyed in 1921, but nevertheless a great deal of work has been done where possible to reconstitute records and the gaps are not nearly as wide as may be supposed.

Perhaps the worst effected in the fire were the Census Returns prior to 1922 and of those remaining, there are twenty-three volumes on County Antrim for 1851, fourteen volumes for County Cavan for 1821 and in six volumes for County Londonderry for 1831. For some curious reason the returns for 1861, 1871, 1881 and 1891 were never preserved.

With regard to the Parish records of Protestants living in the Republic, these should also have been deposited at the Public Record Office. If they had been, they too would probably have been destroyed in the fire. Fortunately however an additional clause in the Act allowed a clergyman in charge of the Parish to retain his records provided he could prove adequate storage facilities. Of the 1,643 Protestant Parishes in Ireland 1,006 of those prior to 1871 were deposited and duly destroyed and the remaining 637 are still retained in their own Parishes or have been deposited at the Public Record Office since the fire. In some cases these registers go back to as early as 1634 but in most cases for the first two centuries they were badly kept but nevertheless useful information can be obtained from them. A letter to the Public Record Office will always give the answer as to whether the records of a certain parish exist and if so where they may be found.

Inquiries with regard to Quakers are well kept and may be referred to by application to:

The Society of Friends,
5 Eustace Street,
Dublin.

Catholic Parish records were not recorded as official prior to 1829 and in fact the keeping of such records at that stage was frowned

141

upon. However, application to the Priest of the relevant Parish could sometimes prove fruitful.

Details with regard to protestant parishes and name of the incumbent can be found by referring to Crockfords Clerical Directory or if a copy is not available a letter addressed to:

The Editor,
Crockford's Clerical Directory,
Oxford University Press,
Amen Corner,
London E.C.4.

or alternatively for catholic parishes, application may be made for similar information from:

The Editor,
Thom's Directory of Ireland,
Alex Thom Co. Pty. Ltd.,
Crow Street,
Dublin.

For information with regard to wills, application should be made once again to the Public Record Office where the collection from 1904 is complete and from 1858 almost complete. In addition there are many abstracts of wills which were originally made for Genealogical purposes, many of which go back as far as 1536. These too are available at the Public Record Office.

The Genealogical Office, Dublin Castle, which is the combined office of the Chief Herald and the Chief Genealogist of Ireland contains all the Heraldic records of the Republic and photo-stat copies of the early Ulster records. Applications to this Office should be sent to:

The Chief Herald of Ireland,
Genealogical Office,
Dublin Castle,
Ireland.

Many of the original Celtic pedi-grees prepared by Roger F. Ferral in the year 1709 are contained in a volume called 'Linea Antiqua'. This publication gives a great deal of reliable information with regard to many of the ancient Irish families whose surmanes begin with 'O'' and 'Mac'. This volume is of course in the Genealogical Office.

Trinity College, Dublin which is the Premier University of Ireland has the largest library in Ireland and references to any of its volumes will be made on behalf of an inquirer if they are sent to:

The Assistant Registrar,
Trinity College,
Dublin.

Furthermore, the University prepares and keeps up a complete list of all admissions to the University. In addition to details of the students, their entry, their University attainments also their father's professions and occupations may be obtained from this record entilted 'Alumni Dublinenses'.

Though it is popularly believed that a Roman Catholic cannot become a Freemason, this statement is completely inaccurate as the ban lies on the Catholic side, on the grounds that Freemasonry is a secret society. Consequently many Irish are Freemasons. Their records are well kept and many Genealogical facts can be brought to light by applying to:

The Grand Secretary's Office,
Freemason's Hall,
17 Molesworth Street,
Dublin.

Printed Sources

'The Origin and Stem of the Irish Nation' published by John

O'Hart in 1875 and generally referred to as O'Hart's Irish Families, gives an extremely ambitious genealogical record of all well known Irish families consisting generally of nothing more than a string of names. This volume must never be taken as reliable unless information taken from it is checked from some other source.

'Burke's Landed Gentry of Ireland' consists of four editions, 1899, 1904, 1912 and 1958. Prior to 1899, the Irish families were included in the English Edition entitled 'Burke's Landed Gentry', established in 1836 by John Burke and carried on by his son Sir Bernard Burke who was Ulster King of Arms.

Other printed sources include Dalton's 'King James's Irish Army List' of 1689, The Freeman's Journal, Walker's Hibernian Magazine (1771 to 1812) and old copies of the newspapers.

If reference is to be made to a Society well versed in searching Irish records there are one or two available. For example:

The Society of Genealogists,
37 Harrington Gardens,
London S.W.7

has a considerable amount of Irish material, but the Society is exceptionally busy and inquiries may take a considerable time to be answered.

Alternatively, the application may be made to:

The Secretary,
The Irish Genealogical Research Society,
82 Eaton Square,
London S.W.1

For additional searchers in Belfast application may be made to:

Messrs. Ellis,
78 May Street,
Belfast.

A certain amount of reliable information with regard to Irish military history may be obtained from:

The Military History Society of Ireland,
1 Northgate Street,
Athlone,
Co. Westmeath.

Search into Irish pedigrees should never be looked upon as being easy. One must possess a considerable amount of patience and not be in a hurry and be thankful when one is able to produce information that gives a reliable answer to one's problems.

Islands, Channel – These Islands consist of a small group of Islands close to the North West Coast of France. The principal Islands are Jersey, Guernsey, Alderney and Sark, and they are the only portions of the Duchy of Normandy which still belong to the British Crown. Acts of the British Parliament do not apply to these Islands without their consent.

Jersey.

Births, marriages and deaths have been officially recorded in Jersey since 1842.

Complete Registers of births and deaths are kept by the Parish concerned. In the case of marriages, two registers are kept, one by the Parish concerned and the other by the Superintendent Registrar. Information may be obtained by applying to:

143

The Superintendent Registrar,
States Building,
St. Helier,
Jersey.

Registration of baptisms and funerals are carried out in the Parish concerned and date from approximately 1542. Inquiries in this case should be sent to,

The Dean,
St. Saviour,
Jersey.

Searches and certificates can be obtained on application either to the Parish concerned or to the Superintendent Registrar.

Copies of Wills and Contracts relating to Real Estate are maintained and the records will be inspected if application is made to:

The Judicial Greffier,
States Building,
St. Helier,
Jersey.

It should be noted that though the national language of the Island is French, English is understood everywhere on the Island, but if copies of documents are applied for, in many cases the language used is French.

Guernsey.

The Registrar General's Office, Greffe, Guernsey maintains registers of births and deaths since 1840. Prior to this date records are maintained by the Parish Churches. Registers of marriages from 1919 onwards are also maintained in this Office, together with registers of all marriages in places other than Churches of the Church of England since 1840. All other records are main-

tained by the Churches concerned.

Alderney.

A number of registers of Alderney were destroyed during the German Occupation, 1940 to 1945, but the following are still available. Births from 3rd August 1850, deaths from 2nd August 1850, marriages from 1st July 1891. Duplicates of the registers of births and deaths from 1925 and of marriages from 1919 are maintained by the Registrar General of Guernsey.

Copies of Wills of Realty are available in the Registrar General's Office while copies of the Wills of Personality are held by:

The Registrar to the Ecclesiastical Court,
9 Lefebvre Street,
St. Peter Port,
Guernsey.

It should be noted that the Channel Islands fall within the diocese of the Bishop of Winchester.

Sark.

The remaining Islands namely Sark, Herm, Jethou and Brecqhou, all fall in the administration of the States of Guernsey and inquiries should be sent to the Registrar General of that Island.

Isle of Man – This Island, which lies approximately half way between England and Ireland, is not bound by Acts of the United Kingdom Parliament unless specially mentioned in them.

The compulsory registration of births and deaths came into operation in 1878 and that of marriages in 1849. The completed registers are deposited with,

The Registrar General,
Government Office,
Douglas,
Isle of Man.

Registrations prior to this date may be obtained from the Parishes concerned.

Wills are recorded in:

The Probate Registry,
Finch Road,
Douglas,
Isle of Man.

and the title deeds to Real Estate are preserved in the Register of Deeds at the same address.

Searches can be made and certified copies of any entries in the registers can be obtained on application to the Registrar General. The fees are exceptionally low.

J

Jamaica – Compulsory registration dates from 1st April 1878 for births and deaths and 1st January 1880 for marriages. Inquiries should be sent to the Registrar General, Kingston.

Jewish Records – There has been a considerable amount of changing of surnames amongst the Jewish population, particularly on their first arrival in England. Jews present in England in 1290 were expelled by Edward I and were not permitted to settle in England again until 1695.

There are two kinds of Jews, the Sephardic Jews who had intermarried with the Spanish and who were recorded as the Aristocracy of the Jewish World and the Ashkenazim Jews who consisted largely of the refugees from oppression in Russia, Poland and Rumania.

Examples of some known peculiarities with regard to changes in Jewish names include the following. Isaac Ben Israel = Isaac son of Israel, Mordecai Hamburger = Mordecai from Hamburg, Zevi became Hirsch, Hirschell, Hart and even Harris. Ben Uri became Phillips and Ben David became Davis.

Jewish records are retained in the synagogues and may also frequently be obtained from:

The Jewish Historical Society,
Yad Washem Building,
Har Hazicaran,
P.O.B. 1062,
Jerusalem,
Israel.

Reference may also be made to:

The Jewish Museum,
Woburn House,
Upper Woburn Place,
London W.C.1.

Judges – The judges are all appointed from members of the bar. They can thus be traced through Inns of Court. In addition all judges of the higher courts are traceable through Foster's ' Judges of England '.

K

Kenya – The Registrar General, Box 231 Nairobi, holds records of births and deaths from 1896 and marriages from 1899.

Knights Fees – Members of the nobility were in the habit of letting out land to men who thus held it directly from them and not from the crown. These holdings were known as Knights fees and called thus because they were designed to support the armed service of a Knight together with, in most cases, a number of his retainers.

This service was generally available for so many days in each year and in this manner the noblemen could be sure of providing an army for himself, or if called upon by the Sovereign. This system operated from circa 1150.

L

Lay Subsidiary Rolls and Hearth Tax Returns – Indicate the existence, locality and to some extent the status of people.

Leeward Islands –

Antigua. Records of Births, Marriages and Deaths dating from 1856 are deposited with the Registrar General.

Montserrat. Civil registration was made compulsory in 1869. Records prior to this date are held by the parish clergy. Inquiries should be made through the Registrar General, Plymouth.

St. Christopher – Nevis. The commencement of civil registration in the Presidency are widely dispersed as follows: St. Kitts, Births 1859, Marriages 1885, Deaths 1859. Nevis, Births 1860, Marriages 1925, Deaths 1861. Anguilla, Births 1901, Marriages 1925, Deaths 1901.

Earlier records are available but are retained by the ministers of the appropriate religious denominations.

Applications should be sent to the Registrar General of the Presidency.

Virgin Islands. Records dating from 1859 are held by the Commissioner. Prior to this date there are Anglican records from 1816, Wesleyan from 1800. Applications to the Registrar General, Tortola, British Virgin Islands.

Lesotho – No details of the registration procedure in this state are available at present.

Library Facilities – The Library at the British Museum receives copies of every book published. This same right is held by the Bodleian at Oxford, the University Library at Cambridge, the National Library of Wales, the Scottish National Library and Trinity College, Dublin. If therefore one wishes to carry out research in any of the numerous publications of assistance to a genealogist and one is near one of these centres, the volumes one requires are readily available there.

Public Libraries are operated by almost every city and town council and many of these hold a number of such volumes but the choice will naturally be limited.

Livery Companies – As early as the 12th century groups of London craftsmen and tradesmen, in association with each other formed guilds for the general protection and assistance of their craft or trade. Many of these livery companies as they came to be called are no longer in existence but 83 of their number still survive.

Many of these livery companies maintain records and assistance can frequently be given to the genealogist with regard to inquiries about a man who followed a particular craft or trade.

M

Malaya – Records of births and deaths in the States of Penang and Malacca date from 1869 and 1870 respectively. Those of the old Federated States date back to 1894 (in Selangor) while those of the old unfederated States were only commenced between 1915 and 1930. Marriage records are held by the Registrar of Marriages, Births and Deaths in each state.

Malta – Registration dates from 1863 and the records are retained in the Public Registry of either Malta or Gozo. Applications should be addressed to the Director of the Public Registry of Malta or Gozo. Earlier records are kept by the parish churches.

Manor Court Rolls – These rolls are to a great extent still privately owned and apart from the difficulty of tracing their ownership, chances of their surviving at all is not great. However, any such Manor Court Rolls in existence have to be registered with:

The Historical M.S.S. Commission,
Manorial Documents Registry,
Quality House,
Quality Court,
Chancery Lane,
London W.C.2.

There is legislation today which guards against their destruction or sale overseas.

Should such Rolls survive you may well be in a position to learn much of your earlier ancestors, and may even succeed in tracing them, even though they were only humble folk, for a couple of hundred years back before the start of Parish Registers.

Marriage by Licence – Marriage has often been by ' banns ', which is a notice of intention to marry, called out three times during Sunday services in the Parish Church in which the bride and bridegroom resided. If for some reason or other the parties concerned wished to dispense with this requirement they could do so by being married by licence. An occasion of this sort might arise if the couple wanted to be married in a hurry and at one stage in history it became a status symbol to be married by licence.

There were many types of licence: if the couple both lived in the same diocese it could be obtained from the bishop of that diocese but if they resided in different dioceses it was necessary to obtain the licence from the archbishop's office. If they lived in two ecclesiastical provinces it was necessary to apply to the Master of Faculties of the Archbishop of Canterbury.

Useful information is contained in what are known as the Allegations. These were statements made by the bride and bridegroom, together with bonds, which were assurances by the bondsmen and were retained in the diocesan register.

A number of marriage licences have been published by the Harleian Society and other bodies and the Society of Genealogists has many Manuscript copies.

Mauritius – Records date from 1712. Prior to 1793 they are held by the parish clergy. After this date they are available from the Registrar General.

Medical Men – If graduates in medicine they can be traced through university records which will give their parentage.

Until 1745 surgeons were linked with the barbers in the Surgeons and Barbers Company, one of the Livery Companies but in 1800 the Royal College of Surgeons was founded.

Many doctors in early times were Licenciates of the Society of Apothecaries (L.S.A.) and that body, from the late 18th century, has detailed records of people admitted. These records are now in the Guildhall Library, London. Later when the Royal College of Physicians was founded records of all doctors were kept by this institution.

Medical men in the services and the East India Company can be traced in the records of the appropriate service.

N

Naval Records – Initial enquiries with regard to naval personnel should be addressed to:

The Admiralty,
Whitehall,
London S.W.1.

New Hebrides Condominium – Applications should be made to the High Commissioner for the Western Pacific, in the case of registrations under the Pacific Order-in-Council, 1893. For registrations under the Pacific Islands Civil Marriages Order-in-Council 1907, inquiries should be sent to The British Resident Commissioner.

Newspapers – A great deal of useful information can be obtained from the newspapers; for example, important marriages are frequently written up giving names of the guests and relationship to the bride and groom, reports of important funerals frequently give the names of relatives attending, etc. Most newspapers have a library which contains complete records of past issues and frequently such information can be obtained on payment of a small fee.

New Zealand – Copies of all registers of births, marriages and deaths are held by the Registrar General, Wellington and date back to January 1848. Prior to this date there are some entries relating to births and marriages between 1840 and 1848, but the records are far from complete. Records prior to 1848 are available in the parish churches.

Marriages of members of the Forces solemnised outside New Zealand are registered with the Registrar General.

Maori births and deaths are registered under the Maori Births and Deaths Regulations 1935, but registration of Maori marriages is not compulsory.

Nigeria – Registers of births and deaths date from 1876 and for marriages from 1886. The Registrar for marriages is the Police Magistrate, Lagos, while the Registrar for births and deaths is the Assistant Director of Medical Services (Health). These officials retain the originals, while copies are forwarded to the Chief Secretary to the Government.

Non-Parochial Registers and Records – The Non-Parochial Registers and Records formerly in the General Register Office were transferred in 1961 to the Public Record Office, where they may be inspected without charge by the holders of Readers' Tickets. Temporary Readers' Tickets and copies of Information for Readers will be sent on request.

For persons unable to make a personal search the Public Record Office can provide the names and addresses of two independent Record Agents who might be prepared to undertake a search. The Public Record Office accepts no responsibility for arrangements made between such agents and their clients, nor can it supply information as to the scales of charges of such agents or offer any opinion of the probable cost of any particular search undertaken by them.

Alternatively the Public Record Office is prepared, for a fee of £3 0s. 0d. (£3 5s. 0d. for correspondents overseas) per search, to search over a period of five years and in up to three registers for an entry relating to the birth (or baptism), marriage or death (or burial) of a particular person, and, if successful, to supply a copy of the record or particulars of the information contained therein.

A list of the two main classes of Non-Parochial Registers – *Lists of Non-Parochial Registers and Records in the Custody of the Registrar General* (London, H.M.S.O., 1859) – may be available at or through a public library. Persons unable to consult this list before applying for searches should bear the following in mind: The Non-Parochial Registers relate only to England and Wales and they do not include Parish Registers of the Church of England. Almost all are from Protestant Non-Conformist Churches, but not all such churches kept their own Registers and many of their members and adherents had their births, marriages and deaths recorded in the Parish Registers: the few Roman Catholic Registers come mainly from the North of England: there are no Jewish Registers: with the exception of the Registers of the Society of Friends (Quakers) there are virtually no marriage registers: few of the Registers are of more recent date than 1837.

There is no general index to the Non-Parochial Registers and no search can be undertaken without knowing the location and preferably also the denomination of the church at which the birth, baptism, marriage, death or burial is likely to have been recorded. For larger towns searches can be undertaken only when the precise name of the church can be given. For London and its environs there are the Registers from over two hundred churches and institutions; search will not be undertaken in these unless the applicant can specify a particular church or the Registers of births either from Dr. Williams' Library (1742–1837, relating to Presbyterians, Independents and Baptists) or from the Wesleyan Methodist Metropolitan Registry (1818–1837).

There can be no guarantee that an entry relating to a particular person will be located. The Public Record Office reserves the right to decline to make a search. When a search has been made the fee will be retained, whether or not any positive result has been obtained.

Applications for searches should be made on the appropriate form. Payments should be made in sterling, and for the exact sum specified, by postal order, or by a cheque drawn on an English account or by

International Money Order payable to the Public Record Office. Up to three applications may be made on any one form; further forms will be sent on request. There may be a delay of some weeks before searches can be undertaken and the results notified to the enquirer.

The Parish Registers often contain entries relating not only to members of the Church of England but also to Dissenters, since the Registration Act of 1695 required notice of all births to be given to the Rector, Vicar, Curate or Clerk of the parish, while Lord Hardwicke's Marriage Act of 1753 virtually restricted marriages to Parish Churches, although it did not apply to Quakers or Jews and was often ignored by Roman Catholics. Many Dissenting Churches, however maintained their own Registers of births or baptisms (particularly after 1785, when the extension of stamp duty to registration in Non-Conformist Registers appeared to give official sanction to them), while a Registry of births for Presbyterians, Independents and Baptists living in and around London was established at Dr. Williams' Library in Red Cross Street in 1742 and the Wesleyan Methodists established their own Metropolitan Registry in Paternoster Row in 1818. Those Dissenting Churches which had their own cemeteries also maintained Registers of burials, while the Quakers and (until 1753) a few other Dissenting Churches maintained Registers of marriages.

In 1836 Commissioners were appointed to inquire into the state, custody and authenticity of these Non-Parochial Registers and their Report of 1838 (*House of Commons, Sessional Papers*, 1837–38, vol. 28) was followed by the Non-Parochial Registers Act of 1840. This provided that those Registers and Records authenticated by the Commissioners, together with certain unauthenticated Registers of baptisms and marriages performed at the Fleet and King's Bench Prisons, at May Fair and at the Mint in Southwark, which had been deposited in the Bishop of London's Registry in 1821, should be deposited in the General Register Office.

A new Commission was appointed in 1857 to consider a number of Non-Parochial Registers which had come to light since 1838. It made its report later in the same year (*House of Commons, Sessional Papers*, 1857-58, vol. 23), and this was followed by the Births and Deaths Registration Act of 1858, which provided for the authentication of these Registers and their deposit in the General Register Office.

The Non-Parochial Registers and Records deposited under the Acts of 1840 and 1858, together with a few unauthenticated Registers deposited subsequently in the General Register Office, were transferred in 1961 to the Public Record Office, where they have been arranged in five classes, comprising some 7,000 volumes and files. They are open to inspection without payment of a fee in the Search Rooms. There is no general index to these classes and for a search to be practicable it is necessary to know at least the approximate locality in which a birth, marriage or death occurred and preferably also the denomination of the church or chapel at which it would be likely to be registered. Extended and speculative searches in these Registers cannot be undertaken by the staff of the Public Record Office.

With one exception (the Register of the Independent Church at St. Petersburg, Russia, 1818–1840) the

Non-Parochial Registers relate solely to England and Wales. Almost all are from Protestant Non-Conformist Churches; they include several Registers of Huguenot and other Foreign Protestant Churches in England and a separate class of Registers of the Society of Friends (Quakers). Indexes to the latter are preserved in the Library of the Society of Friends, Friends' House, Euston Road, London N.W.1. The few Roman Catholic Registers which are included come mainly from the North of England; other Roman Catholic Registers remain in the custody of the present priests-in-charge of the respective churches. A few Registers relate to non-denominational institutions, such as the City of London burial ground at Bunhill Fields and the British Lying-In Hospital, Holborn. There are no Jewish Registers.

Most Non-Parochial Registers relate to the period 1775–1837, although a few do continue beyond that date to as late as 1857 and several go back as far as the middle of the seventeenth century or even, in the case of some Foreign Protestant Churches, to the sixteenth century.

A fuller account of the history of these Registers will be found in Edwin Welch, 'Nonconformist Registers' in the *Journal of the Society of Archivists*, Volume II, No. 9, pp. 411–417.

North Borneo – All registrations prior to the Japanese invasion were lost but efforts are being made to reconstruct the old registers. Registrations from 15th July 1946 are made with the Registrar of each district.

P

Pakistan – Completed registers are deposited with the Registrar General of Births, Marriages and Deaths of the respective provinces. Registration of Christian and most Parsee marriages date back to 1872 and 1865 respectively. There is no registration for Hindu, Moslem or other religious sects.

Parish Registers – These were ordered to be kept by Henry VIII in 1538.

Initially there was considerable opposition against the keeping of Parish Registers, in consequence of which, except in a very few Parishes, they are very haphazard and in many cases almost impossible to read.

Various Ordinances were passed to ensure better maintenance of the Parish records but it was only gradually that the system came to be adopted wholeheartedly.

In 1597 an order was issued by the Archbishop of Canterbury that copies of the registers should be sent each year to the Registrar of each diocese. These came to be known as the Bishop's Transcripts.

Parish Registers, Proceedings for Obtaining Information – The first step is to write to the vicar or rector of the Parish giving him as much information as possible and ask him specific questions to which you require answers.

One must remember that the Parish incumbent is a busy man who is generally poorly paid and one should, therefore, if at all possible, send him the return postage fee.

The standard fees for research are very small (see Fees for Certificates) but as it is not always possible to give an estimate for the number of years to be searched it is perhaps better to offer the incumbent a choice of either the statutory fee or a donation to the Parish funds. In most cases he will elect the latter but one should ensure that by this method he receives at least as much if not more than the statutory fee, plus postage.

The name of the incumbent can always be ascertained from the latest edition of Crockford's Ecclesiastical register.

Parish Registers, Scotland – Scottish Parish Registers commence in the middle of the 17th century. Their origin is obscure and initially they were less well kept than those in England. They are now all stored in the New Register House, Edinburgh and may be searched by personal application. Alternatively, for those living away from Edinburgh an application for search may be sent through the post, though there will be considerable delay before it can be answered.

Professional Help – Very few amateur Genealogists have time available to carry out research into their family history as they would like to and at some time or other it becomes necessary or desirable to arrange for professional assistance.

In a case where the cost is not of vital importance recourse may be made to certain professional bodies to carry out the entire research. Such bodies include:

The College of Arms,
Queen Victoria Street,
London E.C.4.

If one knows one of the Officers of

Arms personally it is better to write to him direct. If not a general letter of application to the College will be dealt with by the 'Officer of Arms in Waiting'.

Society of Genealogists,
37 Harrington Gardens,
London S.W.7.

A letter to the secretary will provide the assistance one requires but owing to a terrific volume of work in hand there may be anything up to nine months' delay before one's application can be dealt with.

Lyon Office,
New Register House,
Edinburgh,
Scotland.

Deals with Scottish applicants and a general letter addressed as above will provide information on how to proceed further.

The Scots Ancestry Research
Society,
22 York Place,
Edinburgh 2.

A non-profit making society which carries out research for its members. A membership fee of two guineas is payable on application after which researches are carried out for a reasonable charge on a rotation basis. There is usually a delay of about three to six months.

Genealogical Office,
Dublin Castle,
Dublin,
Eire.

The office of the chief Herald of Ireland, which came into existence in 1943 will carry out research into Irish families at a moderate fee but

152

there is considerable delay before work can be commenced.

Where an amateur researcher requires assistance from, say, another part of the country or overseas he can then apply to the Society of Genealogists (address given above) for the name of a local researcher who will probably be prepared to try and provide the answer to his query. Negotiation between the applicant and the researcher is left to the applicant. Fees for such researches vary considerably and one is strongly advised to ask the fee before committing oneself to a particular researcher.

Protestation Oath Rolls – These rolls dated 1641–42 are kept in the record office of the House of Lords. They contain lists of people holding office at the time who affirmed their loyalty to the crown. A similar roll named the Association Oath Roll was signed in 1696 and is held at the Public Record Office.

Public Record Office – See Census Returns 1841 etc., Non-Parochial Registers and Records, and Records of Services of Members of the Armed Forces.

Q

'Q' List or Record Publication – A guide to the publications put out by the Record Commissioners and the Masters of the Rolls. This can be obtained free of charge from H.M. Stationery Office.

R

Reasons for Undertaking Research – There are five reasons for wishing to undertake this type of research.

1. Personal, a simple interest in the family pedigree.

2. Personal, to provide a link with an armigerous ancestor with the object of establishing one's own right to use the appropriate armorial bearings.

3. Personal and general, a matter of interest in making a collection of a number of family pedigrees.

4. Professional or semi-professional, carrying out research for other people either on a purely professional basis or to occupy one's time, the other party purely paying the expenses of the research.

5. A combination of two or more of the above.

Now let us consider these in some detail. Most people have an interest in their own family, though this interest varies very considerably in different countries. Possibly the Scots are the most interested and there is an old Scottish saying 'Heredity is a hereditary study'. Because of the clan system, Scottish history goes back a long time before civic records were maintained. The family links are exceptionally strong and it is true to say that where a family history is in existence in connection with a Scottish family it is more often than not accurate.

With regard to the Welsh and the Irish, their early history may or may not be correct. The more prominent families invariably go back to the Welsh Princes or the

Irish Kings, but in the very early days both of these were somewhat numerous and most of the records were handed down by word of mouth, so one cannot vouch for their accuracy. Furthermore, the records, such as they are, pass only from father to eldest son and no details are given with regard to other relatives. Neither is there a record of births, deaths or marriages, except in so far as the really outstanding individuals are concerned.

The English are in many cases somewhat reluctant to delve into the past. There is often the fear of finding an ancestor who was born out of wedlock. There is also a reluctance to bring to light many of the lowly forebears, but if one remembers the old saying that fortunes are made and lost every four generations, then one can more readily accept the good with the bad. After all, in these modern times there is no slur on one's character even if an ancestor, of say, three hundred years ago, was illegitimate or if he earned his living as a crossing sweeper. The fact that we are in better circumstances today should be adequate recompense and we can look back over the years with pride. Conversely, if we find ourselves to be in a more lowly position than that occupied by the ancestor – then we can be inordinately proud of that ancestor.

Records of Service Honourable East India Company and Indian Government – Records of service of European members prior to independence are preserved in the India Office of Records, Commonwealth Records Office, King Charles Street, London S.W.1.

Records of Service of Members of the Armed Forces – Records of service preserved in the Public Record Office include those of members of the British Army before 1900 and those of members of the Royal Navy before about 1910, also those of other ranks (but not officers) of the Royal Marines before 1901 and of members of the Royal Irish Constabulary. They may be inspected without charge by the holders of Readers' Tickets. Temporary Readers' Tickets, valid for 7 days, may be obtained on a personal application at the Enquiries Desk. Application forms for three-yearly Readers' Tickets and copies of Information for Readers will be sent on request.

There is no general index to service records and without a certain amount of preliminary information search is not feasible. In general it is necessary to know the name (and number if possible), service, rank, ship or regiment and dates of service. Where medals are held, this information will be found engraved on the rim. Records of service have been kept in various ways in different services and at different times; for certain periods records of some kinds of service have not survived, while for others, particularly before the nineteenth century, the records of service do not give much information of a personal nature. There can, therefore, be no guarantee that the record of service of any particular person can be traced or that, if it is traced, it will necessarily be complete or supply the particular information sought. The Public Record Office reserves the right to decline to make a search. When a search has been made, the fee will be retained whether or not any positive result has been obtained.

Alternatively the Public Record Office is prepared, for a fee of £3 0s. 0d. (£3 5s. 0d. for correspondents overseas) per search to search for the basic record of service of a particular person or for the record providing a specific piece of information about him and, if this is successful, to supply a copy of the record or particulars of the information therein contained. Estimates of the cost of officially certified copies will be given on request.

Applications for searches should be made on the appropriate form. Payments should be made in sterling, and for the exact sum specified, by postal order, or by cheque drawn on an English account or by International Money Order payable to the Public Record Office. Up to three applications may be made on any one form; further forms will be sent on request. There may be a delay of some weeks before searches can be undertaken and the results notified to the enquirer.

Recussant Rolls – Give the names and residence of people found guilty of nonconformity either Roman Catholics or Protestant dissenters and there is a useful return of all convicted recussants giving their status and place of abode in August 1677 in the British Museum Manuscripts Department. (Add M.S. 20.739).

S

St. Helena – Civil registration commenced in 1852 and applications for information must be sent to the Registrar. There are no earlier records.

Sarawak – Records are held by the Director of Health and Medical Services. Those for European births date from 1910 and for Asiatic births from 1924 and Asiatic deaths from 1925. The Marriage Registrar in each district holds details of all church and civil marriages back to 1931. All Sarawak records have unfortunately been subject to the Japanese occupation and for this reason some gaps exist. Applications to the Directory, Kuching, Sarawak.

Scotland – There are quite a lot of differences between English and Scottish Genealogy which must be understood by the inquirer of Scottish origin if he is not to be beset by pitfalls. Apart from anything else, most Scottish records began later than those in England, primarily due to the turmoil in Scottish History.

It is as well to understand something of Scottish History before attempting research into Scottish genealogy. First of all one must realise that the Highlanders and Lowlanders belong to a completely different group of people. The Highlanders were of Celtic origin while the Lowlanders were of Germanic origin; in fact similar in every respect to those who overran the Roman Province of Southern Britain.

Another fallacy believed by most people is that everyone bearing the name of a clan is descended from the same stock. This is brought out very clearly by the fact that many people who took refuge in Scotland and in some cases the survivors of Scottish family feuds invariably placed themselves under the protection of another family or clan and adopted the same name as their protectors.

It is a good idea for the researcher into Scottish genealogy to obtain a copy of a Scottish Clan Map and study this in conjunction with such a book as ' Scottish Clans and their Tartans ' or ' The Clans, Septs and

Regiments of the Scottish High-
lands' both published by Messrs.
W. & A. K. Johnson of Edinburgh
as they will help considerably to
clarify the position.

Compulsory registrations of births,
marriages, and deaths was instituted in Scotland in 1855 and since
that time all the records have been
kept at:

The General Register Office of
Births, Marriages and Deaths,
New Record House,
Princess Street,
Edinburgh 2.

The fees for research and Certificates are basically the same as those
in England.

Strangely enough all the ancient
Parish registers prior to 1855 are
also maintained in the same building but they do not go back much
beyond 1700. One must of course
realise that the established Church
of Scotland is the Presbyterian
Church. Application to H.M. Registrar General will also provide information with regard to the Parish
registers, though one must be exceptionally careful that the Parish concerned is named and spelt correctly.
The reason for this is that the
Registry Clerks will not guess at a
name. Unless correctly spelt the
reply will come back as ' Unknown '
or, ' No Record '.

Census records are available for
the years 1841, 1851, 1861, 1871,
these are also maintained at New
Record House.

Testaments or Wills were proved
before the Commissariat Courts and
the following dates give the earliest
entries available.

1514	Edinburgh.
1715	Aberdeen.
1674	Argyll.
1576	Brechin.
1661	Caithness.

1637	Cumfries.
1539	Dumblane and Perth.
1867	Dunkeld.
1547	Glasgow.
1564	Hamilton and Campsie.
1630	Inverness.
1661	The Isles.
1663	Kirkcudbright.
1595	Lanark.
1561	Lauder.
1684	Moray.
1644	Orkney and Shetland.
1681	Peebles.
1802	Ross.
1549	St. Andrews.
1607	Stirling.
1700	Wigtown.

The Registers of the four Scottish
Universities, Glasgow, Edinburgh,
St. Andrews and Aberdeen will provide useful information in the case
where an ancestor matriculated at
one of the Universities. In most
cases in addition to the names of
the entrants, names of the parents
are given as well.

There are a number of Societies
in Scotland designed to help with
the study of family history. The
chief amongst these is:

The Scots Ancestry Research
Society,
20 York Place,
Edinburgh 2.

The Society was founded in 1945
as a non profit making organisation
and considerable help has been
given to inquirers of Scottish descent
both at home and overseas.

The application form supplied by
the Society asks for the following
details:

Name of persons about whom
search is being made.
Date of birth.
Place or Parish in Scotland where
born.

156

If married, name of spouse.
Date and Place of marriage.
Place of death (if in Scotland).
Was the person the owner or tenant of any land or house property in Scotland. If so give address.
What was his profession or trade.
Was he or she resident in Scotland in or after 1841. If so, where and when.

There is also:

The Society of Genealogists,
37 Harrington Gardens,
London.

which has a very excellent Scottish Library and it is frequently worth making application to the Research Section of the Society for assistance.

There are a number of printed works which may assist the researcher. These include the following:

'Scots Peerage.' (Sir James Balfour).
'A Guide to the Public Records of Scotland' deposited in H.M. Register House, Edinburgh. (Livingstone).
'The Surnames of Scotland, Their Origin, Meaning and History.' (George Black).
'Scottish Family History. A Guide to works of reference on the History and Genealogy of Scottish Families.' (Margaret Stuart).
'Fasti Ecclesiae Scoticanse.'
'Register of Deeds 1661 to 1811.'
Scots Magazine 1739 to 1826.
Kirks Session Records.
The Register of Tailzies. In England these are known as entails. First formally legalised in 1685 the register runs through to 1903.

A most important Office in connection with Scottish genealogy is the Lyon Office, Edinburgh.

Lord Lyon King of Arms is a very powerful Officer of State in Scotland and has the last word with regard to everything which concerns Scottish heraldry. The bearer of a Coat of Arms holds his Grant for himself for life and for his eldest son, but the younger sons may not bear Arms unless they have been matriculated at Lyon Office and provided with the appropriate difference marks for their particular branch of the family. These differences are decided by Lord Lyon. An extremely useful book on the subject of Scottish Heraldry is that written by Sir Thomas Innes of Learney, the late Lord Lyon which is called 'Scots Heraldry.'

Two other useful sources of information are the National Library of Scotland and:

The Scottish Genealogical Society,
21 Howard Place,
Edinburgh.

Seychelles – The Chief Civil Status Officer holds the records which for births date from 1794 and marriages and deaths from 1808.

Sierra Leone – The Registrar General holds the Marriage Registers which date from 1796, which the Chief Registrar of Births and Deaths, Medical Department, Freetown, Sierra Leone holds records of births and deaths from 1854.

Singapore – Civil Registration of births and deaths commenced in 1872, the records are held by the Registrar of Births and Deaths. The Registrar of Marriages holds the records of marriages which commenced on the following dates:

Marriage Registry	1880
St. Andrews Cathedral	1890
Presbyterian Church	1859
Cathedral of the Good Shepherd	1899
Church of St. Joseph (Portuguese Mission)	1899
Methodist Church	1890

Solicitors – Can frequently be traced through the Law Lists from which, by patient research, one can generally establish a date of death.

Somerset House – A large building overlooking the Strand in London which was built on the site of a palace originally designed for the Duke of Somerset during the reign of Edward VI but as he ended on the scaffold the proposed palace was never built. Somerset House is the home of a vast collection of records the most important of which, so far as the Genealogist is concerned, is the record of births, marriages and deaths which was started on the 1st July 1837 and covers details for England and Wales.

For procedure with regard to obtaining information from Somerset House see Somerset House, Method of Obtaining Information.

Somerset House, Method of Obtaining Information – By far the best method of obtaining information from Somerset House is to make a personal application. A search ticket can be obtained which enables one to search unrestricted for a whole day. This, however, is not a satisfactory method as research of this nature is a very tiring business; particularly when one realises that each volume measures about two feet by eighteen inches and weighs somewhere in the neighbourhood of ten or eleven pounds. By careful thought one can generally limit the area of ones search to a period of a few years and by so doing one lessens the cost and lightens the task.

If it is impossible to get to Somerset House one can apply for certificates by post though the cost is naturally slightly higher and it is necessary to give rather fuller information than one needs when undertaking ones own search. In a case of this sort the Officials of Somerset House will undertake a search covering a period of five years.

Southern Rhodesia – Official registration only began in 1904, but there are some records of deaths and marriages from 1891. Records are with the Registrar of Births and Deaths, Salisbury. Records of Marriages are held by the Secretary, Department of Home Affairs, Salisbury.

Surnames, Adoption of – English surnames date back in many cases to the 13th and 14th centuries. Welsh surnames are of considerably later origin but the Welsh were in the habit of giving a string of names with the word ap, meaning 'son of' in between; thus we can find David ap Rhys ap Guillim ap Morgan, meaning that David was the son of Rhys who was the son of Guillim who in turn was the son of Morgan and this system was used in lieu of surnames.

Surnames, Irish – Many Irish names date from before the conquest of England. In the reign of Henry II an army was sent to conquer Ireland for the English King. Many of the Irish Barons who led this enterprise remained in Ireland and established themselves.

Many of the old original Irish names were anglicised at the same time.

Surnames, Scottish – In Scotland the system of naming was different.

Life was hard and men could only live and bring up their families in safety by being banded together. These groups came to be known as 'clans' and they took the clan name as their surname.

Trinidad and Tobago – Civil registration dates from 1848. The records are held by the Registrar General, Red House, Port of Spain, Trinidad, B.W.1.

Turks and Caicos Islands – Records which date from 1863 are held by the Registrar General, Grand Turk.

T

Tanzania – Applications must be made to the Registrar General of Births and Deaths, Dar-es-Salaam. The records were only commenced on 1st April 1921, but there are some records available from 28th August 1917.

With regard to the records of Zanzibar, information may be obtained from the Custodian of Registers of Births and Deaths (Administrator General). The following records are available:

Births: Zanzibar from 1st July 1909, Pemba from 1st January 1925.
Deaths: Zanzibar from 1st March 1906, Pemba from 16th March 1907.
Marriages: from 26th August 1907.

In addition there are some records available prior to civil registration.

Births: British Consulate Books, Zanzibar from 19th July 1868 to 13th June 1913. Pemba from 26th July 1900 to 16th November 1923.
Deaths: British Consulate Books 20th May 1868 to 23rd January 1914.

Tonga – Records of births and deaths commence from 1867 and for marriages from 1892. Applications to the Registrar of the Supreme Court, Nukú alofa.

U

Uganda – The Records of births, marriages, deaths and adoptions date from 1st January 1905, though there are details of marriages for nine months earlier. These are kept by the Registrar General. In addition the Vice-Consulate at Entebbe holds a register of births which precedes civil registration.

United Empire Loyalists – Records of members are preserved in the Public Archives of Canada, Ottawa.

University Entrance – Records of all entrants to Oxford and Cambridge may be found in Alumni Oxonienses and Alumni Cantabrigienses which are available at many of the larger libraries.

Other universities issue Calendars which have the names of graduates for each year. Some of these are collected together into volumes as for example at London University and Trinity College, Dublin.

One must, however, remember there were only two universities in England until 1900, when London University was founded.

United States of America – The following information is extracted from U.S. Public Health Service December 1961).

159

For every birth and death, an official certificate should be on Publication 630A–1. (Revised record in the place where the event occurs. These certificates are prepared by physicians, funeral directors, other professional attendants, or hospital authorities. They are permanently filed in the central vital statistics office of the State, independent city, or outlying area. Information contained in the certificates is useful for many purposes and can be obtained by requesting certified copies of these original records.

To obtain a certified copy of a certificate, write to the vital statistics office in the place where the birth or death occurred. Addresses of these offices and fees charged are listed on the following pages.

In writing for a certified copy, it is suggested that a money order be enclosed with the letter together with the cost of return postage. Fees listed are subject to change. The letter should state the purpose for which the copy is needed.

The letter should give as much as possible of the following facts:

1. The full name of the person as given on the birth or death record,
2. Sex and race.
3. Parents' names, including maiden name of mother.
4. Month, day and year of the birth or death.
5. Place of birth or death (city or town, county, and State; and name of hospital, if any).

When a birth was not recorded with the vital statistics office either of two courses of action may be taken by the individual to prove birth facts:

1. Younger persons should apply to the vital statistics office at the place of birth for forms and instructions for filing a delayed certificate of birth because they will probably be asked for copies of the record on many occasions throughout life.
2. Older people should ask the agency needing evidence of birth facts what records other than the birth certificate will be accepted. Persons nearing retirement may save time by using records already in existence instead of filing a delayed record. Also, some agencies need to see such other records whether or not a delayed certificate has been filed.

An official certificate filed at or near the time of birth is the first and best proof of birth facts. However, if the birth was not recorded, two or more of the following records may be useful in establishing date of birth, place of birth, and parentage.

Records may be obtained as follows:

Hospital record of the birth – Request a certified statement from the person who has charge of the official hosiptal records.

Physician's record of the birth – If the physician who delivered the baby has a record of the birth, obtain a statement certified by him.

Baptismal or other church records – If the baby has been baptised, or has undergone some other church rite, request an official statement from the custodian of the church records.

School records – It may be possible to obtain an official statement from the person in charge of the school records, giving age (or birth date) and parent's names.

160

Insurance records – If application has ever been made for insurance, request an official statement from the insurance company of the birth facts as given on the insurance records.

Selective service records – (1) Veterans registered during World War I should write to the Federal Records Centre, 221 St. Joseph Street, Eastpoint, Georgia; (2) Veterans registered during and since World War II should write to the Selective Service Board of the State where they were registered. In either case, be sure to provide the following information: name of the person when registered, where registered, and date of birth as given on the registration.

Census Records – The Personal Census Service Branch, Administrative Service Division, U.S. Bureau of the Census, Pittsburg, Kansas, will search decennial population census records for information about age and place of birth, Request form 10-611, 'Application for search of Census Records.'

Other Federal records – The National Archives and Records Service General Services Administration, Washington 25, D.C., maintains many records which may prove a person's age or citizenship, for example: homestead applications, ship passenger lists, seamen's protection-certificate applications, pension applications, and personal records.

Other personal records – Records such as applications for motor vehicle operators permits, marriage records, employment records, and records of fraternal organisations usually include one or more facts of birth.

In obtaining these records to prove age or place of birth, remember that records created nearest the date of birth usually are the most helpful.

State	Address of Vital Statistics	Remarks
Alabama	Bureau of Vital Statistics, State Dept. Health, Montgomery 4, Alabama	State Office has records since 1908.
Alaska	Bureau of Vital Statistics, Alaska Dept. of Health & Welfare, Alaska Office Building, Juneau, Alaska	State Office has records since 1913.
American Samoa	Registrar of Vital Statistics, Pago Pago, American Samoa	Records on file since 1900.
Arizona	Bureau of Vital Statistics, State Dept. of Health, Phoenix 18, Arizona	State Office has records since 1st July 1909, also all original records filed in counties before that date.
Arkansas	Bureau of Vital Statistics, State Board of Health, Little Rock, Arkansas.	State Office has records since 1st Feb. 1914. Verification of information from this file costs 50 cents. For records before 1914 in Little Rock, Fort Smith or Texarkana, write: City Clerk in place where birth or death occurred.

162

California	Bureau of Vital Statistics, & Data Processing, State Dept., Health 631J St. Sacramento 14. California	State Office has records since 1st July 1905. For records before that date write to County Recorders in county of event.
Canal Zone	Vital Statistics Clerk, Health Bureau, Balboa Heights, Canal Zone	Central Office has records since May 1904.
Colorado	Records & Statistics Section, State Dept. of Public Health, 4210 East 11th Av., Denver 20, Colorado.	State Office has records since 1907. For records before 1907 write to County Clerk in county where birth or death occurred.
Connecticut	Public Health Statistics, Section, State Dept. of Health, State Office Building, Hartford 15, Connecticut	State Office has records since 1st July 1897. For records before that date write to Registrar of Vital Statistics of town or city where birth or death occurred.
Delaware	Bureau of Vital Statistics, State Board of Health, Dover, Delaware	State Office has records beginning with 1861 but no records available for 1863-1881.
District of Columbia	D.C. Dept. of Public Health, Vital Statistics Section, Room 1028, 300 Indiana Av., NW Washington 1, D.C.	Death records on file beginning with 1855 and birth records beginning 1871 but no death records were filed during the Civil War.

163

State	Address of Vital Statistics	Remarks
Florida	Bureau of Vital Statistics, State Board of Health, P.O. Box 210 Jacksonville 1, Florida	State Office has some records since 1865 and majority of records since 1917.
Georgia	Vital Records Service, State Dept. of Public Health, 47 Trinity Av., SW, Atlanta 3, Georgia	State Office has records since 1st Jan. 1919. For records before that date in Atlanta or Savannah, write City Health Officer in place where birth or death occurred.
Guam	Office of Vital Statistics, Division of Public Health, Dept. of Medical Services, Govt. of Guam, Agana, Guam.	Records on file since 26th October 1901.
Hawaii	Office of Health Statistics, State Dept of Health, Punchbowl and Beretania Streets, Honolulu 1, Hawaii.	Has records since 1853. 'Certificates of Hawaiin birth' (in effect, delayed certs) on file in office of Lt.-Governor of Hawaii.
Idaho	Burea of Vital Statistics, State Dept. of Public Health, Boise, Idaho.	Has records since 1911. For records from 1907-1911 write to the County Recorder in county where birth or death occurred.

164

Illinois	Bureau of Statistics, Illinois Dept of Public Health, Springfield, Illinois	Has records since 1st July 1915. For records before that date (and for copies of State Records since 1st July 1915) write to County Clerk of place where birth or death occurred.
Indiana	Division of Vital Records, State Board of Health, 1330 W. Michigan, St. Indianapolis 7, Ind.	Has records since 1st Oct. 1907. For records before that date write to Health Officer of city or county where birth or death occurred.
Iowa	Div. of Vital Statistics, State Dept. of Health, Des Moines 19, Iowa	Has records since 1st July 1880.
Kansas	Div. of Vital Statistics, State Board of Health, Topeka, Kansas	Has records since 1st July 1911. For records before that date, write to County Clerk in county where birth or death occurred.
Kentucky	Bureau of Records and Statistics, State Dept. of Health, 275 East Main St. Frankfort, Kentucky	Has records since 1st Jan. 1911, and for Louisville before that date. If birth or death occurred in Covington before 1911 write to City Health Dept.

165

State	Address of Vital Statistics	Remarks
Louisiana (except New Orleans)	Div. of Public Health Statistics, State Board of Health, 325 Loyola Av., P.O. Box 630, New Orleans 7, Louisiana	Has records since 1st July 1914. For records before that write to Parish Clerk or Parish Clerk or Parish where birth or death occurred.
New Orleans	Bureau of Vital Statistics, City Health Dept., 1W03 City Hall, Civic Center, New Orleans, Louisiana	Has birth records since 1790 and death records since 1803.
Maine	Division of Vital Statistics, State Dept. of Health & Welfare, Augusta, Maine	Has records since 1892. For records before that year write to Town Clerk where birth or death occurred.
Maryland (except Baltimore)	Division of Statistical Research & Records, State Dept. of Health, 301 West Preston St., Baltimore 1, Maryland	Has records since 1898.
Baltimore	Bureau of Vital Records, City Health Dept., Municipal Building, Baltimore 3 Maryland	Has records since 1875.

Massachusetts (except Boston)	Registrar of Vital Statistics, 272 State House, Boston 33	Has records since 1850. For records prior to that year write to City or Town Clerk, where birth or death occurred.
Boston	City Registrar, Registry Division, Health Dept. Room 1004, City Hall Annex, Boston 8, Massachusetts	Has records since 1639.
Michigan	Vital Records Section, State Dept. of Health, Old deWitt Road, Lansing 4, Michigan	Has records since 1867. Copies of records since 1867 may also be obtained from County Clerk. Village and City Clerks have records of births and deaths since 1906. Detroit records may be obtained from City Health Dept. for births since 1893, deaths since 1897.
Minnesota	Section of Vital Statistics, State Dept. of Health, 469 State Office Building, St. Paul 1, Minnesota	Has records since 1900. Copies may be obtained from Clerk or District Court of county where birth/death occurred. For records in St. Paul, Minneapolis, or Duluth, write Health Officer of city where birth or death occurred.

State	Address of Vital Statistics	Remarks
Mississippi	Division of Public Health Statistics, State Board of Health, Box 1700, Jackson 5, Mississippi	State Office has records since 1st November 1912.
Missouri	Bureau of Vital Statistics, State Dept. of Public Health and Welfare, Jefferson City, Missouri	Has records from Jan. 1910. If birth/death occurred in St. Louis (city), St. Louis County or Kansas City before 1910 write City or County Health Dept.
Montana	Registrar of Vital Statistics, State Board of Health, Helena, Montana	Has records since late 1907.
Nebraska	Bureau of Vital Statistics, State Dept. Health, State Capitol, Lincoln 9, Nebraska	Has records since late 1904. If birth occurred before that date, write State Office for information.
Nevada	Division of Vital Statistics, State Dept. Health, Carson City, Nevada	Has records since July 1911. For earlier records write County Recorder where birth/death occurred.

New Hampshire	Division of Vital Statistics, State Dept. Health, 61 South Spring Street, Concord, New Hampshire	Copies of records may be obtained from State Office City/Town Clerk where birth/death occurred.
New Jersey	State Registrar of Vital Statistics, State Dept. of Health, Trenton 25, New Jersey	State Office has records since 1848.
New Mexico	Division of Vital Statistics, State Dept. Health, Box 711, Santa Fe, New Mexico	State Office has records since 1st Jan. 1920.
New York	Office of Vital Records, State Dept of Health, Albany 8, New York	Has records since 1880. Prior to 1914 in Albany Buffalo, and Yonkers, or before 1880 in any other city, write to Registrar of Vital Statistics in city where birth/death occurred. For rest of the State, except New York City, write to State office.
New York City Bronx Borough	Bureau of Records and Statistics Dept. of Health of New York City, 1826 Arthur Av., Bronx 57	Records on file since 1898 records from 1866–1897 on file Manhattan Bor.

State	Address of Vital Statistics	Remarks
Brooklyn Borough	County Clerk, Kings County Historical Division, 360 Adams St., Brooklyn 1, N.Y. Bureau of Records and Statistics Dept. of Health New York City, 295 Flatbush Av. Ext., Brooklyn 1 N.Y.	Records for deaths on file from 1847–1865. Records on file since 1866.
Manhattan Borough	Bureau of Records and Statistics Dept. of Health of New York City, 125 Worth St., New York 13, N.Y.	Records since 1866, for Old City of NY (Manhattan and part of Bronx) death records from 1847–1865 write to Municipal Archives and Records Retention Centre of N.Y. Public Library, 238 William St., N.Y. 38 (No Fee.) Records since 1898.
Queens Borough	Bureau of Records and Statistics Dept. of Health New York City 90–37 Parsons Boulevard Jamaica 32, New York	Records prior to that year are on file with State Dept. of Health.
Richmond Borough	Bureau of Records and Statistics Dept. of Health New York City 51 Stuyvesant Place, St. George, Staten Island 1, New York	Records since 1898. Prior to that year are with State Dept. of Health.

North Carolina	Public Health Statistics Section, State Board of Health, P.O. Box 2091, Raleigh, Nth. Carolina	Records since 1 Oct. 1913 and some delayed records prior to that date
North Dakota	Division of Vital Statistics State Dept. of Health, Bismarck	Records since 1908. Some from 1893–1908.
Ohio	Division of Vital Statistics State Dept. Health G-20 State Dept. Building, Columbus 15, Ohio	Records since 20/12/1908. Before that write Probate Court in county where b/d occurred. Records since 1908.
Oklahoma	Division of Statistics, State Dept. Health, 3400 North Eastern, Oklahoma City 5, Oklahoma	
Oregon	Vital Statistics Section State Board of Health, 1400 SW 5th Avenue, Portland 1, Oregon	Records since 1903 excluding those of Portland for 1903–1915. For these write Portland City Health Dept.
Pennsylvania	Division of Statistics and Records, State Dept. Health, Health and Welfare Building P.O. Box 90, Harrisburg, Pen.	Records since 1/1/1906. Before that date write Clerk of Orphan's Court in county where b/d occurred. For b/d in city of Philadelphia from 1860–1906 apply Vital Stat. Section Dept. Health, City Hall Annex, Philadephia 7, Pennsylvania.

State	Address of Vital Statistics	Remarks
Puerto Rico	Bureau of Demographic Registry and Statistics, Dept. of Health, San Juan, Puerto Rico	Central Office has records since 22/7/1931. Prior to that date write local registrar (Registrador Demografico) where b/d occurred or central office.
Rhode Island	Division of Vital Statistics, State Dept. Health, State Office Building, Room 353, Providence 2, Rhode Island	Records since 1852. Prior that year write Town Clerk where b/d occurred.
South Carolina	Bureau of Vital Statistics State Board of Health, 1821 Pendelton St., Columbia, S.C.	Records since 1/1/1915. City of Charleston has birth records from 1877 and death records from 1821. City of Newberry has listings of b/d from late 1800s. Copies are only obtained from Charleston County Health Dept. and from Newberry County Health Dept.
South Dakota	Division of Public Health Statistics, State Dept. Health, Capitol Building, Pierre, S.D.	Records since 1/7/1906. Also access to other records for some b/d before that date.

Tennesse	Division of Vital Statistics, State Dept. of Health, Cordell Hull Office Building, Nashville 3, Tennessee	Records since 1/1/1914 and 1908–1912, also prior to 1908 for Chattanooga, Knoxville, Nashville. If b/d occurred Memphis before 1914 write to Memphis-Shelby County Health Dept.
Texas	Bureau of Vital Statistics, Dept. Health, 410 East 5th St., Austin 1, Texas	Records since 1903.
Trust Territory of Pacific Islands	Clerk of Court (district where event occurred)	Courts have records since 21/11/1952. Beginning 1950 a few records for various islands temporarily filed with Hawaii Bur. Vit. Stat's.
Utah	Division of Vital Statistics, State Dept. Health, Salt Lake City, Utah	Records since 1905. If b/d occurred 1890–1904 in Salt Lake City or Ogden, write City Board of Health. For records elsewhere in State 1898–1904 write County Clerk in county where b/d occurred.

State	Address of Vital Statistics	Remarks
Vermont	Secretary of State, Division of Vital Stat., Montpelier, Vermont	Certified copies issued by Town and City Clerks where b/d occurred or by office of Secretary of State. For information on registration procedures, how to correct a record etc., write Dept. of Health.
	Public Health Statistics Division, Vermont Dept. of Health, Burlington, Vermont	
Virginia	Bureau of Vital Statistics, State Dept. of Health, 1227 West Broad Street, Richmond 20, Virginia	Records 1853–1896 and since 14/6/1912. Between these dates write Health Dept. where b/d occurred. Birth records from 1/7/1906, death from 1/1/1906.
Virgin Islands (US) St. Thomas	Registrar of Vital Statistics, Charlotte Amalie, St. Thomas, Virgin Islands	
St. Croix	Registrar of Vital Statistics, Christiansted, St. Croix, Virgin Islands	Records on file since 1873.
Washington	Public Health Statistics Section, State Dept. Health, 214 General Administration Building, Olympia, Washington	Records from 1/7/1907. In Bellingham, Seattle, Spokane, Tacoma a copy may be obtained from City Health Dept. Before July 1907 write Auditor of county where b/d occurred.

West Virginia	Division of Vital Statistics, State Dept. Health, State Office Building No. 3, Charleston, West Virginia	Records since 1917. Prior to that year write Clerk of County Court where birth or death occurred.
Wisconsin	Bureau of Vital Statistics, State Board of Health, State Office Building, Madison 2, Wisconsin	Records since 1840.
Wyoming	Division of Vital Statistics, State Dept. Public Health, Cheyenne, Wyoming	Records since July 1909.

175

Useful Printed Sources for Research –
'Complete Peerage', edition by Edward Cockayne.
'Peerage of England'. Collins.
'The Scots Peerage' by Sir James Balthes.
'Burkes Peerage'.
'Debretts Peerage', first published 1803.
'The Landed Gentry of Ireland from 1899'.
'The Landed Gentry of Great Britain 1898', with an Irish Supplement 1937 and American Supplement 1939.
'Complete Baronetage 1900 to 1906'.
Fox Davies' 'Armorial Families'.
Burkes 'Family Records'.
Walfords 'County Families 1864 to 1920'.
Kellys 'Handbook to Titled, Landed and Official Classes'.
'The Upper Ten Thousand'.
'Dictionary of National Biography'.
'Who's Who'.
'Who Was Who'.
Gentleman's Magazine first published 1731, useful to 1868, contains many notes re distinguished people, clergy, service personnel, farmers and artisans.
United Services Journal from 1829.
Naval and Military Gazette.
Alumni Oxoniensis, by John Foster in two sections 1500 to 1714 and 1715 to 1886.
Alumni Cantabrigiensis 1751 to 1900.
The above are particularly useful in respect of clergymen who will be found referred to as 'Clerk in Holy Orders' or 'Clerk' for short.
Crockfords Clerical Directory from 1858.
'Index Ecclesiasticus' by John Foster 1800 to 1840.

Information with regard to Roman Catholic Priests is best sought through their own Church Authorities.

W

Wales – Prior to 1284 which was the year in which Edward I of England had conquered Wales and annexed it to his dominions, the basis of old Welsh Genealogy lay in tenure of land. At that time the Welsh held their land through their family groups. There was no servility, there were merely Kings and Nobles, and the mass of the Welsh freemen who were known as 'Bonheddig'.

All classes of Welsh take tremendous pride in their pedigrees, primarily because they had to, as it was through the pedigree that they claimed their right of land and many other rights and privileges.

The old Welsh pedigree may be divided into four principal sections:

1. The Biblical Section. These were people who claimed to be able to trace their pedigrees back to Biblical figures and there is reputed to have been one family which even produced a pedigree back to Noah in the Ark.

2. The Classical Section. These people claim ancestry amongst the Greek and Roman Gods and in fact the names of some of the Roman Rulers of the Government in Britain during the Roman occupation are frequently found. Descent from Knights of King Arthur's Round Table is also not a rare occurrence and in fact these two forms of pedigree vie well with many of the old Irish Family Trees.

3. The Dynastic Section. These contain many genuine names and simple pedigrees go back as far as the sixth century and represent a number of old traditions. Those in this category from the ninth century to 1284 are comparatively reliable.

4. The Bonheddig Section. These cover a wide range of princes, lords and lesser families from the period of A.D. 900 to A.D. 1200 and are also generally accurate. It is from this group that the majority of the Welsh aristocratic families emanate today.

Between 1284 and 1542, when Henry VIII imposed a new administrative system on Wales, the system remained virtually the same, but was probably a little more efficiently carried out.

From 1542 up to 1837 Welsh records may be compared with those in England. In other words, records of births, marriages, and deaths, or perhaps it would be more correct to say baptisms, marriages and burials will be found in the ecclesiastic parish records. In the earlier days they were badly kept but as time went on the general efficiency improved.

From 1837 all Welsh records of this nature are available in Somerset House.

Before dealing with the research into a Welsh family it is necessary to have some idea with regard to Welsh surnames. For example: When surnames were first adopted by the Welsh, which was rather later than in England, many of them took the English counterpart of their Christian names, thus John became Jones, William became Williams, Hugh became Hughes etc. Prior to this the Welsh had used a system of names something after this style. John ap Griffiths ap Morgan ap Rhys. In other words, John son of Griffiths son of Morgan son of Rhys. In this way the Welshman recited his pedigree through a number of generations, every time he gave his name.

For those people who are lucky enough to be able to get hold of the last definitive edition (1952) of 'Burkes Landed Gentry' there is a very careful account of Welsh genealogy written by Major Francis Jones, one of the leading Welsh scholars of the present age.

Great changes were produced in Wales during the time of Henry VIII and it was at this time that the Welsh were made aware of the College of Arms through the medium of Visitations and the great interest which the English Heralds took generally in Welsh pedigrees, and it is interesting to note in this connection that a number of Welshmen were appointed deputy Heralds.

There is a most important collection of manuscripts available for the genealogist in the National Library of Wales of which the address is:

The National Library of Wales,
Aberystwyth,
Wales.

This is one of the libraries founded by Royal Charter, granted in 1907 and like that of the British Museum it is entitled amongst other things to receive a copy of all books printed in Britain.

There are many collections of manuscripts of the older Welsh families and for those who think their family might be amongst them a letter to the library is an advisable move.

Other places where useful material can be found are the Bangor University College Library, the Cardiff Public Library, the Bodleian Oxford Library, and there are quite a number of Welsh genealogy records to be found in the Harleian manuscripts which are in the British Museum.

A very good Welsh section is also available at:

The Society of Genealogists,
37 Harrington Gardens,
London S.W.7, England.

A letter to the Secretary will always produce a courteous reply.

Welsh wills are now available at the Bishoprics, namely at Bangor, Llanduff, St. Asaph (now deposited at Bangor) and St. Davids at Caermarthen.

The Public Record Office in London contains the Equity Records, Common Law Records, including the Fines and Recoveries of the time of Henry VIII to William IV Jail Files for the period and the Plea Roles from 1485 onwards and in addition a number of miscellaneous or general records.

It is true to say that the genuine inquirer into Welsh genealogy has a far greater chance of success if he understands Welsh, as much of the old material has never been translated into English.

Wills – A will can be a most valuable document and it can equally be a most frustrating one. At its best it will give a great deal of information with regard to the testator's family together with some interesting bits of history which would probably not be found anywhere else.

Since 1858 Wills and Administrations in England and Wales present no difficulty because from that time onward they have been proved either in the Principal Registry at Somerset House or at one of the District Probate Registries. Wherever proved the printed will and administration calendars at Somerset House and at District Registries list them.

Wills prior to 1858 present more difficulty as their proving was in the hands of the Church. If a man had property in two or more diocese his will would have to be proved in one of the archbishop's courts either the Prerogative Court of Canterbury or the Prerogative Court of York and if property was held in both the provinces of York and Canterbury the proof would be found at Canterbury.

In cases where property was held in only one Archdeaconry the executors could prove his will in that Archdeaconry, but there was no bar to its being proved in a higher court and this alternative was frequently adopted because of the reluctance in having family affairs dealt with locally.

An excellent publication dealing with the whereabouts of wills is ' Wills and Their Whereabouts ' by Anthony J. Camp.

Wills, Scotland – Scottish Wills were proved before the Commissariat Courts and 1514 is the date of the earliest entry. The wills have all been indexed. An enquiry with regard to a Scottish will should be sent to H.M. Registrar General, New Registrar House, Edinburgh.

Windward Islands –
Dominica. Records date from 1860. Information may be obtained from the Registrar General.
Grenada. Records of marriages date from 1841 and births and deaths from 1866. Applications with regard to these should be sent to the Registrar General. Records prior to these dates, and some do exist, are retained by the clergy of the various denominations, the

178

oldest being in the parish church of St. George, from 1784.

Saint Lucia. The Registrar of Civil Status holds the records which date back to 1869 with a few baptismal registers to 1806.

Saint Vincent. The records are maintained by the Registrar General, Kingstown, St. Vincent and date from 1st July 1863. Some earlier records are kept by the clergy.

Writing up the Pedigree – One should never be too long before putting the results one has achieved from ones research into some sort of logical form on paper.

A family pedigree may be written up in various ways and to illustrate the different systems, the Banks family history has been set out.

First of all there is a narrative system as used in 'Burkes Peerage' and 'Burkes Landed Gentry', etc. This system is not always easy for the inexperienced genealogist to follow, but providing one keeps a clear head and a logical sequence, it is undoubtedly the most compact method and it is a system which lends itself to reproduction by means of a typewriter or photostat process.

It should be noted particularly when writing up a pedigree by this system that the sons are all listed first, followed by the daughters. Secondly, in order to keep the head of the next generation in his correct position in the chart, one uses the words 'of whom presently' against his name and on completion of the details of that generation one starts off the next generation by referring to him not only by name, but giving his position in the family, for example: 'The Eldest Son' or 'The Third Son' whichever it may be.

It is also of great importance in this type of recording if one has to clear the details of a particular branch of the family one must place a figure and a letter before each name using if necessary a mixture of Roman and Arabic figures with the letters a, b, etc. (to denote the different generations). This could be easily understood by referring to Chart No. 1. Sons are listed first commencing with figure 1, the second son is 2 and so on. This is followed by the daughters who also commence at 1. Issue from this generation became 1(a), 2(a), and the issue from generation (a), became 1(b), 2(b), etc.

The second system and one of which we are all familiar is the chart system as used in many history books. This system is undoubtedly the best when preparing the original material, but in a case where for example, say, three sons in one family each marry twice and each produce ten children, the chart will very soon become unwieldy and it will be almost impossible to keep the generations on the same line which is always preferable if it can be managed. Once again we can refer to the Banks family in Chart II and this system can easily be understood.

In addition to a chart of this nature, supposing branches of the family have moved to different parts of the world each branch can then be kept as a separate chart, if necessary on separate sheets of paper.

An alternative method, but still in the form of a chart and once again showing the Banks family is that given as Chart III. This system is best used either in the early stages of the compilation of a pedigree or in families where the number of issue has been relatively small. It is essential to keep each generation in its logical place in the chart. In a Chart of this kind each generation is headed A, B, C, etc. and beside the chart a list of notes should be set out to include information not given on the chart.

When one is collecting material to make up the details of a pedigree, one will always acquire many interesting additional scraps of information with regard to ones ancestors. This will always be of great interest to later generations and unless preserved it is the sort of information which easily becomes lost. This should be collected and may either be set out in the form of legend notes at the foot of the chart or may be written up in narrative form as a separate document. The system decided upon will depend largely on the amount of information given and on the personal whim of the narrator.

Z

Zambia –
Northern Rhodesia. The filled registers are deposited with the Registrar General, Lusaka and date from 1902. Some of the records of the British South Africa Company dating back to 1898 have also been preserved.
Nyasaland. Records of marriages have been kept from 1903 and births and deaths from 1904. There are available from the Registrar General, Births, Marriages and Deaths at Zambia.

BANKS CHART I.

Richard Banks (of the ancient family of Banks, Barons of Bally-hauris) of Kanturk House and Springfort Co. Cork Temp. Charles II m. Miss Butler and had issue,

1. John b. 22nd January 1687.

2. James b. 22nd November 1692.

3. William b. 23rd November 1694.

4. Richard of whom presently.

1. Sarah b. 1st October 1696.

2. Mary b. 3rd July 1698.
The 4th Son.
Richard Banks of Kanturk House and Springfort b. 16th July 1703 m. Jane dau. of Richard Goodwin of Coomhooly and Reindesart, Co. Cork and had issue, seven sons and two daus.

1. Richard (Rev) b. 1728. Scholar Trinity Coll. Dublin 1747, m. 1762 Catherine Grove of Bully Rimmock, Co. Cork and d.s.p. 12th August 1797.

2. William b. 20th September 1730; d. at St. Helena 16th June 1753.

3. Percival b. 23rd September 1731; killed at the Storming of Bellisle.

4. James b. 5th June 1733; d. 5th October 1801.

5. John b. 12th May 1735; d. in Portugal 29th August 1759.

6. Thomas b. 3rd June 1738; d. 24th July 1775.

7. Goodwin b. 8th December 1739.

1. Catherine b. 10th July 1732.

2. Mary b. 18th May 1734.

The youngest Son.

Goodwin Banks J.P. of Kanturk House, b. 8th December 1739; m. Mary Allan (whose family had property near Kanturk, Co. Cork), and had issue:

1. George.

2. Richard, Major North Cork Militia.

3. James.

4. Goodwin, Major 31st Regt.
The eldest son.
George Banks, J.P. of Glannanore, Castletown Roche, near Fermoy, Co. Cork; m. 1791 Mary dau, of Rev. Edward Delaney, Rector of White church or Templegall, Diocese of Cloyne and d. 29th January 1830 having had issue by her (who d. 22nd May 1837) four sons and five daus.

1. James George (Rev) of Glann, Vicar of Worminghall, Co. Buckingham; m. 17th April 1820, Letitia, dau. of Francis Talbot (of the Wexford Talbots) of Foxboro House, King's Co., by Mary his wife, widow of Robert Norton, K.C. and dau. of John Eiffe, and d. 7th November 1843 having by her had issue,

1(a) George, his heir b. 12th January 1827; m. Eliza Hamilton and d.s.p. 18th September 1871.

2(a) Francis Talbot (Rev), Vicar of Edstaston, Co. Salop b. 30th January 1833; m. 5th October 1858, Fanny Jane dau. of Edward Keane, Capt. R.N. by Sarah Ladd Peake his wife and grand dau, of Michael Keane, uncle of 1st Lord Keane and had issue.

1.(b) James Edward b. 20th April 1866.

2.(b) John Norton b. 20th November 1870.

1.(b) Letitia Sarah, b. 1st January 1860; m. 3rd July 1883 Rev.

Victor Reginald Banford, Vicar of Wigginton, Staffordshire, who d. 24th August 1920 leaving a dau.

2.(b) Frances Isabella Mary, b. 25th February 1862.

3.(b) Agnes Talbot, b. 23rd April 1864.

4.(b) Eleanor b. 13th July 1868.

5.(b) May Eiffe b. 22nd April 1873; d. 14th December 1896.

1.(a) Bridget Francis b. 9th February 1821; d. 19th March 1821.

2.(a) Mary Georgina b. 11th April; d. May 1822.

3.(a) Mary Anne Bridget b. 4th August 1823; d. August 1850.

4.(a) Francis b. 20th October 1824; d. May 1825.

2. Charles Percival of whom presently.

3. George of Kenmare, Co. Kerry.

4. Goodwin (Rev), Vicar of Charlesworth, Co. Derby; m. 1st Sarah dau. of Joseph Lea, of Davenham, Co. Chester and had two sons and one dau.,

1.(a) Joseph who d.s.p.

2.(a) James of Carringmore House, Co. Kerry b. 1840; m.1875 Elizabeth, dau. of John Dickinson of Wembrick House, Ormskirk, Co. Lancashire and has a son,
Goodwin b. 1875.

1.(a) Anne, m. 24th August 1881 Henry Daniel Connor, K.C. of Manch House, Co. Cork and has issue.
He m. wndly Elizabeth Latouche. He d. 1877.

1. Mary m. 5th August 1819 Rev. Joseph Rogerson Colter, Rector of Donoughmore Co. Cork, Senior Prebendary of Clayne, and Rural Dean, grandson of Sir James Colter of Rockforest, near Mallow Co. Cork, and d. 15th April 1851 having had issue.

2. Jane m. William Delaney of Conwaymore Co. Cork and had issue.

3. Anne m. Rev. James White, Vicar of Inchegeela, Co. Cork and had issue.

4. Susan m. Robert Bullen of Ballythomas House, Mallow Co. Cork and had issue.

5. Catherine, d. unm.
The second Son.
Charles Percival, b. 1806 m. 16th January 1840 Sarah Holmes of Maiden Hull Charleville, Co. Cork, later emigrating to Australia. He d. at Ballaret, Victoria, 5th August 1874 having had issue.

1. George Charles of whom presently.

2. Godfrey Holmes b. 3rd November 1849.

1. Susan Low b. 9th June 1842.

2. Sarah b. 10th March 1849, d. 1849.

3. Sarah b. 20th October 1850.
The Eldest Son.
George Charles b. 29th October 1840; m. Emmie Lording and by her had issue,

1. Charles George of whom presently.

1. Emmie.

2. Mary Helen.

3. Dora Susan.

The Son.
Charles George Banks, b. 30th August 1875; m. Amelia Allan, he

182

d. 14th June 1959 having had issue, Allan George b. 27th January 1912. m. 12th August, 1939 Myrtle Anne Madden and has issue,

1. Roger Howard, b. 6th October 1942.

2. Rowan Wesley, b. 13th April 1946.

1. Gail Patricia, b. 24th August 1940.

2. Glenrose Lorraine b. 22nd February 1948.

Ellen Mary b. 11th July 1908.

Note: The above is a genuine pedigree but for obvious reasons the name has been changed.

BANKS.

of the ancient family of Banks, Barons of **Ballyhauris**.
Co. Cork, Ireland temp. Charles II.

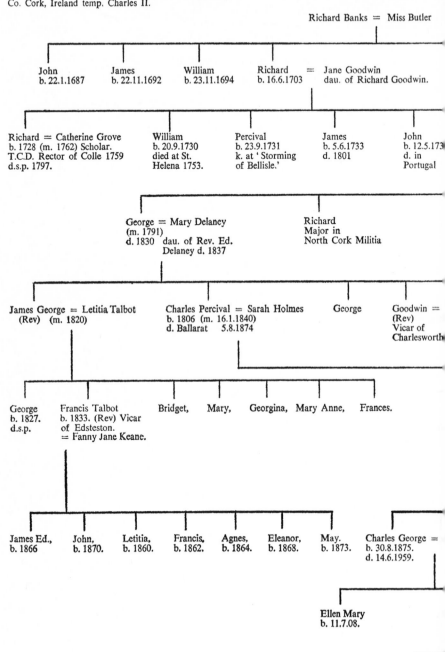

Richard Banks = Miss Butler

John
b. 22.1.1687

James
b. 22.11.1692

William
b. 23.11.1694

Richard = Jane Goodwin
b. 16.6.1703   dau. of Richard Goodwin.

Richard = Catherine Grove
b. 1728 (m. 1762) Scholar.
T.C.D. Rector of Colle 1759
d.s.p. 1797.

William
b. 20.9.1730
died at St.
Helena 1753.

Percival
b. 23.9.1731
k. at ' Storming
of Bellisle.'

James
b. 5.6.1733
d. 1801

John
b. 12.5.173
d. in
Portugal

George = Mary Delaney
(m. 1791)
d. 1830   dau. of Rev. Ed.
Delaney d. 1837

Richard
Major in
North Cork Militia

James George = Letitia Talbot
(Rev)   (m. 1820)

Charles Percival = Sarah Holmes
b. 1806 (m. 16.1.1840)
d. Ballarat   5.8.1874

George

Goodwin =
(Rev)
Vicar of
Charlesworth

George
b. 1827.
d.s.p.

Francis Talbot
b. 1833. (Rev) Vicar
of Edsteston.
= Fanny Jane Keane.

Bridget,   Mary,   Georgina, Mary Anne,   Frances.

James Ed.,
b. 1866

John,
b. 1870.

Letitia,
b. 1860.

Francis,
b. 1862.

Agnes,
b. 1864.

Eleanor,
b. 1868.

May.
b. 1873.

Charles George =
b. 30.8.1875.
d. 14.6.1959.

Ellen Mary
b. 11.7.08.

Gail Patricia
b. 24.8.1940.

CHART II.

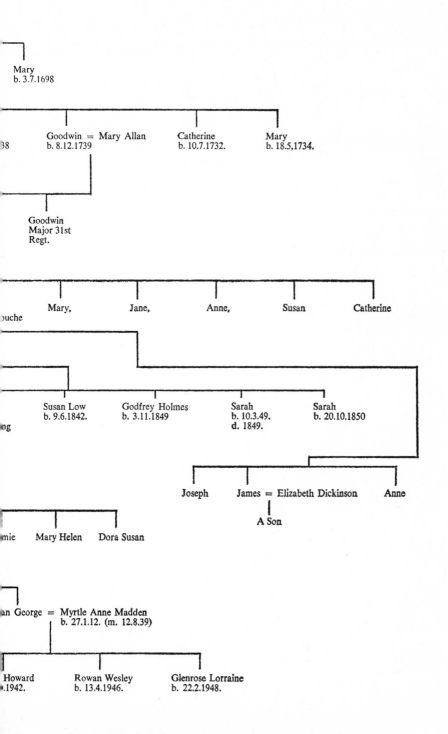

Mary
b. 3.7.1698

Goodwin = Mary Allan   Catherine   Mary
88   b. 8.12.1739   b. 10.7.1732.   b. 18.5,1734.

Goodwin
Major 31st
Regt.

Mary,   Jane,   Anne,   Susan   Catherine
ɔuche

Susan Low   Godfrey Holmes   Sarah   Sarah
b. 9.6.1842.   b. 3.11.1849   b. 10.3.49.   b. 20.10.1850
ng   d. 1849.

Joseph   James = Elizabeth Dickinson   Anne

A Son

mie   Mary Helen   Dora Susan

an George = Myrtle Anne Madden
            b. 27.1.12. (m. 12.8.39)

Howard   Rowan Wesley   Glenrose Lorraine
1942.   b. 13.4.1946.   b. 22.2.1948.

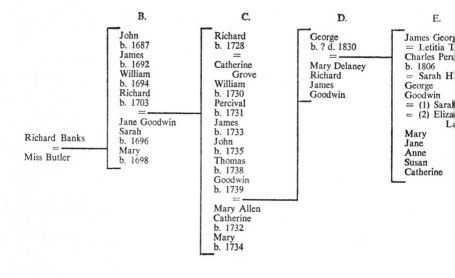

	B.	C.	D.	E.
	John b. 1687 James b. 1692 William b. 1694 Richard b. 1703 = Jane Goodwin Sarah b. 1696 Mary b. 1698	Richard b. 1728 = Catherine Grove William b. 1730 Percival b. 1731 James b. 1733 John b. 1735 Thomas b. 1738 Goodwin b. 1739 = Mary Allen Catherine b. 1732 Mary b. 1734	George b. ? d. 1830 = Mary Delaney Richard James Goodwin	James Geor[= Letitia T Charles Perc b. 1806 = Sarah H George Goodwin = (1) Sara[= (2) Eliza L. Mary Jane Anne Susan Catherine

Richard Banks
=
Miss Butler

Notes

Generation.

A. Richard Banks of the ancient family of Banks,
    Barons of Ballyhauris of Kanturk House and
    Springfort Co. Cork, Ireland, Temp. Charles II.

B. Jane Goodwin dau. of Richard Goodwin.

C. Richard, Scholar Trinity Coll. Dublin, Rector
    of Coole 1759, d.s.p.
    William d. St. Helena 1753.
    Percival d. at Storming of Bellisle.
    John d. in Portugal.
    Goodwin, J.P. of Kanturk House, Co. Cork.
    George, J.P. of Glannanore, Castletown Roche.

CHART III.

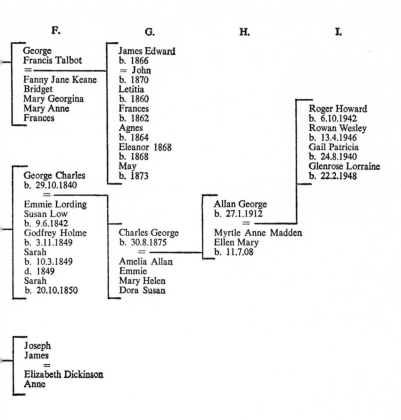

PART THREE

ARMOUR AND ARMS

ARMOUR AND ARMS

A study of armour and arms is one of the subjects closely related to Heraldry. It is not long after commencing to learn about Heraldry that one begins to be fascinated by the different shapes of shield, by the introduction of the surcoat and the reasons for it and the various ways in which the Knights of the Middle Ages displayed their armorial bearings for all to see.

Immediately there is an interest aroused in the mind of the student with regard to the peculiar shaped pieces of metal with which the early fighters clad themselves to go into battle. How they could move at all, let alone fight their enemies, with so much ironmongery around them.

This Dictionary of Armour and Arms has been allied to a similar work on Heraldry to provide a natural outlet for this interest and to give the student of Heraldry an easy means of egress to the meaning of many of the terms which he may find in books on Heraldry.

I have included a short reference with regard to all the various pieces of armour and the arms of the period which the student may find referred to. In fact I have gone further, as I have made the work as comprehensive as possible though I have only given in general terms the descriptions of the various items and their uses together with the approximate dates when the various items were used.

Much of my information has been obtained from or verified in ' Armour and Blade ' by Ellacott, ' Arms and Weapons ' by Martin and the ' Dictionary of Chivalry ' by Uden all three of which are most interesting and valuable references and to which I give grateful acknowledgement.

191

A

Aalspiess – This was a colloquial name for the thrusting-lance which should not in any way be confused with either the mounted man's lance or the soldier's pike, though frequently it could resemble and even be mistaken for the *plançon à picot*. It was designed entirely as a striking weapon, particularly for thrusting and in order to protect the hand it was fitted with a guard-rondel at the socket. It had a much shorter shaft than the man at arms' lance. The adoption of the aalspiess coincided with the knightly practice at the time of fighting on foot.

Ailette

Ailettes – A curious accessory used by the Nobility between the years 1270 and 1350. They consisted of a pair of small vertical plates either oblong or square which were secured to stand up on the shoulders. They may have been designed as additional protection for the neck but in this respect can have been of very little use as they were made of material far too flimsy to provide adequate protection. They may have been purely decorative because invariably they were painted with the armorial bearings of the wearer.

Aketon – A knee length shirt-like garment stiffened with vertical quilting. The sleeves varied between short and wide and long and tight and there was an upstanding collar. It was used principally by foot soldiers as a form of non-metallic defence but later many mounted men used it as a lining for the hauberk.

All-round Cuisses – A type of plate armour designed to enclose the thighs completely. They were introduced early in the 16th century particularly for the protection of those fighting on foot.

Almain Rivets – A type of light armour, first used in Germany, which consisted of plates sliding on rivets set in slides to ensure greater flexibility. Almain is derived from the early name for Germany. Eventually this type of armour was made in other countries and records show that Henry VIII sent to Milan for five thousand suits of Almain Rivets.

Angon – A type of spear almost exactly similar to the Roman 'pilum' which was developed by the early Frankish tribesmen. It was used to hamper their opponents' movements and was in use about A.D. 450.

Archer – The origin of the archer is obscure but they appear to have been first used by the early Egyptians. For many years only a short

192

bow of approximately four feet in length was used giving a range somewhere between 150–200 yards.

The Greeks developed a special tactic for the archer by mounting two on a chariot. At the time this form of warfare had tremendous impact upon their enemies.

The Romans surprisingly enough did not develop archery any further and in fact made little use of the weapon. However, by the Norman era the bow had become popular again though it was shortly replaced by the cross-bow.

In 1272 Edward I introduced the long bow, which had been developed in Wales, giving his troops a weapon with greater fire power and a longer range and in later years it was the English archers who were primarily responsible for the victories of Crécy and Agincourt.

Armed Cap-à-pie – Virtually armed from head to foot.

Armet – This was a type of helm originating in Italy spreading through other continental countries and eventually arriving in England

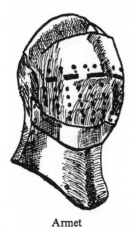

Armet

about 1450. It never became as popular with Englishmen as it was

in other countries. It was vastly superior to the early bascinet as it was both lighter to wear and it gave better protection. The principal difference between the armet and earlier types of helm was that the latter had to be put on by lowering them over the head, which incidentally had to carry most of the weight. However, the lower parts of the armet were made to open out on hinges so that it could be closed around the head thus transferring the weight to the shoulders.

Arm Guards – Various types of protection were developed through the ages to protect the arm. The earliest of these being the ordinary chain mail, which in various forms was in existence until the 15th century. During the 14th century, plates were introduced to cover both the upper and lower arm and these were strapped on top of the undercoat of mail. At the same time plated gauntlets were introduced with protection over both wrist and fingers.

From time to time additional pieces of armour were added to protect the elbow, the shoulder and the various slits through which the lance might penetrate when the arms were bent. During the 16th century a more complex system of plates was developed, though mail was still used to protect the gaps between the plates at vital spots such as the bend of the elbow. This form of protection lasted until the decline of armour.

Arming Cap – Initially this consisted of a kind of skull cap of leather reinforced with an iron covering which in turn was protected by a mail hood. Later, however, the same name was given to a kind of quilted roll worn around the head under the helm and with a broad chin strap to protect the cheeks from being rubbed.

Arming Doublet – This was a kind of under garment developed on the lines of the Aketon which was designed for use under the more comprehensive type of mail in use in the 15th century. In addition to its quilted material it had pieces of mail laced to all the vital points which were not covered by plate or where the plates might allow the lance to penetrate.

Arming Sword – During the 15th century Knights used two types of sword one long and one short. The Arming Sword was the short sword he wore on his belt when on horseback, while the long sword was attached directly to the saddle. Thus if dismounted at any time he was still sure of having a weapon.

Armour – Refers to the defensive covering worn by a fighting man. In early days it was made of toughened leather or quilted material somewhat similar to canvas but later it was generally constructed of metal either in the form of mail or plating.

There is an interesting point in connection with mediaeval armour: at the time no one talked of a 'suit of armour' as it is referred to today. Instead both the Knight and armourer referred to it as 'an armour' or 'harness'.

The separate types and parts of armour are discussed in the relative alphabetical position.

Armour, Articulated – A system devised in connection with plate armour using rivets and sockets designed to make armour more flexible at specific places, such as the elbow, the knee, and the foot. In addition a particular type of articulated gauntlet was devised in order to give the hand complete freedom of movement.

Armour, Body – A general term covering all types of armour protecting the body.

Armour, Custom Made – Owing to the vast difference in the size of individuals, it was as important for armour to be made to fit the individual as it is today with tailor-made suits.

Armour, Gothic – Gothic armour is particularly noteworthy for its stylised elegance and it was at its peak during the second half of the 15th century. Many of the Gothic styles were reproduced in the Italian workshops, largely because they catered for the export trade whereas the German armourers were kept busy enough fulfilling the requirements within their own country.

Armour in the German Style – A general term embracing all Germanic armour from the Gothic style to the later Maximilian armour.

Armour, Krebs – The name given to a form of armour considerably lighter in weight from the early rigid plates. The system consisted of several overlapping lames somewhat similar to the shell of the crayfish. It was particularly popular in Poland and Hungary when used for cavalry.

Armour, Maximilian – It was the youthful Arch-Duke Maximilian, a contemporary of Henry VIII, who, as the result of his wealthy marriage, was able to display a keen and early interest in the production of the best armour. His generous support of numerous armourer's workshops stimulated German output.

The Maximilian type in general is looked upon as the armour with the closely fluted plates, and it was always highly decorative.

Armour, Parade – Most members of the Nobility were satisfied to use ordinary undecorated armour in times of war, however, it became the custom for each to possess a highly decorated armour for parade and ceremonial purposes. During the 16th century much of this was constructed in the Greenwich workshop instituted by Henry VIII.

Armour, Plated – Refers to the later types of armour as opposed to the time when mail was used.

Armour, Tonlet – Consisted of rigid imitation pleats, with cut away portions in front and at the back to enable the wearer to mount his horse.

Armourers – Some of the better known armourers included Tomasso Missaglia, who was knighted by Duke Filippo Maria Visconti in 1435, Desiderius Helmschmied, whose name actually meant 'Helmet-maker', and Negroli, the latter's principal competitor.

Arrow – A straight shaft with a metal point at one end which was generally barbed at the tip and had a flight of three feathers at the other end.

During the days of the short bow arrows were no more than two feet in length. However, when the long bow came into being arrows were normally three feet in length.

Articulated Plates – See Armour, Articulated.

Artists – With the great increase in the decoration of armour it became necessary for artists of the time to provide the designs to which the armourers worked.

Some of the better known artists who worked in this connection include Hans Burkmair, Andrea del Castagno, Albrecht Dürer, Hans Holbein, Leonardo da Vinci and Raphael.

Arquebus – A kind of early carbine first introduced in the mid 16th century.

Attic Helmet – Introduced by the Greeks as a lighter and less cumbersome form of helmet than had been used earlier. It consisted of a round metal cap with protruding defence for the neck, cheek and nose, the ears being left free. The cheek pieces were generally decorated and in many helmets they could be pushed up on hinges when not required. In addition it possessed a triangular fronted ornamental band for protection of the forehead. A crest was mounted consisting of a horse hair fan which ran over the central portion from slightly forward of the perpendicular to the neck protection.

The early Romans copied the

Attic Helmet

Greek style of helmet but introduced two additional plumes. This was discontinued during the 1st century A.D.

Aventail – Consisted of a tippit of mail attached to the lower edge of the bascinet and hanging over the shoulders. It was in use about 1330.

Aventail

Axe – One of the principal Knightly weapons but always subsidiary to the lance and sword. Many Nobles in fact preferred the axe above all other weapons.

There were several types in use at various times some with long handles and some with short handles but in every case it was essential that perfect balance was obtained in its structure.

B

Back Plate – This refers to the first and subsequent rigid defence designed to cover the back in a similar manner to the breastplate covering the chest.

Back Sword – A single-edged sword.

Baldric – A bandolier type belt for carrying the sword. It dates back to antiquity and has its modern counterpart in the shoulder strap of an army officer's sam browne belt.

Banner – There were three principal types of flag carried during the Middle Ages, the banner, the standard and the pennon. The banner may be described as the principal battle flag. It was square or rectangular in shape and bore the arms of the Nobleman for whom it was carried and was always of considerable importance, not the least being that it provided a rallying point for the Noblemen's retainers. One of the principal banners of France was the Oriflamme which was captured at Agincourt.

Barbut – A barrel type helmet with solid cheek pieces extending round the face but leaving a 'T' shaped opening in front for the eyes, nose and mouth. It was not attached to an aventail.

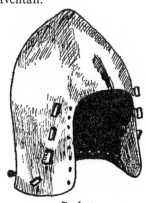

Barbut

Bard – A general term used to cover both the armour and trappings of a horse. The earliest form of bard consisted of mail covering over the head, neck and body down to below the stomach. In addition four mail 'Trouser legs' hanging to knee level were used. This must have been of great weight and for that reason is was seldom used.

A later form of horse armour consisted of a series of plates over the neck and head while the body was covered with a form of short caparison. These were known as the chanfron. After a few years the peytral and crupper were added which consisted of solid plates of cuir bouilli or in some cases metal.

Barrel Helm – A mediaeval form of helmet called thus because of its simple barrel shape which often had a flat top. It gave complete covering to the head, which with the aid of lining and some sort of skull cap, took the full weight.

Bascinet – A basin shaped helmet originally open at the front but later fitted with a snout type visor terminating in a long point. This was in use circa 1390.

The great bascinet introduced some 30 years later had a heavier plated rounded visor and was often used in tournaments.

Bassilard – A sharply tapering two edged dagger which had its popularity in the 13th and 14th centuries. Occasionally worn with armour but it was of more general use in civilian dress and was quite frequently carried by ladies attached to their girdles.

Bastard Sword – A sword with a shortened blade sometimes known as the 'hand-and-a-half' sword.

Battering Ram – A crude but usually effective means of breeching the walls of a castle or city. It generally consisted of a tree trunk to which an iron head was fixed and it was generally swung to-and-fro by a team of men working on either side. It was generally brought to the wall or gateway under cover of a strong team using timber mounted on wheels designed to give temporary cover to the operators.

Types of Battle Axe

Battle Axe – A well balanced axe generally with a splayed out head and curved blade. In addition there was a point on the end of the shaft and the back of the blade. Particular attention was paid to its balance.

Battle Sabre – A heavy type of curved sword generally used for cutting purposes by cavalry. It could also be used for thrusting.

Bears' Feet – An unusually wide form of sabaton believed to have been adopted by the French Knights with a view to concealing a physical deformity of Louis XII.

Beaver, Bevor – A piece of armour designed to protect the lower part of the face. It could either form part of the helmet or be fixed to the breastplate. It could be raised or lowered according to its type thus allowing the wearer to eat or drink.

Belt – Various types of belt have been in use throughout the ages either worn round the waist or slung bandolier-wise over the shoulder and not infrequently a combination of the two. These have almost invariably been designed as a means of carrying sword and dagger.

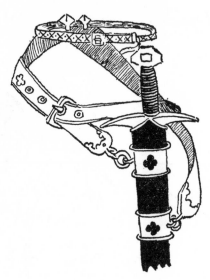

Belt circa 1323

Besague – A circular plate attached to the bracer and laced to the front of the shoulder and the outside of the elbow. These were in use circa 1320.

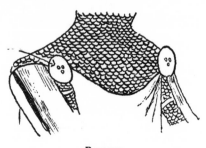

Besague

Bicoquet – A form of closed helmet consisting of several pieces of metal which enclose the head, neck and chin. It was fitted with a rounded visor hinged on pivots.

Bill – A mediaeval pole weapon pointed at the end with a spike at the back and a short curved blade in the front.

Body Armour – See Armour, Body.

Bonnet – A type of padded skull cap over which was worn a metal covering generally used by foot soldiers during the 16th and early 17th centuries.

Bordon, Bourdonass – A light hollow lance generally made of poplar and designed to shiver easily against the opponent's armour. In the early tournaments the principal object was to knock the adversary from his horse. This was difficult to achieve owing to the high projections both at the front and the back of the saddle. With the bordon however, honour was satisfied if the lance was shivered.

198

Boss – A term used for the projecting knob in the centre of early shields, also for the ornamental stud on a bridle.

Bouché – The notch at the top or near the right hand top of a shield designed to take the lance.

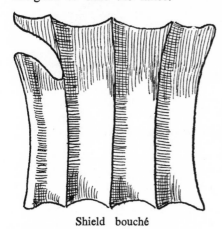

Shield bouché

Bourd – A system of broad strips of leather or wood fastened to the pommel of the saddle designed to afford protection for the abdomen, knees and legs of the rider. This was introduced in the latter half of the 14th century.

Bow – The weapon used by an archer or cross bowman.

Bracae – Padded extensions to the short trousers worn by Roman soldiers in about the 1st century A.D. Bracae did not actually cover the knees but protected the upper half of the knee-cap and lower thigh.

Bracer – Originally the name given to the leather cuff worn on the left forearm of an archer to protect against the rub of the bow-string in shooting.

After 1300 the name was given to an assembly of plates curving round

the forearm and upper arm with the cup-like couter for covering the elbow and a similar plate known as the spaudler attached to the shoulder. The whole assembly was attached to the hauberk.

Braconnière – A system of lames designed to cover the lower abdomen.

Braquemart – An accessory made by continental armourers and designed like the cod piece in civilian dress to replace the mail.

Breastplate – A rigid curved plate designed for protection of the chest. It was attached to the back plate and had a number of accessories attached to it.

Breastplate

Breech – A kind of mail trousers for protection of the lower body and legs.

Brigandine – Somewhat similar to the coat of plates but its plates were very much smaller and consequently gave greater flexibility. It was used fairly extensively by archers and other light troops.

In the mid-15th century equipment was based on the brigandine to which additional pieces were strapped.

Broad Sword – The double edged sword of the 17th and 18th centuries, the guard of which was formed by a basket of open iron work which enclosed the entire grip.

Brocas Helm – One of the tilting helms to be seen in the tower of London armouries. It dates from circa 1500 and is considered by many to be one of the finest examples surviving. It weighs 22½lbs. and still possesses the original staples and locking bars both back and front for fastening it down securely on the shoulder and chest.

Bronze – A metal much used by the early Egyptian warriors. It was used to make helmets, breast and back plates and the early type of greaves.

Bronze was also used in connection with weapons for the heads of spears and for swords, though the latter were shorter in length and had to be used purely for thrusting as a slash with a bronze sword would have broken it.

Buckler – A small round shield used for fighting on foot.

Buff Coat – A stout leather coat with deep skirts, originally made of buffalo hide to which various armoured accessories were strapped. During the 17th century these coats replaced the arming doublet.

Buffe – A kind of beaver used as a face guard on the burgonet.

Burgonet – An open peaked helmet used originally by the Burgundian troops. It had cheek pieces, sometimes with an adjustable buffe, and there were a number of different shapes, some with an almost flat top, others rising to a fan-like crest.

Burgonet

Burnie – A type of leather jerkin covered on the outside by overlapping plates of iron, copper and in some cases horn. This form of reinforced jacket originated during the Roman era and was noteworthy for the flexibility of movement it allowed, at the same time offering ample protection from sword cuts, spear thrusts and even arrows. During the Norman era the same name was given to the jacket constructed completely of mail.

It is interesting to note that in the scenes of the Battle of Hastings on the Bayeaux tapestry the horse and foot soldiers are both shown wearing the burnie.

C

Cabacete or cabasset – A type of light helmet worn by the Spaniards. It consisted of a tall narrow piece with a turned down brim that came to an upturned point fore and aft. It was frequently worn with a large beaver which practically covered the face and its gorget plate extended well down over the chest.

Caligae – A form of leg covering worn by Roman soldiers circa 1st century.

Caliver – A hand gun, lighter than the musket, which was fired without a gun rest.

Camail – A form of mail cape which was suspended from the bottom of the helmet and was designed to cover the chin, neck and shoulders.

Canon cars – One of the earliest types of armoured fighting vehicle which was used in the early 16th century. It was hand propelled by four men each side and was completely protected by a turret and deflecting surface over the top.

Caparison – Originally designed as a form of protection for the horse to meet attacks against the underbelly and legs. For battle purposes it was made of toughened leather which was followed later by the light linen covering of the same design generally emblazoned with the rider's coat of arms.

Caparison

Capeline – Sometimes called the 'lobster-tailed pot'. A helmet with a hemi-spherical skull piece fitted with a visor which comprised an adjustable rod forming a nose

guard, hinged cheek pieces and extending to a broad neck guard of overlapping and articulated plates. Introduced about 1620.

Carbine – A name given throughout the ages to many light types of hand gun or rifle. It was originally introduced in the 16th century as a form of small wheel-lock gun.

Case Hardening – A process instituted from the 15th century for hardening armour, probably by means of heat in contact with charcoal.

Case of Rapiers – The rapier was the most commonly used weapon for duelling and they were originally packed two in a case so that each contestant could use an identical blade, however, when duelling became more intense it was not uncommon for each contestant to use two blades one in either hand. The term for this form of bout was 'to fight with a case of rapiers'.

Cassis – The type of helmet worn by the later Roman troops. Its design combined that of the attic helmet and the 5th century jockey cap. It possessed a frontal band, a prominent neck guard and hinged cheek pieces and it possessed a small attachment at the top to which a plume could be fixed for ceremonial purposes.

Cassis

Cataphractus The Roman mail armour designed to protect the horse. See ' Bard '. The name was also used in connection with the troops thus equipped.

Catapult – One of a group of missile throwing engines used principally in siege warfare. The catapult was used principally for hurling stones, darts and fire brands.

Cavalier – One of the continental names for Knight. Generally refers to any form of horseman.

Cavalry – A general term applying to horsed troops.

Cementation – A lengthy process designed to produce steel for sword blades.

Centuries – Roman units consisting of sixty men.

Ceremonial Armour – See Armour, Parade.

Cervellier – A light iron skull cap worn by English long bow-men.

Chanfron – A form of head armour for the horse which was introduced during the 13th century.

Chanfron

Chandelier – A shafted weapon with an exceptionally long spike intro-

duced originally during the 13th century in Flanders and still in use as part of the equipment of the foot soldiers of various countries during the next century.

Chape – The small metal sheath at the bottom of a scabbard designed to strengthen it.

Chapeau de Montauban, Chapel de Fer – A kind of head piece derived from the round hat worn in civilian dress during the 13th century and particularly popular amongst fighting men. It was sometimes made of steel and possessed a brim which could be of varying width, slightly curved towards the back.

Chauses – Strips of mail introduced about 1150 for the protection of the front of the leg for mounted men. These were provided with laces for fastening. Another form consisted of a complete mail stocking. In either case the chauses were braced up to the waist and they were often gartered below the knee.

Cheek Pieces – These were first introduced by the early Greeks in approximately 600 B.C. as a rigid attachment to the helmet.

The Romans continued to use cheek pieces but smaller in design and generally hinged so that they could be raised when not in use.

During the Norman era cheek pieces were only noticeable amongst some of the troops during the Battle of Hastings and after a few years they were discarded in favour of the ventail (q.v.). When the more solid type of armour was introduced cheek pieces were generally incorporated in the construction of the helmet, though frequently they were hinged for removal when not required. Alternatively they were part of the visor. However, in 1450 we see the Italian barbut which returned to a style similar to the early Grecian helmet of the 6th century B.C.

Children's Armour – Armour specially designed for children who were eventually destined to become Knights.

Chin Straps – Used in connection with the arming cap and any other padded head piece worn under the helmet. In later years the width of the chin strap was increased to prevent the cheeks from becoming rubbed under the helmet.

Chivalry – A general term used to cover the whole of the Knightly system of the Middle Ages and for the particular conditions and virtues which governed their conduct. See also 'Code of Chivalry'.

Chlamys – The voluminous cloak generally caught up at the shoulder by a brooch which was worn by the Roman soldiers.

Cinquedea – A dagger with a short but broad blade, waisted near the hilt and five fingers' widths across, hence the name.

Claymore – The original Claymore was a long two-handed sword with very simple quillons, however, by the 17th century it had become a moderately broad-bladed double-edged weapon, the guard of which was formed by a basket of open ironwork which enclosed the entire grip.

Cloak and Sword – A form of fighting during the 16th century when the cloak was used instead of a shield. The object was to render the adversary's sword arm useless by throwing the cloak over his blade.

Close Helmet – A type of helmet which was much used towards the end of the 16th and during the 17th centuries. It was derived from the great bascinet and it fitted much more closely to the shape of the head.

Coat Armour – A general term applying to coats of arms or armorial bearings.

Coat Emblazoned – The original surcoat used by the crusaders was emblazoned with the appropriate cross of the army to which the wearer belonged. In addition, strips of coloured material were stitched to the surcoats of particular leaders. Subsequently these surcoats were reduced in length and emblazoned with the arms of the wearer.

Coat of Mail – A general term covering the mail garment worn by the later Romans and the Normans until solid armour was introduced.

Coat of Plates – Consisted of a leather or canvas garment, some-

Cinquedea

203

times quilted, to which small plates were laced as a means of body protection. The plates were so arranged that there was always a double thickness of metal.

Code of Chivalry – It is almost impossible to reconcile the code under which the Knights of the Middle Ages lived and fought and the nearest we can come to it is by referring to Leon Gautier, a French scholar who devoted the greater part of his life to the study of the literature of chivalry. From his researches, Gautier worked out what he described as his ten commandments of Knightly conduct. These were:

1. Unswerving belief in the Church and obedience to her teachings.
2. Willingness to defend the Church.
3. Respect and pity for all weakness and steadfastness in defending them.
4. Love of country.
5. Refusal to retreat before the enemy.
6. Unceasing and merciless war against the infidel.
7. Strict obedience to the Feudal overlord, so long as this duty did not conflict with duty to God.
8. Loyalty to truth and to the pledged word.
9. Generosity in giving.
10. Championship of the right and the good in every place and at times against the forces of evil.

Cod Pieces – The front part of the skirt of the armour which was often replaced by a piece of mail.

Coif – A kind of aventail made of leather or canvas. The name coif has also been given to the close fitting mail hoods worn at the time of the Battle of Hastings. These were generally made in one piece with the hauberk.

Cohort – A Roman unit of 600 men.

Collar – Generally constructed of plates, it replaced the gorget during the 16th century.

Conical Helmet – Generally refers to the Norman type helmet, either of pointed or flat-topped design.

Conical Helmet

Contours of Armour – It was essential to the armourer, in order to make his product so that it would protect the wearer and yet not hinder his movements, to have a sculptor's understanding of human anatomy. He had to understand the play of every muscle and the hinging of every joint both human and in the metal. As the result the contours of armour followed those of the figure it was designed to protect.

Copper – Between the age of the stone weapons which terminated about 5000 B.C. and the inception of bronze about 200 B.C. the only metal available for weapons was copper. This material, in very rough form, was used both for swords and daggers, the blades of which had to be riveted to the handles and the weapons could only be used for thrusting purposes as they were not strong enough for cutting.

Cored Blade – An early idea of the Greeks was to provide cored blades to their daggers. This provided a long socket in which a shaft could be fitted, thus turning the dagger into a spear.

Corinthian Helmet – A solid armoured helmet produced by the Greeks, circa the 6th century. It had solid defence over the neck and cheeks but an opening in front allowed the wearer to see and eat his food.

Corseque

Corinthian Helmet

Coronel – A crown shaped head fitted to the point of a lance for use in tournaments.

Corseque – A shafted weapon with a long point at its head and two smaller points at the neck.

Couching the Lance – The original position of holding the lance under the armpit supported in the rider's right hand. This position could only be adopted immediately prior to meeting the enemy, thus conversing the bearer's strength.

This system was discontinued in favour of the lance rest or queue thus taking the strain from the rider. Originally introduced as a single hooked rest about 1390, the second, reversed hook came in about a century later.

Coudieres – Special plates of leather or metal in various shapes and sizes designed to protect the elbow in a suit or armour. Those for right and left arms occasionally varied in style and when the shield was discarded as a means of defence, that on the left arm was necessarily made larger and stronger.

Couteau de Breche – This was a shafted weapon very similar to the fauchard with which it was often confused. It consisted of a long shaft with a large knife type blade which was richly adorned with ornamental engraving. It was occasionally used in combat for thrusting

205

rather than for cutting, but more generally it was reserved as a weapon carried by such troops as palace guards, etc.

Couter – A form of elbow guard introduced about 1260.

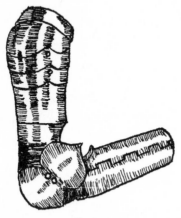

Couter

Craniquin – An instrument working on the same principal as a lifting jack which was used to load certain types of cross bow.

Crécy, Battle of – One of the more famous victories in early English history. It took place on the 26th and 27th August 1346 when the French Knights under Philip VI attacked the English who were located between the villages of Crécy and Wadicourt. The English had taken up a position on a low ridge with woods on their right and behind them. It is estimated that the French army consisted of something over 40,000 while the English only had about 13,000, of whom about 3,000 were Knights and men-at-arms and well over half the remainder were archers. The French army lacked discipline, which was one of the principal features of the English and, because of this, the Battle was

joined shortly before sundown on the 26th August instead of waiting until dawn on the 27th as Philip had intended. There was considerable shouting and jumping in the air by the French forces which was greeted by complete silence in the ranks of the English. Suddenly, however, when the French were in comfortable bow shot, the English archers took a pace forward and firing four or five times faster than their adversaries literally shot the French army to pieces.

This virtual slaughter was followed by an attack by the close-ranked Knights of France, which was met with the same repetition – the step forward, followed by the ruthless whistling of arrows aimed at the horses, and once the Knights were unseated they were easy prey to the swords and axes of the English. The battle ended soon after midnight when the surviving French wandered away in the darkness.

The French casualties were put at somewhere in the neighbourhood of between 13,000 and 30,000 whereas the English losses, ascertained from all available records, did not exceed 50.

Crest – The emblem worn on the top of the helmet as a further means of identification of a leader in addition to his coat of arms.

Crested Armour – A kind of ridged or fluted armour developed towards the end of the 15th century.

Crinet – A protective armour for the horse's neck. It was constructed of a series of overlapping plates to allow free movement.

Cross Bow – One of the earliest forms of shooting weapon. It was not, however, recognised as a weapon suitable for warfare until

Crest

the 12th century. It was used extensively during the third crusade and King John is recorded as having paid his cross bowmen three pence per day for foot soldiers and seven pence halfpenny per day if they were mounted.

The cross-bow had a very short life in England as it was replaced about 1272 by the long-bow.

Crinet (worn with Chanfron)

Crupper – In early days a protection for the hind quarters of a horse. The word has now come to mean the leather loop passing under the tail of a horse and round its hind quarters which is fastened to the saddle to keep it from slipping forward.

Crusades – A number of expeditions which the European continental countries including Britain, France, Germany, Austria, Italy and Spain undertook against the followers of Islam in an endeavour to regain and protect the Holy Land in general and the Holy City of Jerusalem in particular.

The crusades were instrumental, as are all wars, in improving and generally advancing armour and weapons.

Cuirass – A general term first applied to the chest and body armour of the Greek soldier of the 5th century B.C. Since then it has come to be applied in almost every century to the armour of the chest, stomach and the back and is even worn today by members of the household cavalry.

In its earliest form it consisted of toughened leather and *cuir boulli* a light material laced with small plates and finally the solid form of breast pate.

Cuirassine – A form of under garment worn under the armour, usually without a back plate. It was rather similar to the brigandine in appearance and was designed as a strongly reinforced doublet as a protection against sword and dagger thrusts.

Cuir Boulli – Leather material, frequently hardened with hot wax, which was used extensively in connection with protective garments from early Roman times until the end of the 14th century, in Europe and even later in the east.

207

Cuisse – An extra protection designed to cover the thigh of the mounted man which was his weakest point.

Cutlass – A comparatively short but very stout sword which was particularly popular in naval establishments. First introduced in the 16th century.

D

Dagasse – A broad knife with a double edged blade similar to the braquemart.

Dagger – A weapon introduced to the Knightly classes during the 13th century where it was exceptionally popular. There have been many types some similar to a short sword, tapering and double edged and the other with a single edge, more or less similar to the modern carving knife. Some types reached as much as two feet in length and were frequently mistaken for small swords.

Demi Greaves – Light metal plates which protected the front of the legs only.

Demi Lancer – A lancer of the period circa 1550 who carried a lance only eight feet in length.

Destrier – A very powerful type of horse used exclusively by Knights in the Middle Ages. They were carefully bred and trained and reserved for use in *tournaments*.

The name is said to have been derived from the Latin dextra, right hand from which it is believed that the horse was trained to lead with his right leg, thus ensuring that if he swerved he would do so to the right, thus avoiding a collision with the adversary.

Development of Armour – Armour in some form has been in existence since the early Egyptians about 1500 B.C. but it was of simple construction and consisted, for the archers, of a corselet of glued flax with a padded felt helmet and for the spearmen, a fabric coat to which bronze scales were laced.

The early Greeks during the 6th century B.C. wore plates, again of bronze beaten to the shape of the body, to cover the chest and back. On their otherwise bare legs they had plated greaves, again beaten to the contour of the legs, and worn on the head was the Corinthian helmet with its solid cheek and nose pieces. The Greek warrior also carried a large round shield.

A hundred years later the solid breast and back plates were exchanged for a leather jacket with bronze scales, somewhat similar to the early Egyptian spearmen but to this he added comparatively solid metal shoulder guards which were attached to the breast and back plates. He also changed to the Attic helmet, which though somewhat similar to the Corinthian helmet, provided more comfort to the wearer.

The Roman soldier of the 4th century B.C. really showed little improvement on the Greeks of 100 years earlier as his armour was virtually copied from the Grecian style. However, by the 1st century A.D., though he had discarded the bronze scaled jacket in favour of a slightly longer leather jacket reinforced by circular plates, laced to fit the body and shoulders, he had introduced a form of tough leather armour covering the thighs, known as bracae and caligae to protect his legs, instead of the early greaves. These latter were of thick fabric and cross gartered over the top.

Passing to the Saxon era we find the introduction of mail, which at the time was more or less universally adopted. The Saxon warrior also carried a round shield and used a tight fitting metal skull cap.

The Normans of the 11th century relied almost entirely on mail with the long mail hauberk which hung down to their knees and mufflers and mittens which covered the arms and hands. This was reinforced with the pectoral covering the chest and the coif which fitted the neck, ears and over the head, either under or over the helmet.

The helmet was originally of conical shape and was worn over the coif but later became flat-topped to be worn under the coif.

In 1066 the Normans carried the unwieldy kite-shaped shield which, by the beginning of the 13th century, had been shortened, widened and curved to fit the body.

This form of armour was used in the early crusades with the addition of the surcoat.

By the end of the 13th century the mail coif was discarded in favour of a more comprehensive steel helmet and a few years later certain elements of plate were added to the mail, namely sabatons, schynbalds and poleyns to cover the feet, legs and knees. Bracers and couters for the arm, plated gauntlets for the hand and the aventail, which joined the helmet, to cover the neck. At the same time the shield was made considerably smaller.

By the beginning of the 15th century we find the more solid plate introduced in the form of breast and back plates, plates for the lower abdomen and also the lower leg. By this time the visor had become established.

A century later the warrior was completely clothed in steel with all the added extras such as stop ribs, haute pieces, and though mail still existed it was only used to protect parts of the body which plate could not cover or where gaps were likely to appear.

The 16th century shows armour at its peak when the armourers of Italy and Germany led the field to be copied later in Henry VIII's Greenwich workshop. This was the great Maximilian age.

From this time onward body protection was forced to comply with the increasing efficacy of small arms and armour was thickened to withstand the musket ball. Eventually this competition reached a stage of absurdity and the soldiers refused to use armour.

This decline was gradual as a cuirass and a helmet were used for some time as a partial protection but eventually it was all discarded.

In the 20th century the only armour remaining is in the form of a steel helmet worn in battle by fighting services and units of the civil defence and in various forms of bullet proof waistcoat, which appear from time to time.

Double Axe – A double headed form of battle axe used occasionally by the Romans.

Double Frog – Introduced circa 1740 was used to carry both sword and bayonet.

Double Knot Decoration – A particular method of decorating armour during the 16th century. First originated in Milan it was copied by English armourers.

Duelling – Prior to the introduction

of the rapier, duelling was very much a matter of chance and fair play was hardly considered. When the rapier came into use, however, strict rules for the conduct of duels was introduced. Duelling was made illegal in England during the 18th century, but was still carried on until the early middle part of the 20th century in Germany, particularly amongst students.

E

Elbow Gauntlet – A particular type of gauntlet, with a long reinforced extension reaching to the elbow, used by light cavalry circa 1645. It was worn with the buff coat.

Elbow Gauntlet

Elbow Pieces – Articulated metal sections designed to cover the elbow and allow free movement.

Embossed Armour – A type of highly decorative armour introduced by Italian and German armourers during the 16th century.

Enarmes – The name given to the straps inside the shield by which it could be slung over the arm or held in the hand.

Epaule de Mouton – A special piece of armour so named from its shape attached to the right vambrace, thus giving protection to the bend of the arm against lance thrusts. Eventually the name was corrupted to the word pauldron by which this piece of armour is probably better known.

Epée – A type of small sword with a shell guard protection designed entirely for thrusting. Used extensively for duelling, particularly in France.

Estoc – An alternative name for the arming sword.

Etched Decoration – A system of decorating armour which was carried out by means of acid biting into the metal, the surface of which was otherwise protected by wax. It was first used at the end of the 15th century.

F

Falchion – A type of sword used during the 16th century.

Fauchard – A weapon similar to the couteau de brèche which was particularly popular amongst the Princely Houses of Italy for arming their palace guards. It was never popular in France but was used in Germany, Spain and England up to the end of the 17th century.

Fauld – A kind of skirt made of plates used as part of the armour during the 15th century.

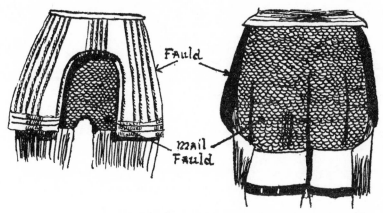

Faulds (front and back view)

Fencing – In early days fencing was a means of practising sword play amongst the knights and esquires. As time progressed, however, it was used as a method of settling private grievances between two people and then came to be known as duelling. Various weapons have been used for duelling the most popular of which was undoubtedly the rapier.

Though duelling was always an indictable offence in England it was quite common during the 18th century and until a comparatively late age, swordsmanship was a prerequisite of a gentleman and consequently a number of fencing academies were in existence to teach swordsmanship.

Fencing is still practised in the Olympic Games.

Field Armour – A specially strongly constructed form of armour designed for use on the battlefield. It was generally devoid of a decoration which was reserved for parade armour.

Finger Rings – An addition added to the rapier to strengthen one's control of the weapon. Introduced circa 1600.

Rapier

Flail – One of the crueller weapons of the Middle Ages. It was somewhat similar to the hinged flail used by country men for thrashing corn but with the shorter arm having instead a chain with a spiked ball on the end. The slang name for the flail amongst the soldiers of the time was the 'Holy Water Sprinkler'.

Flanchard – Flank protection for the horse.

Flat Topped Helmet – Introduced by the Normans early in the 13th century. It was generally used in conjunction with the mail coif and ventail.

211

Fluted Armour – Introduced by Maximilian during the 16th century.

Foils – A form of fencing weapon which were 1lb small swords with a guard button on the point.

Fortasse – Part of the armour attached below the fauld. The lower hoop was separated into two parts by a semi-circular gap in front and further divided at the sides. A single half round narrow plate formed the rear of this lower hoop and all three plates were attached to the hoop above them by straps and buckles. The two front sections were called foretasses and the rear plate was the hindtasse. In later years the name tasset was given to the foretasses.

Fork – A popular weapon used by foot soldiers from the 12th century onwards. It was based like many other weapons of the time on implements used by the country men. There were different designs, usually of three prongs, and different lengths and some had hooks in addition designed for pulling a horseman from the saddle.

Fourche Ferrée – The name given to a particular type of fork.

Francisque – Originally a shafted weapon deriving from the axe and serving as a tool as well as weapon. It did not carry any form of attachment enabling it to be used for thrusting and remained in existence only until the 10th century.

Frog Head Helmet – A particularly heavy reinforced helmet characteristic of the end of the 15th century.

Fuller – The groove provided on each face of a sword blade to lighten it without weakening it.

Fyrd – A general term given to the levies in early England.

G

Gadlings – Short spikes sometimes attached to the knuckle plates on the gauntlet assembly.

Gambeson – A form of quilted coat sometimes worn by mounted men over the aketon.

Garde Braces – An additional form of plate fitting partly over each pauldron and bearing the haute pieces.

Gauntlets – An assembly covering the hand instead of the old mufflers

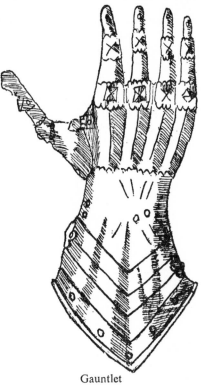

Gauntlet

212

which were an extention of the coat of mail covering the wrist and hand and tied at the sleeves. The gauntlets consisted of a fabric glove originally with a single plate for the back of the hand fastening to the fabric and with small overlapping plates for the fingers, thus enabling them to move easily. With some types spikes of iron called gadlings were fixed to the knuckles and joints, thus converting the gauntlet into a formidable weapon of offence.

At a later stage the solid plate protecting the back of the hand was extended round the wrist.

By the middle of the 17th century a special elbow gauntlet for the left arm only (see elbow gauntlet) was developed while that for the right arm consisted of a reinforced leather glove.

Genouillières – A general term covering armour for the knee caps. In early times they were made of cuir boulli or leather but eventually they were constructed of metal in various shapes.

Guisarme

Gisarme, Guisarme – A mediaeval pole weapon terminating in two prongs one straight and the other curved.

Gladiator – A Roman professional swordsman reserved primarily for purposes of entertainment. He wore a high crested, broad brimmed helmet with a perforated visor, a greave on his right leg and articulated metal lames on his sword arm and on his left arm he carried a small round shield.

Roman Gladiator

Gladius Ibericus – A short broad bladed Roman sword.

Glaive – A mediaeval pole weapon consisting of a broad pointed blade with a long spike attached opposite the front of the blade. This spike was approximately $\frac{2}{3}$ the length of the blade.

Goedendag – There seems to be considerable discrepancy in the description of the goedendag amongst his-

213

torians but all agree that it must have been a most terrible weapon whose effects during the 14th century gave it a proverbial reputation for its efficacy.

Some writers describe it as being similar to the mace which was a club-like weapon with spikes on its ball-shaped head. Others describe it as a pole weapon terminating in a long metal spike with, approximately 18 inches from the end, a sharpened blade similar in shape to the pick-axe attached to it.

Gonfannon – Sometimes known as gonfalon. Probably derived from the Norse ' gunnefane ' or war flag. It was used extensively by the Normans with whom it had a square body with three or more tails. Later it was used more by the Italians than in any other country.

Gorget – Consisted of a solid caped collar covering the lower part of the face and extending over the shoulders.

Goupillon – A short shafted weapon headed by an articulated joint from which were attached one or more short chains. At the end of each chain was a wooden ball fitted with spikes.

Grand Guard – A large additional piece of plate fixed to the left of the breastplate extending over the right side. Used specifically for jousting.

Grand Phalanx – A Greek military unit containing well over 1600 hoplitai.

Great Bascinet – The name of a new type of helmet developed from the tall pointed bascinet to which the beaver had become an integral part. This was developed during the early 15th century.

Greaves – The early greaves introduced by the Greeks during the 6th century B.C. consisted of plates extending round part of the legs. During the time of the early Romans greaves were extended by Gorgans which fitted over the knees. They were then discarded for many years but returned about 1250 in the form of the schynbald (q.v.).

Greave

Greek Armour – This consisted of a kind of plated cuirass with plated guards strapped over the shoulders. The metal used in all cases was bronze.

Greek Sword – A short but broad bladed weapon of bronze which was riveted to the handle. It could only be used for thrusting as it had insufficient strength to be used as a cutting weapon.

Greenwich Armour – In 1519 Henry VIII established a chain of workshops in Greenwich, chiefly staffed by German and Italian armourers, for the manufacture of high quality armour. This armour was made available to members of the nobility at exorbitant prices.

214

Grey Goose Feather – Used exclusively for the flights of arrows for the long bow.

Grip – The name given to the handle of a sword, by which it is held.

Grunenberk's Wappen Buch – Published in Munich about 1483, is one of the finest records of German armour of the time that is still available today.

Guige – A belt used for carrying the shield when it was not in use.

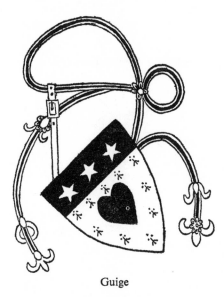

Guige

Gussets – Attachments of mail used by armoured men to guard the joints of plate equipment.

H

Halberd – A long shafted weapon which may be found in many different forms but generally consisting of a spike at its head and an axe blade, either square or curved, concave or convex, particularly for parade use. Its counterpart used in war was generally only five or six feet in length. The most advanced types could hook, trip, pierce and cut.

Half Armour – So called because it generally only protected the body and head and sometimes the arms.

Hammer, or War Hammer – A weapon in shape somewhat similar to the modern craftsman's claw hammer but with a handle heavier in weight and at least twice the length. Frequently it was fitted with a spike at its head for use as a thrusting weapon.

Hand Guard – A general name given to the form of protection for the hand on a sword.

Haqueton – A close-fitting garment of cloth or leather generally covered by a knee-length tunic bearing the overlord's colours. The arms were protected by leather or cloth with padding at the shoulders, and the legs by strips of leather reaching to the ankles.

Harness of Mail – A form of hauberk designed for the horse.

Hastings, Battle of – The battle fought in 1066 between the invading Normans under Duke William and the defending English under Harold.

A fine record of the battle may be found in the Bayeaux Tapestry (q.v.).

Haubergeon – A shortened form of hauberk generally with cut away sides.

215

Hauberk – A garment of mail which fitted over the whole body and which was generally made in one piece with the mail coif or hood.

Haute Piece – By 1430 the inner edges of the pauldron had been turned up as a form of protection for the neck. A few years later these were attached to the guard braces.

Haute Pieces

Heater Shield – The type of shield that succeeded the kite shaped variety used by the Normans. It was rather similar to the bottom of a flat iron but shaped to the body.

Heaume – The continental name for a helmet.

Helm – The particular pattern of helmet used in a tournament. This had a jutting lower half of the part covering the face which slightly overlapped the upper half and there were narrow slits for vision. It appears almost impossible to have been able to see out of a helm but, providing the shoulders are hunched and the head slightly bent forward as though charging with a lance, visibility is comparatively good.

Helmet – A general term embracing all the various types of head covering from the earlier Greek and Cretan helmets of various shapes, sizes and patterns, first constructed of padded leather and then of bronze, followed by the famous Attic Helmet, into the Norman era when either a conical or flat topped helmet was combined with the mail coif and ventail, to the various types of metal helmet including the bascinet, the snout type, the great bascinet, the barbet armet, sallet, morion and burgonet.

Hindtasse – Worn on the opposite side of the leg to the foretasse (q.v.).

Hood of Mail – The mail coif.

Hoplitai – Part of the Athenean army consisting of free citizens who formed the main phalanx of the heavy infantry of the early Greek army.

Horse Armour – The first attempt at horse armour consisted of the mail barding used by the Roman catafractus in the 4th century. This was not successful and was discarded. The next attempt in the early 14th century consisted of metal plates over the head, neck, chest and flanks. These included the chanfron, crinet, peytral, crupper and flanchard which were generally used in conjunction with the caparison or trapper as it was sometimes called. Later on, much of this was discarded but the neck plates and chanfron were retained for another century or two.

Hosting Harness – In this sense hosting means ' Battle ', therefore the expression refers to battle armour.

216

used for the tournament was the great bascinet. Other types were also used but in general the protection afforded by the jousting helm was greater than that in the more ordinary types.

I

Infantry – A general term referring to foot soldiers.

J

Jack – A rough canvas garment with plates of metal or horn sandwiched between layers of material and stitched in. Worn particularly by infantrymen.

Jaserenc – A very early name for the mail hauberk.

Javelin – Derived from the lance. The javelin was a very light type of spear designed to be thrown from a fairly considerable distance. Its point was barbed thus rendering it more deadly.

Jousting Armour – The tournament was always looked upon as a great ceremonial occasion and for that reason jousting armour was considerably more decorative than battle armour. Furthermore, it was greatly reinforced and specific items such as the stop ribs were introduced specifically for jousting. It should be remembered that knights spent far more time in jousting than in battle, hence the importance of special armour to avoid accidents.

Jousting Helm – A popular helm

Jousting Helm

Jousting Saddle – This was made to a particular pattern. The front of the pommel was raised considerably, with the object of covering the lower abdomen and affording additional thigh protection for the rider.

Jupon – An alternative name for the surcoat when reduced in size to thigh length.

K

Kettle Hat – A type of helmet used principally by foot soldiers. It resembled the British steel helmet of the first World War with padded lining and a chin strap.

Kidney Dagger – A kind of dagger

217

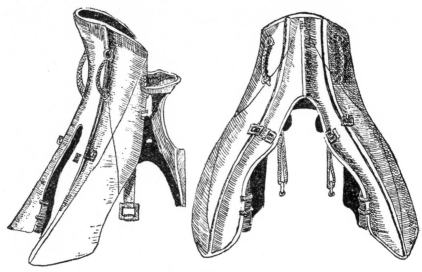

Jousting Saddle (circa 1430)

so-called from the kindey-shaped lobes at the base of the handle.

Kidney Dagger

Klappvisior – A traditional German type helmet the front of which lifted on a hinge set in the brow. It possessed long horizontal sights and air-holes. It was from this helmet that the visor was developed.

Knee Pieces – The earliest form of protection for the knee was provided by gorgans attached to the greaves used by the early Romans about 400 B.C. The later Roman soldiers used padded material which was an extension of the short trousers but which did not connect with the caligae worn on the legs. These were called bracae.

The next step in the early 14th century were the poleyns which were plated knee pieces strapped to the greaves. This form of knee protection continued with minor amendments until the decline in armour.

Knight – In the earliest days of the mediaeval period all members of the Nobility were termed Knights and it was not until some years later that other ranks graded above the Knights were introduced. The whole basis of chivalry revolved round the Knightly classes.

Knights were divided into Knight bachelor, which is in fact, the lowest rank and Knights banneret who were selected as leaders. In addition there were certain orders, two of which evolved from the crusades. These were the **Knights Templars** and the Knights Hospitallers. In addition to these almost every country possessed their own Orders of Knighthood.

Knuckle Bow – The curved portion round the grip of a sword designed to protect the knuckles.

L

Lambriquin or **Mantling** – A short shoulder length cape designed to hang from the top of the helmet for the protection of the head and neck. This was brought into use during the crusades as a protection against the sun.

Mantle or Lambriquin

Lamellar Armour – Small metal plates laced together upon a leather or fabric base. Used extensively in the east.

Lames – The small metal plates laced to leather or fabric in certain types or armour.

Laminated Plates – Small reinforcing plates used to fill the gaps or protect vital joints in plate armour. They were designed to overlap the principal pieces of armour thus giving movement in addition to protection.

Lance – The principal weapon used by the Knightly class and the one most used in the tournament. There were many types and sizes of lance and they were of various lengths.

Generally the shaft was of plain wood but at one stage it was of metal splayed out towards the handle to give protection. Behind the hand hold it was thickened considerably to give balance. This type was considerably heavier and necessitated the use of a lance rest.

Lance Rest – With the increased weight of the metal lance it became necessary to introduce a rest in conjunction with the armour. Consequently two hooks, one of which

Lance rest

was reversed, were fastened on the side of the breastplate. The lance rested on top of the front hook and was supported by the rear one, thus the weight was taken by the body instead of the arm and shoulder.

Leg Lames – Articulated plates used particularly in the leg armour and in the sabetons.

Legion – A Roman unit consisting of between 4,500 and 6,000 men.

Legionary – The ordinary Roman soldier.

Lobster Tail – A name given to one of the kinds of helmet used in the middle of the 17th century. It derived its name from the tail piece extending over the neck which looked like a lobster's scales.

Locked Helmets – These were used principally by the German foot soldiers and consisted of a helmet with a locking device for affixing it to the remainder of the armour.

Long Bow – The famous bow introduced originally by the Welsh circa 1272 which was primarily responsible for the victories of the English armies at Crécy and Agincourt against the French armies, which were of vastly superior numbers.

The long bow could be fired rapidly at an effective range of 400 yards and it used a three foot arrow, popularly known as the grey goose shaft.

Long Shield – A name sometimes given to the kite-shaped shield used by the Normans.

Long or Kite-shaped Shield

Long Sword – Originally used by the Merovingians and Franks, was also adopted by the Normans. It consisted of a sword with long broad blade and cross shaped quillons. In some cases the handle was extended and the sword was used as a two-handed weapon.

M

Mace – A club-like and very vicious weapon of which there were numerous shapes. Most had a short-ish handle and were headed by either a spiked metal ball or various types of fan-like protuberances extending from the head.

Types of Mace

It was a particularly favourite weapon with soldier-churchmen, such as Bishop Odo of Bayeaux the brother of William the Conquerer who fought at Hastings, because the mace was looked upon as a bruising weapon rather than a blood drawing weapon and they were thus able to argue that they were not shedding blood.

Macedonian Phalanx – A Greek unit consisting of approximately

16,000 foot soldiers in 16 ranks deep, armed with a 24 foot spear.

Mail Leggings – The mail covering for the foot and legs popular during the Norman era.

Mail Shirt – Another name for the coat of mail worn in the Norman era.

Main de Fer – A rigid defence for the hand and forearm strapped to the left side of the cuirass or brigandine.

Maine Gauche – A type of dagger designed specifically for a left handed man.

Malchus – A short bladed sword with a slight curve in the blade which had a single cutting edge.

Mameluke Sword – A curved Turkish sword the hilt of which had a peculiar snake-like form.

Maniple – A division of the phalanx designed for more rapid movement particularly with a view to reinforcement when necessary.

Manteau d'Armes – A rigid cape-like plate extending from the centre of the chest to cover the shoulder and left upper arm. It was designed primarily as a protection against lance thrusts.

Maul – A particularly unpleasant type of percussion weapon which was fitted to the end of a shaft. It was used in France circa 1381.

Measurements of Knights – As it was of vital importance that armour fitted the wearer it was essential that armourers took careful measurements of their customers, thus ensuring adequate movement and protection.

Mêlée – A free for all fight in the lists between two teams of Knights. They were supposed to be friendly contests but accidents were frequent, for example, in a mêlée in the year 1240, 60 Knights were killed.

Misericorde – A straight thin bladed dagger, so called because it was frequently used to give the final ' mercy ' stroke to wounded Knights.

Mittens – The name generally given to the mail covering for the hand. This was generally tied at the wrist.

Mitten

Morgenstern – A popular German and Swiss weapon consisting of a shaft about six feet in length bearing a hexagonal head bristling with spikes. It was still in use in some districts in Switzerland in the 17th century.

Morion – A form of helmet used at the end of the 16th century with strongly curved brim and a comb-like structure which ran across the top of the head from side to side.

Moulded Cuirass – An early Greek form of body armour consisting of a bronze plate hammered to fit the contours of the body.

221

Muffler – A mail covering for the back of the hand with leather inset for the palm and an under slit for freeing the hand when required.

Munition Armour – A low quality form of armour introduced about 1500 for the infantry and light cavalry.

Musket – The early 17th century form of small arm.

Musketeer – Infantry soldiers armed with an arquebus or musket. They wore a broad brimmed hat or morion with no visor or neck guard.

N

Nasal – The small metal strip extending from the brow of a helmet to cover the nose. It was used extensively during the Norman era and it also appears in the early Corinthian helmet but was later discontinued and was subsequently replaced by the visor.

Neck Guard – Throughout the ages the neck has been protected by various means. The early Greeks and Roman helmets had a protective strip extending from the back of the helmet. In Norse and Norman times the neck was protected by the ventail and after the inception of the solid helmet the neck was taken care of by part of the helmet.

An additional part of the neck protection was provided by the haute pieces introduced in the early 16th century.

P

Pansiere – Part of the defences for the lower abdomen.

Pas d'Ane – A special ring guard extending down the blade of a rapier circa 1600.

Passage at Arms – A fight or encounter. A favourite method adopted by the Knight Errant was to pick a narrow bridge and endeavour to hold it against any other Knight that wished to pass that way. Sometimes they would camp out for days waiting for a chance adversary.

Pass Guard – A large extra defence for the left elbow generally worn with a main de fer.

Pauldron – A large curved plate attached to the breastplate which extended over each side of the chest and back.

Paunce – An additional plate or sometimes strip of strengthened leather used below the breastplate for the protection of the lower abdomen.

Pavise – A type of shield used particularly by long bowmen who could shelter behind it when not actually shooting.

Peascod – A civilian garment which played an important part in the design of the breastplate.

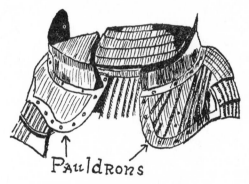

Pauldrons

Note: Left side larger for greater protection, right side cut away allowing room for lance.

Pectoral – A reinforced plate used to cover the chest. It was first used about 900 B.C. and again during the Norman era with mail.

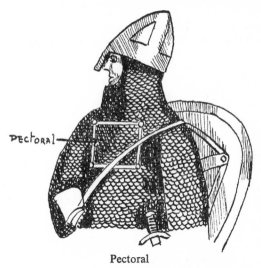

Pectoral

Peltast – A general name given to mercenaries formed into light infantry units circa 500 B.C.

Pennon – A small twin tailed flag carried either by a Knight or one of his retainers on his behalf and emblazoned with his badge and livery colours but not with his coat of arms.

Peytral – Chest protection for the horse.

Phalanx – See Macedonian Phalanx.

Phalerae – Medallions denoting military honours used by the Romans. They were fastened to the cuirass.

Picadils – The extended scalloped edges of the fabric or leather linings worn under the pauldrons.

Pieces of Advantage – Additional pieces of armour added to the ordinary harness for special protection

223

during the tournament. Initially only the left side was reinforced, as that was the more vulnerable, but gradually they spread to other parts of the armour. Introduced in the middle of the 16th century.

Pike – One of a number of pole weapons employed by the foot soldier primarily against horsemen. Its shaft was approximately 15 feet and in battle it was held inclined forward with the butt of the pole inserted in the ground and held firm by the soldier's foot.

Pikeman – A general name for soldiers armed with shafted weapons.

Pilum – The Roman javelin adopted in preference to the spear. The shaft was about 7 feet in length.

Pizaine – A stiffly made mail collar with stout rings which was used with the haubergeon.

Plackart – Another name for paunce.

Plançon – A group of weapons including the plançon à picot, plançon à broche which were forbidden by the statutes of the Lille Magistrature as being prohibited weapons during the 14th and early 15th century. This was because they were particularly vile weapons.

Poignard – One of the numerous types of dagger.

Pommel – The circular knob on the handle of a sword designed particularly to give it balance.

Pot Helmet – The type of broad brimmed metal helmet worn with a face guard and the lobster tail by light horsemen circa 1645.

Poleyn – A quilted cover for the knee worn above the schynbald circa 1250.

Pour Point – A general term for any quilted protection.

Q

Queue – The lance rest (q.v.).

Quillons – The cross guards of a sword.

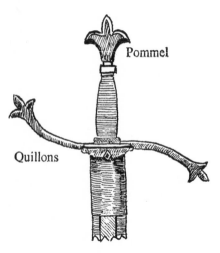

Italian Sword circa 1530

Quilted Fabric – Various types of quilted fabric were used in connection with armour. In the early days it was used instead of armour, later with plates laced to it and later still as a lining, thus acting as a kind of shock absorber against blows received on the plates of the armour.

Quintain – An apparatus used by horsemen for practice. It consisted

224

of a pivoted horizontal arm mounted on a tall post. At one end of the arm was the target and at the other end a sand bag. Providing the rider hit the target, the sand bag was whirled round by the blow thus knocking him from the saddle unless he was quick enough to avoid it.

Quiver – A sheath or case slung on to the belt or baldric for carrying arrows.

R

Ram – See Battering Ram.

Ransom – A sum of money or quantity of valuables payable by a prisoner in exchange for his freedom.

Generally speaking the ordinary soldier stood very little chance of having his life spared if he was captured unless, of course, he could be sold into slavery.

Higher-ranking prisoners were almost invariably spared as they were normally in a position to pay adequate ransom.

Rapier – A slender and finely-pointed type of sword used for thrusting and parrying instead of cutting and hewing with its edge. It was used extensively for duelling.

Rerebrace – Originally referred to the plated covering at the back of both the upper and lower arm, but later generally referred to both plates on the upper arm.

Resistance of Armour – The story was the same in the Middle Ages as it is today and where today it is a constant struggle between the penetration power of modern weapons and the effectiveness of the armour on tanks etc., so in the Middle Ages it was a constant struggle between the armourer and the constantly improving weapons which they were protecting against. By the beginning of the 17th century, in order to protect against the improved power of the musket, armour had become so heavy that the fighting men either refused to wear it or demanded extra pay for wearing it at any other time than when actually fighting.

Rondache – The general name given to any circular shield carried by horsemen in the 16th century and from the next century by foot soldiers. It was frequently made entirely from iron or steel and served as a lance or sword breaker.

Rondle Dagger – A dagger used almost exclusively by military personnel. Its pommel and hand guard were formed of roundles consisting of flat discs or plates of various shapes set horizontally to the blade.

Rowel – A spiked wheel or disc on a spur as opposed to the plain pointed type.

S

Sabatons – A system of overlapping horizontal lames introduced early in the 14th century to cover the shoes.

Sabre – The cavalry sword designed principally for cutting but also for pointing. It was a stout weapon with a particularly fine edge and a curved blade.

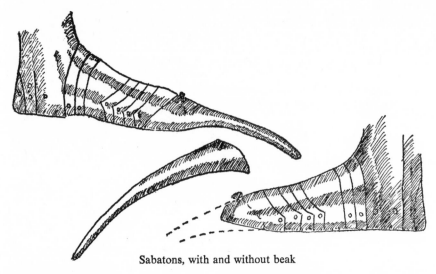

Sabatons, with and without beak

Saddle-bow – The front part of a saddle which during the 12th century was developed in height thus protecting the rider and assisting him to resist the shock of any blows made at him.

Saddle Tree – The wooden framework of the saddle.

Salade Helmet – Sometimes called Sallet. A popular helmet at the end of the 15th century. It rested entirely on the head and was not attached to the body armour. There were various shapes, but the later types all carried a movable visor.

Samurai – A class of Japanese professional swordsmen who came into being during the 12th century.

Saracenic Armour – A mixture of mail and subsidiary pieces of plate, in some cases the plate being inserted in the mail. There was very little change in this armour between the time of the later crusades and when the British fought in the Sudan in 1898.

Saxe or Scrammer Saxe – The sword used by the Franks which had a single cutting edge but a very sharp point.

Scabbard – The cover for sword or bayonet.

Scale Armour – Refers in general to all types of armour of which the make-up is primarily of small scales of metal.

Scaling Fork – A particularly long shafted weapon with prominent hooks, sometimes carried on scaling ladders for the purpose of dragging defenders from the battlements.

Schynbald – Long strips of plate covering the front of the chausses. Introduced about 1350.

Scimitar – A curving sword, generally broader towards the point, with a single cutting edge on the convex side.

Scutum – A large square, curved type of Roman shield on which they

226

emblazoned the insignia of their unit. By standing a number of scuta together the Romans formed a kind of defensive wall.

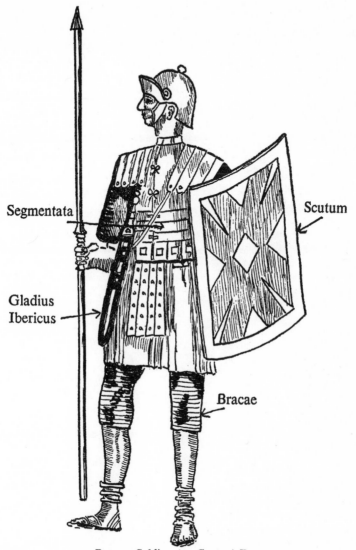

Segmentata

Gladius
Ibericus

Scutum

Bracae

Roman Soldier 1st Cent. A.D.

Segmentata – Refers to the long narrow plates laced round the body of a Roman soldier.

Shaft – Refers to the handle of certain types of weapon including lance, pike, halberd, axe, etc.

Shafted Weapons – These have been described under the alphabetical name of each weapon.

Shield – Throughout the ages the shield has taken many forms. The early Egyptians carried a shield approximately the same shape as the modern Heraldic shield though up-side-down. The Greeks and

Knight 1220 with 'heater' shield

Bronze Age tribesmen used a round shield; in the case of the Greeks it was generally emblazoned with some monster or animal. The Romans preferred the square scutum which stood about three feet high and was slightly curved. These were frequently used in batches to form a protective wall. The early Saxons used a round shield named 'target' which was generally painted in different coloured roundles and from which the word target of today is derived.

The later Saxons and Normans used the long kite shaped shield which was perfectly sensible for foot soldiers but extremely awkward to handle on horseback.

About 1200 the shape of the shield changed to what came to be known as the 'heater' type. This was shorter than the kite shield and considerably wider and curved to fit the body. It was upon this type of shield that the early coats of arms were emblazoned.

By the late 13th century the size had been much reduced and the curve of the shield was nothing like so pronounced.

This was followed in the 14th century by a type which did not follow the conventional shape, it was nearly rectangular, pointed at the base and carried a notch in the left hand corner (from the viewer's point of view) for the lance.

By 1600 the shield had almost disappeared in European countries in favour of improved armour for the left side of the body. The one exception to this being the round target shield with central spike carried by the clansmen during the Jacobite rebellions.

Shrimp – A type of small armoured barrow with two light guns pointing forward through a tapered shield and a cluster of curved blades in the front. This was used at the siege of Boulogne 1543.

Shoulder Pieces – A general name given to armour specifically designed for the protection of the shoulder.

Skirt – A skirt shaped piece of plate armour designed to cover the abdomen and hips. This has been variously designed to fit closely to the contours of the body and to be flared out.

Skull Cap – The strengthened leather cap fitting close to the head which preceded the introduction of the helmet.

Soleret – Flexible armour for the foot generally made of steel plates or cuir boulli. They were frequently fastened by straps which could be cut if it was necessary for the wearer to fight on foot, thus removing the projecting point to permit easier walking.

Spaudler – A series of small overlapping plates to protect the shoulder.

Spear – A general term embracing weapons with a pointed head on a long shaft. Used both by foot soldiers and cavalry though for the latter it was generally termed lance.

Spearmen – Foot soldiers armed with a spear.

Spontoone – A half pike retained until the beginning of the 18th century and carried by officers, primarily to denote their difference in rank from ordinary soldiers.

Spurs – An essential part of the Knight's equipment when on horseback. There were many different designs which frequently displayed superb craftsmanship.

Kinght's Spur with Rowel

Stiletto – A needle sharp dagger of Italian origin.

Stirrup – First adopted during the 8th century particularly against the incursions of the Hun. They were designed to allow the horseman to brace his feet and legs forward, thus securing more power to strike with his weapons.

Stop Rib – Small metal projections added to plate armour to prevent an attacking lance head from sliding between joints. Originally used around the neck but later spreading to other vital joints.

Studded and Splintered Armour – The name sometimes given to the type of armour worn during the transitional period of 1330-1360. In it there were many varieties and combinations of mail and plate.

Surcoat – The light linen coat worn over the armour adopted during crusades for protection against the sun and rain. Later shortened in size and emblazoned with coats of arms and used to assist identification on the battlefield during the 14th and 15th century.

Swingle – A weapon fitted with sharp spikes which was attached to the shaft by an articulated joint, thus enabling the bearer to strike a two-handed blow to the head of an opponent.

Sword – The types of sword have been discussed under their separate alphabetical headings.

Sword Belt – Originating of a bandolier or sling type worn over the right shoulder. It has also included the waist belt type and the combination of the two culminating in the sam browne belt of today.

Sword Breaker – A comb shaped bladed weapon designed to catch the blade of an adversary's sword and with a sharp twist to break it.

Sword-breaker

Sword Smith – An armourer specialising in making swords. His craft has been of paramount importance from the early Saxon time.

T

Taces – A name given to gaps likely to appear between plates in armour and which were generally protected by strips of mail.

Tang – The projection from the blade of a sword on to which the grip and handle furniture are attached.

Target – A type of shield (q.v.).

Tassets – Small metal strips strapped to the fauld to provide additional protection for the thigh.

Three Quarter Armour – A system introduced during the 17th century for cavalry providing armour down to the knee and leather riding boots for the feet and legs.

Tilting Armour – Specially protected armour designed for use in tournaments. It was generally decorated but not so generously as that used for ceremonial parades.

Tonlets – Rigid imitation pleats cut away fore and aft which formed the skirt. Circa 1511.

Tonlet

Tournament – A meeting held during the Middle Ages at which knights proved their skill by jousting or tilting. There were various types of bout, the 'mêlée' in which teams of knights fought against each other and the 'lists' at which two knights fought each other in single combat. Originally the object was to unhorse the adversary but later a system was developed whereby points were obtained by merely breaking lances.

In early days there was very little control kept during these bouts but latterly a system of rules was rigidly enforced.

A tournament was always a gala affair, combined with banquets and jollifications and invariably a local beauty was selected as Queen of the Tournament.

Trotting Armour – A kind of half armour used in Germany, so named because it gave the horsemen more mobility.

Turban Helmet – An eastern innovation, about half-way between a turban and a helmet. Constructed of metal, sometimes pointed and flat topped, it had flutings round the circumference representing the folds of the turban.

230

Two Handed Sword – A very large type of sword popular during the 15th century. Its size and weight necessitated the use of both hands to wield it. It could not be used in close formations and was generally designed for huge, horizontal cutting sweeps. The grip was elongated and the blade was generally over four feet in length, though some specimens have been found up to six feet over all.

Two-handed Sword

U

Upper Canon – A name given occasionally to the pair of plates enclosing the upper arm, similarly the pair for the forearm were known as the Lower Canon.

V

Vambrace – The name originally applied to the frontal plates on both the upper and lower arm. A little later it was applied to both front and rear plates of the forearm, and finally the name was given to cover the defences of the whole arm.

Vamplate – The circular disc used to protect the hand on the shaft of a lance. It did not appear until the early 15th century.

Velvet Covering – About 1400 it was the custom in Italy to cover the body defences with a short velvet jacket rather similar to the jupon but not decorated with any form of armorial bearings.

Ventail – See Aventail.

Vizor, Visor – The name covering various types of defence for the front of the face. It was first seen in the gladiators' helmets during the 1st century. It was not used by the Normans who preferred the nasal and the aventail. It was, however, reintroduced during the 14th century.

There were many types and shapes of the vizor but basically the mechanics were the same in each

Lances with Vamplates

231

case, namely that when not in use they could be raised over the forehead, where a clip held them in position.

Types of Vizor

W

Waistcoat Cuirass – Introduced in 1580, it was another example of making armour to resemble the civilian garment. It generally had hinges at the back which permitted it to open in front where it had fastenings in stud form. A row of steel imitation buttons down the front completed its decoration.

Waist Plate – A form of metal belt used in Germany to wear over armour. Circa 1520.

War Hammer – See Hammer.

War Scythe – A form of shafted weapon whose design was based on the implement of the countryside but stronger in construction and of better balance.

Wearing of Armour – Naturally it was impossible for a Knight to spend day after day dressed up in his plate armour. Frequently even in battle they preferred to wear the more flexible shirt of mail. For many years, too, mail was retained as useful in an emergency. It was carried in the saddle bag and could be donned in a hurry if the Knight ran into trouble in town or along the road.

Weight of Armour – Some comparative weights of armour are given in the following:

Complete Armour		lb	oz
Italian Field Armour	(c. 1450)	57	0
German Field Armour	(c. 1525)	41	13½
English Field Armour	(c. 1590)	71	14
Jousting Armour	(c. 1500)	90	1½
Mail			
Long Hauberk	(14th century)	31	0
Short Hauberk	(14th century)	20	11
Helmets			
Black Prince's Helmet		7	2
Bascinet (visored) and camail	(c. 1390)	12	9
Sallet	(c. 1470)	5	0
Jousting Helm	(c. 1480)	23	8

Wheel Lock – A more advanced type of musket than the matchlock.

White Armour – Sometimes called Alwyte Armour. Up to the early 15th century it had been the custom to cover armour with a surcoat or jupon. At about this time, however, this outer garment ceased to be worn and the Knight thus appeared with his armour uncovered, cased virtually in glittering steel from head to foot. This was known as white or alwyte armour.

White Harness – An alternative name for White Armour.

Wrapper – A form of reinforcing beaver designed to fit around the cheek pieces of the armet and covering part of the chest. A strap and buckle secured this piece of the helmet. Introduced in the middle of the 15th century.

PART FOUR

HISTORICAL AND MISCELLANEOUS

HISTORICAL AND MISCELLANEOUS

THIS SECTION is designed to incorporate a number of items which do not correctly belong to one of the other three parts in the book.

The Historical references, whether referring to a particular King or to a battle, have been chosen because they are of significance in-so-far as Heraldry is concerned and they are references which will occur from time to time in the reading carried out by any keen student of Heraldry.

The items which are non-historical are also items which are better grouped together on their own, rather than being classified as Heraldry, Genealogy, or Armour and Arms.

A

Agincourt – A battle fought on the 25th October 1415.

On the days prior to the battle the English army of some 5,000 men at arms and archers had been dogged by a vastly superior French army estimated at approximately 50,000. On the evening of the 24th October, Henry V who led the English army decided to bring the French to battle on the following day. He personally spent the night in careful reconnaissance of the ground and in prayer and, by exercise of the strictest discipline, maintained almost complete silence in the lines of the English troops. The French army, at the same time, spent most of the night in rowdyism and drinking.

Early on the morning of the 25th October Henry lined up the English army on a funnel shaped piece of ground bordered on both sides by thick masses of trees. In front of the English positions the soldiers set six-foot stakes which were pointed at both ends, into the ground. These were pointed forward at a height of about five feet.

By midday nothing had happened and the two armies still stood and looked at each other. On the command 'Banners Advance' the English army moved forward about 200 yards and replanted their stakes. As the afternoon wore on the French decided to attack.

The French army, which consisted almost entirely of knights and mounted men-at-arms, all wanted to be in the van. They had very little discipline and as they rode into the gradually lessening area between the trees they were bumping and boring each other and when some 200 yards from the English positions they met a hail of arrows from the English archers. From then onwards all was pandemonium. Those of the French Knights who managed to reach the English positions could not

237

avoid riding on to the stakes. These wounded their horses and unseated the riders who were quickly despatched by the English axemen. This continued with a mounting pile of dead and wounded bodies in front of the stakes until the French had completely lost heart and fled.

The casualties were estimated at over 10,000 Frenchmen and under 1,000 Englishmen.

It is interesting that shortly after the battle Henry V knighted a number of his followers and confirmed the armorial bearings of all those who had borne them during the battle.

Armourer's Company – One of the earlier craft guilds of the city of London which is believed to have been established at the beginning of the 14th century and which was given its original charter by Henry VI in 1453. During the years a number of allied crafts were incorporated with the company including the Heaumers (who made helmets), the Garnishers and Repairers and the Bladesmiths. More recently it was amalgamated with the Braziers and it survives today under the name of the Worshipful Company of Armourers and Braziers. Its earlier surviving record, dated 1413, shows that the company had the right to examine any weapon or armour offered for sale in the city of London and if it reached the required standard of workmanship it would be stamped with their official mark which was the cypher ' A ' and a crown.

Athelstan – One of the early Kings of the west Saxons and Mercians who lived from 895–940. He is said to be the first man given the accolade of Knighthood by his king, using a sword to confer the honour. The King conferring the honour was Alfred, who was also his grandfather.

B

Baldwin of Flanders 1058–1118 – The first titular King of Jerusalem. During the first Crusade 1096–1100, which was the only successful crusading expedition, Antioch was captured after an eight month siege in 1098, and the Holy city was captured in the summer of the following year. Godfrey de Bouillon was in reality the first Christian King of Jerusalem but he refused to accept a crown and merely retained the title of Count. However, on his death in 1100, Baldwin succeeded him as a properly crowned King.

Balista – A siege engine which looked something like a giant cross bow worked by tension. It could project stones against defences but was more often used to hurl great metal shafts and bolts, which were frequently combined with incendiary material, with the object of setting fire to the area besieged.

Banners, Standards, Guidons and Colours – Standards and ensigns go back to the very earliest days and they are referred to in numerous books of the Bible. Initially introduced as emblems of a tribal chief, they became objects of veneration. As such, besides adorning the chief's dwelling, they were carried into battle where they became not only the rallying point of the force, but one of its principal factors in the maintenance of morale. So long as the ensign or standard was flying the battle was not lost.

During the Roman era we know

that the standard was an important feature in the army and the standard-bearer was invariably an officer of importance.

Referring to the Bayeaux Tapestry, we see that both standards and banners were carried by the forces of both sides, though the emblems used appear childish and it is doubtful if they had as much meaning as did those in Roman times.

Passing to the mediaeval period we find a much more concrete system introduced which coincided with the growth of heraldry. At this time land was generally granted to the king's favourites or supporters or, in fact, to anyone who did a service to the crown, particularly during a campaign. Frequently a title was included, but in return, the nobleman, be he baron or knight, was required to raise a force of so many fighting men, according to his rank, who could be called upon to fight for the king in case of invasion from abroad or expedition against a foreign country.

Each of these landowners had taken, or very soon took, a suitable coat of arms. At the same time, it became the custom for each to carry a banner decorated with his house arms thereon in exactly the same form as were borne upon his shield, surcoat and caparison. The banner was generally square, though occasionally it was to be found greater in depth than in length. The lowest rank to use a banner was the Knight Banneret. Other and lesser knights and their retainers invariably followed somebody else's banner. These lesser knights, each carried a pennon or small swallow-tailed flag attached to the head of his lance. This too was emblazoned with the arms or badge of its owner. If the knight was promoted banneret for his prowess in the campaign, the tails of the pennon were ceremoni-

ously cut off, thereby converting it to a temporary banner which was used thus until he was able to provide a banner of the correct size and form. The esquires used a small triangular pennon. The banner and pennons of the Middle Ages can be seen reflected in modern times in the flags flown on the ships of the more senior naval commanders and vehicles of the commanders in the other two services.

An example of the beautiful banners of today are those of the Knights of the Garter and the Bath to be found hanging in St. George's Chapel, Windsor Castle and Westminster Abbey, respectively. These personal banners show the arms of the Knights to whom they belong and they remain in position during the lifetime of the owner.

The origin of 'Colours' also dates back to the Middle Ages. As the feudal forces were replaced by the standing army of the King, it became the custom for individuals to be entrusted with the task of raising regiments. They in turn deputed to others the task of raising companies. Thus each company became accustomed to fighting under its own captain. This system was virtually similar to, though a definite step forward from, the feudal system referred to above. Here the service was paid, and not given in exchange for the right to a piece of land or by virtue of being some nobleman's serf. Many captains possessed arms and soon each company fought under its captain's banner. Frequently the regiment divided into two sections, the Right Wing and Left Wing, one under the colonel and the other under the Lieutenant-Colonel. This, therefore, meant two or more regimental banners, sometimes there was division into three parts; thus the Major too had a banner. Many of these captains did not possess an entitlement to bear arms and it became the custom for these non-armigerous officers to adopt flags of distinctive colours which, owing to their varied hues, came to be known as 'The Colours'.

From then onwards, there was a gradual process of evolution and, to quote Edwards' 'Standards, Guidons and Colours': page 14, 'By the end of the sixteenth century continental armies were throwing off their loose character as regards formations and adopting a systemised arrangement. One of the pioneers of this movement was Gustavus Adolphus, King of Sweden, who regimented his troops for the Thirty Years' War in Germany (1618–1648). His regiments of Horse and Foot were divided into a regular number of units, each composed of a definite number of men. Each unit had its Standard (Cavalry) or Colour (Infantry), and all the units were of the same general pattern.'

To confirm the trend of opinion at the time we find in Ward's 'Animadversions of Warre' published in 1639, where he sets out the duties of a Colonel of a Regiment. 'He ought to have all the Colours of his Regiment to be alike both in colour and in fashion to avoide confusion so that the soldiers may discerne their owne Regiment from the other Troopes; likewise, every particular Captaine of his Regiment may have some small distinctions in their Colours; as their Armes, or some Emblem, or so that one Company can be discerned from the other.'

In 1660, when Charles II came to the throne, one of his first tasks was to raise a standing army. At the same time, he issued a Royal Warrant giving instructions for the appropriate colours to be made in consultation with 'our trusty and well-beloved servant Sir Edward Walker, Knight, Garter Principal King-of-Arms.' As a result, we find 'The Colonel's colour in the first place, is of pure clean colour, without any mixture. The Lieutenant-Colonel's only with St. George's Armes in the upper corner next the staff; the major's the same, with a pile wavy flottant, and every captain with St. George's Armes alone, but with so many spots or several devices as pertain to the degrity of their several places.' (Capt. Thomas Venn, 1672.)

This reference to 'Garter' is interesting because it was not until 1806, that the Office of Inspector of Regimental Colours was inaugurated, since when it has always been held by an officer of the College of Arms who has invariably become Garter during his tenure of it. (See below.)

At the same time, we find that in the greater part of the army in existence, other than as part of the Standing Army, 'the infantry, and some of the cavalry, bore on their Colours the armorial devices of the Colonels in some shape or other.' ('Standards and Colours of the Army'. Samuel Milne Milne.)

The Colonels practically owned their regiments and the badges and crests frequently changed when the Colonels changed.

In the early eighteenth century (1707), when the infantry arm was re-organised for tactical reasons the number of colours, except in regiments of the guards, where company colours are still in existence, was reduced from twelve to three; presumably the Colonels, the Lieutenant-Colonel's and the Major's remaining.

In 1747, we see the introduction of the present system of Regimental Colours with Regulations to govern them, the first four paragraphs of which are given below:

'No Colonel to put his Arms, Crest, Device or Livery on any part of the Appointments of the Regiment under his command.'

'No part of the Cloathing or Ornaments of the Regiments to be altered, after the following Regulations are put into execution but by His Majesty's permission.'

'The King's or First Colour of every Regiment or Battalion is to be the Great Union.'

'The Second Colour to be the colour of the Facing of the Regiment with the Union in the upper canton. In the centre of each Colour is to be painted or embroidered in gold Roman characters the number of the Rank of the Regiment within a Wreath of Roses and Thistles on the same stalk; except the Regiments which have Royal Badges or particular ancient Badges allowed them; in these, the number of the Rank of the Regiment is to be towards the upper corner. The length of the Pyke and the Colour itself to be of the same size as those of the Royal Regiments of Foot Guards. The Cords and Tassels of all Colours to be crimson and gold.'

These regulations were promulgated a second time in 1751, in almost identical wording, but in the form of a Royal Warrant. Exactly why this was done is not entirely clear unless it was thought advisable to elevate the regulations to the status of a Royal Warrant, and, of course, the Warrant included regulations for Cavalry standards, Guidons and Drum Banners which had not been included in the earlier regulations.

Standards were authorised for Regiments of Household Cavalry and for the Dragoon Guards, while the lesser horsed regiments (the Dragoons) carried guidons. Thus,

once again we see the mediaeval difference in seniority reflected in modern times, the standard arising out of the nobleman's banner and guidon from the lesser knight's pennon. The actual word 'Guidon' is, of course, derived from the French 'guide Homme' which was the name given to the flag carried by the leader of a French Regiment of Horse.

Barbican – A special fortification built to protect the gateway of a castle which was one of the greatest weaknesses in the castle's defence. The barbican generally consisted of strong towers, a drawbridge and a portcullis.

Beauchamp, Richard, Earl of Warwick 1382/1439 – One of the most colourful figures in history and a member of one of the most famous of English families. He was a Knight of the Garter, and of the Bath and on June 26th 1403, at the age of 20, he successfully jousted at the coronation of Joan of Navarre, Queen of Henry IV. In 1408, he travelled to Jerusalem to visit the Holy Sepulchre and on the way was challenged to perform a feat of arms at Verona where he gained victory. He was Lord High Steward at Henry V's coronation and held other various important commands under him in France and by the King's wish had care of the infant Henry VI. His effigy which is one of the most splendid and important in England is in the Beauchamp chapel in the Church of St. Mary in Warwick.

Bohemund of Tarantum – One of the leaders of the first crusade who, after the capture of Antioch, remained as ruler of the Principality of Antioch.

241

Book Plates – This was a very popular method of Heraldic display particularly during the Victorian era. Book plates are designed to incorporate the armorial bearings of the owner together with his name. They may, of course, be in colour or black and white and of any convenient size.

Brandon, Charles, First Duke of Suffolk (Temp. Henry VIII.) – A famous soldier and Earl Marshal of England. He was squire to the Royal body of Henry VIII, and held several important military commands under the King. He had a considerable reputation for jousting and in 1514 appeared with the Marquess of Dorset as the champion of England at the tournaments held in Paris celebrating the marriage of Henry VIII's sister Mary to Louis VII. He rode in the famous tournament held at Westminster in 1511 in honour of Queen Catherine of Aragon and ran eight courses against the King.

Brass – A memorial tablet generally set in stone which attempts to give some sort of pictorial representation of the person commemorated. The metal is sometimes known as Latten which is a corruption of the French 'Laiton' meaning brass but it actually consists of an alloy composed of copper, lead and tin.

Brasses provide invaluable sources of information concerning contemporary costume and armour. Over 7,000 survive in England of a probably original figure in the neighbourhood of 150,000.

While many brasses are devoted to commemorating civilians, undoubtedly the most popular are those portraying Knights and esquires complete with their armour and weapons. One of the most famous being that of Sir John

Brass—Thomas de Berkeley, 1243 in the wall of South Aisle in the Choir of Bristol Cathedral

d'Abernon (circa 1277) in the church at Stoke d'Abernon in Surrey.

A particularly popular hobby amongst many people is that of brass rubbing which is now forbidden in many churches owing to the very considerable wear of the metal and consequent defacement of the memorial.

C

Castles – The castle was developed as a natural means of fortification for man to protect himself and his possessions.

Examples exist in a few cases of fortifications existing in Britain in the pre-Roman era but from their position, generally on top of a hill and the consequent difficulty in providing their inhabitants with water, it is not likely that these fortifications were ever intended to be manned for lengthy periods of time. An excellent example of one of these is Maiden Castle near Dorchester, whose defences extend $\frac{2}{3}$ of a mile in length and $\frac{1}{3}$ of a mile in width. Part of this structure dates back to approximately 2,500 B.C., and it was extended and improved in about 250 B.C.

Roman fortifications consisted more generally of fortified walls to their camps and an excellent example may be seen in the remains of the early fortifications of cities and towns such as York, Colchester, etc. and Hadrian's Wall.

During the troubled time between the Roman occupation of Britain and the Norman conquest the principal defences lay in the old Motte and Bailey type castles.

After the Norman conquest a great many castles were erected in various parts of Britain, there were various types and designs consisting generally of outer walls protected by towers and a moat. The gateways were protected by a barbican or gatehouse with drawbridges and a portcullis. Inside the outer crust the area where garrison lived was frequently divided into two or three defensive areas each of which possessed its own defences and this in turn culminated in the ' keep ' which initially was built as a square tower and later changed to a round tower.

It was in the keep that the castellan and the principal members of his force lived and it was to the keep that the remainder of the garrison retired when the outer defences had fallen.

The early Norman period was the time when most of the English castles were erected and by the time of King John there were as many as 127 in existence in England and Wales.

Château Gaillard – One of the most famous of the castles built by Richard I on the model of some of those great fortresses in the Holy Land. It had three baileys in a line with deep moats between each. The Château was the scene of a bitter siege in 1203/4 when Roger de Lacy, holding the castle on behalf of King John, was besieged by Philip II of France.

Chatelaine – The wife of a castellan, mistress of a castle or château.

Children's Crusade – A disastrous expedition undertaken by thousands of French and German children in an effort to rescue the Holy Land. The crusade was preached by Stephen a 12-year-old boy who promised his followers that the seas would dry up before them, as they had done before the Israelites. By the end of 1212 approximately 30,000 children of the age of 12 or less had gathered at Vêndome and accompanied by a few Priests they started their southerly trek with Stephen their leader riding in a cart covered by a canopy to shelter him from the blazing sunshine.

Before long, due to shortage of water and food, many had dropped out. At Marseilles the remainder were disappointed to find that the seas remained stubbornly impassable. However, two merchants hired a total of 7 ships to take the children to the Holy Land. After they had sailed nothing more was heard of them for a period of 20 years when the news gradually leaked out that two of the ships had been wrecked off Sardinia and the remaining 5 captured by a Saracen squadron and the children sold to slavery.

Concentric Castle – A type of fortress popular in the late 13th and early 14th centuries, consisting of an outer and inner ring of defences. Harlech and Caerphilly are two of the more famous surviving examples.

Council of Westminster – Summoned by Ansel in 1102. One of its important decisions was that Bishops and Abbots would cease from having the power to make knights.

Crécy – Fought on the 26th and 27th of August 1346 when the chivalry of France under Philip VI, consisting of approximately 40,000 Knights, men at arms and archers, attacked and were defeated by an English force consisting of 13,000 of whom about 3,000 were Knights and men-at-arms and the remainder archers.

The success of the battle was due to the rigid discipline exercised by the English army as compared with the complete indiscipline of the French.

Crusades – The name given to the military expeditions carried out by the Christian countries for the recovery of the Holy Land from the Saracens.

Then there were a number of small and insignificant expeditions eight of which are generally distinguished by the name Crusade. The first, from 1096–1100, was the only expedition which could be termed successful and which resulted in the capture of Jerusalem. The last was that led by St. Louis, King of France 1270–72. The most important from the English point of view was the third crusade led by Richard I.

E

Edward I, 1239–1307 – Is generally looked upon as one of the greatest soldier Kings of England. He was a very tall man and his great length of leg earned him the nickname of ' Longshanks '. He was famous in the tournament and as a hunter, yet he loved music, poetry and chess. In 1271 he joined the crusade defeating the Saracens at Haifa where he made a ten year truce. He was accompanied on the expedition by his wife Eleanor of Castile who was herself the daughter of a crusading King. When Edward was struck down by a poisoned Saracen dagger she saved his life by devoted nursing and it is believed that she personally sucked the poison from his wounds.

Edward II, 1312–1377 – He was the grandson of Edward I and like him was also renowned as a soldier but less for his Kingship. During his reign the English won the battles of Crécy and Poitiers.

It was this King who founded the Order of the Garter.

Edward Prince of Wales 1330–1376 – Better known in history as the ' Black Prince '. He was one of the greatest heroes of English chivalry. He commanded the vanguard at Crécy 1346 while still only 16 years of age and was responsible for the rout of the French at Poitiers 10 years later. In spite of his Knightly courtesies he was frequently ruthless and cruel in his campaigns.

The effigy of the Prince may be seen in Canterbury Cathedral.

Eglinton Tournament – An attempt made by Archibald William Montgomerie 13th Earl of Eglinton to revive the splendours of the days of chivalry by staging a tournament at Eglinton castle.

A great deal of money was spent on the arrangements which would probably have been a great success but the whole process was ruined by a fantastic downpour of rain which started shortly before the tournament was due to begin and which resulted in turning the whole area into a sea of wet, slimy mud.

The whole of the story is very thoroughly described in ' Knight and the Umbrella ', by Ian Anstruther.

Escalade – One of the methods of close assault of castles by means of scaling ladders.

F

Field of the Cloth of Gold – The renowned meeting which took place in June 1520 between Henry VIII of England and Francis I of France. The two monarchs vied with each other in the richness of their retinues and their lavish hospitality. A temporary palace was erected, specially for the reception of Henry VIII, which had fountains spouting wine in front of it. Besides this some 2,800 tents were needed.

A week was spent in tournaments, both Kings taking the field with their Knights.

Flags – Flags are so ancient that their origin is unknown. They are alluded to in many ancient writings and their use is always taken for granted.

Flags have taken many forms from the early standard referred to in the Bible to pennons carried on the tips of lances, banners of the Nobility carried in battle, regimental colours, flags of countries, flags of schools, institutions and other bodies, house flags of the mercantile marine, flags used for signalling purposes by the fighting forces on both land and sea, even down to bunting used for purposes of decoration.

Flags in their various forms have been of many different shapes and sizes but are generally of a standard size in every particular section in which they are used, thus signal flags are the same size, regimental colours are the same size, and so on.

Flanking Towers – Towers set at intervals in the walls of a castle which projected outwards. These were designed so that the defenders could shoot down along the wall, particularly at attackers trying to make a breach at the base or to mine under the walls.

Frederick of Barbarossa – Emperor of Germany 1155–1189 – He was a fine monarch possessing all the qualities most admired in the age of chivalry. He set out with an army to join the third crusade but was drowned when crossing the River Calycadnus.

Free Course – One of the methods of combat in a tournament but run without the centre barrier. The chief object of the contest was to shiver one's lance against the adversary's shield or armour.

G

George, St. – The patron saint of England and hero of one of the most famous legends of the Middle Ages. The real St. George, George of Cappadocia was a Christian soldier who was martyred in A.D. 303 after imprisonment and torture in defence of his faith.

The council of Oxford of 1222 ordered that 23rd April should be maintained as a national festival in honour of St. George but it was approximately 100 years later when Edward III nominated him as patron saint of England.

Godfrey of Bouillon – One of the leaders of the first crusade who became the first ruler of the Holy Land. He refused to wear a crown or to use the title King. His sword and spurs are preserved in the Latin Sacristy in the Church of the Holy Sepulchre at Jerusalem.

Golden Fleece – The second most famous order of Knighthood in Europe coming after the Order of the Garter. Founded in 1430 by Philip, Duke of Burgundy it was probably named from the fleece or sheep wool that was the foundation of the wealth of Burgundy.

Guillam, John 1665–1621 – One of the best known early writers on Heraldry. His book ' The Display of Heraldry ' published in 1610 was the first serious treatment in English of the subject, and he was also an officer of arms.

H

Henry V. 1413–1422 – Not only was Henry V a cultured, handsome and really Christian type of man, but he was one of the finest generals that Britain has ever known. He personally planned and organised the whole of the expeditionary force which left England on the 14th August 1415 for France. Prior to their departure, every inlet and creek along the Hampshire coast opposite the Isle of Wight had been packed with shipping. The largest ship of the fleet was the *Trinité Royale* which was Henry's flagship. This ship had a crew of 300 under her master Stephen Thomas and a portage of 500 tons.

The programme of loading and the loads of each vessel were planned by the King who personally exercised supervision throughout.

Following disembarkation in France the army carried out a siege against the small but defended sea port of Harfleur, after which they marched towards Calais. In the vicinity of Agincourt (q.v.) they brought the French army to battle and, in spite of overwhelming odds against them, the English army defeated the French.

Prior to and during the battle Henry V's generalship stood out, yet he found time in which to pray and to give his troops adequate time and encouragement to do so.

After Agincourt he married Catherine of Valois, daughter of Charles VI King of France, but unfortunately died in 1422 at the age of 34.

In spite of a short life it had not been in vain as he bequeathed England something far more valuable than foreign territory. His life and achievement awakened Englishmen to the truths of unselfishness and inspiration and also to a great awareness of their country.

Henry VIII. 1491–1547 – Probably best known for his matrimonial problems but a good king and, though vain and greedy, he was valiant and in his early days good looking.

As one of the principal parties in the Field of the Cloth of Gold (q.v.) he took a very active part in the tournaments and the following extract may be found about him in the Hollinshed Chronicles 'Acquitting himselfe so worthily that the beholders tooke passing pleasure to see his valaunte demanoure in those martiall feates '.

Heraldic Stationers – The name given to a number of firms and small businesses who provide bogus heraldry.

In general terms they offer to supply your 'coat of arms according to your name' and to applications by the general public they make the broad statement, either that anybody can assume arms at will or if his name is the same as a previously recorded armiger they may use his arms.

This is of course completely incorrect and these places should be avoided.

Nobody is entitled to bear arms unless they have been granted by the College of Arms, Lyon office Edinburgh, the Chief Herald of Ireland or by the Heraldic authority of the country from which the armiger originated, or they can trace lineal male descent, which must be conclusively proved, from a properly registered armiger.

Heraldry in Wartime – As armorial bearings worn on the surcoat and the shield provided means of recognition in battle in the Middle Ages, so in modern day warfare members of the British army wear certain insignia on their sleeves to denote the unit and formation to which they belong. These formation emblems are also borne on all unit and formation vehicles.

A form of Heraldry is also used by the Royal Navy and the Royal Air Force in the form of ships' and squadron badges, which are designed in conjunction with the Officer of Arms responsible at the College of Arms.

In addition, regiments of the British army possess guidons and colours for cavalry and infantry respectively which are carried on all ceremonial occasions in peace time. These too come under the inspector of regimental colours who in this case is generally Garter Principal King of Arms.

Holy Land – Equally revered by both Christians and Saracens but for different reasons. It was the site of most of the crusades and during the Middle Ages was regarded as a place of pilgrimage for both men and women.

I

Inn Signs – The Middle Ages and Heraldry in general are constantly illustrated in many of the varied Inn Signs of England, examples being 'The Trip to Jerusalem' and the many Saracen's and Turk's Heads, reminding one of the days of the crusades, others include the Black Prince, George and Dragon, the Castle, The Five Arrows etc.

Others incorporate the arms of some of the more famous English families such as the Granville Arms, the Abergavenny Arms, The Earl of March, etc. Others are named after the various Royal badges, including the Swan, the White Hart, the Lion, the Lion and Unicorn, the Red Dragon, etc.

Italian Course – A form of tournament run with a central barrier which was constructed of wood some five feet in height. The Knights rode on either side, left hand to left hand. Originally the object was to unhorse one's adversary but later the system was devised that only the shivering of one's lance on his shield or armour scored winning points.

J

Japanese Mon – Almost all of the better class families in Japan use the 'mon'. This is a design which is generally, but by no means always, circular in shape and which is frequently based on the blossom of one of the many flowers growing in Japan.

Jerusalem – The capital of the Latin Kingdom, Jerusalem which was captured from the Moslems during the first crusade but lost again in 1187. Richard I came within striking distance of it during the third crusade but owing to the insufficient size of his army was compelled to refrain from trying to retake the city. It was temporarily recovered again in 1222 but was lost again 15 years later, and it was nearly 700 years later, during the first World War, before the city was entered again by a Christian army.

Joan of Arc – Who was sometimes known as the Maid of Orleans was perhaps France's best known figure of the Hundred Years War. She claimed that she had a divine mission to lead the armies of France to victory. Initially she was looked upon with complete scorn but her simplicity, directness and complete sincerity eventually overcame the doubters and the King gave her a military entourage. On the 27th April 1429 she left Blois to keep her promise which was to raise the siege of Orleans. It was a strongly fortified place which had been under siege by the English for many months and was reaching a stage of desperation for lack of food and water. On the 29th April she crossed a flooded river and with a force of about 200 lances and carrying quantities of provisions she rode straight through the English lines into Orleans. Naturally this raised the morale of the French and approximately a week later she launched an attack against the English army which was completely successful. Joan was always in the forefront of the battle with her pure white armour and riding a black horse and she possessed three banners which she is said to have treasured more than her sword, and in fact she was never known to have shed blood.

Her career was short because, after fulfilling her promised mission to relieve Orleans and having had one or two other smaller successes, she was captured on the 25th May 1430 and a year later was burnt at the stake as a witch.

Jousting Checks – Strips of paper or parchment which were marked with the points scored by combatants during a tournament. Scores were kept generally by pricking the parchment or marking with a small stroke as each Knight scored a winning hit. Few of these survive today and those there are, are in the College of Arms in London.

K

King John – Mediaeval people forgave their Kings much, because the worst King was better than the shortest spells of anarchy. 'King John in the sparkle of his intelligence was a true Plantagenet, excelling in military and diplomatic tactics, a great charmer of women, a fine hunter but cruel and mean'. Thus he is described by Andre Maurois.

He was his father's favourite and in the early years was popular with his brothers. He was born in 1167 near Oxford. At first he received no share in the great family inheritance which was divided between Henry, Richard and Geoffrey his elder brothers, hence he acquired the nickname 'Lackland'. This, however, was later remedied when his father, King Henry, gave him the county of Mortain in France.

He was originally affianced to Alice of Savoy, though the marriage never actually took place. However, in early days affiancement was generally looked upon as equivalent to a marriage and many historians describe Alice of Savoy as John's first wife.

His first official marriage took place in 1189, his wife being Isabel, daughter of William Earl of Gloucester. However, after ten years of childlessness he divorced her, much to the annoyance of the English nobility, and a year later married Isabella daughter of Aymer, Count Angoulême. Isabella was only twelve years old, while John was 32, and six weeks later she was consecrated Queen of England.

John's reign is remarkable on the one hand for his acts of brilliance and on the other by the utter cruelty and ruthlessness. Nevertheless, primarily by diplomacy, he managed to remain on the throne until he died at the age of 48 in 1216.

Knights of St. John of Jerusalem – One of the great monastic orders of knighthood which largely grew out of the crusades. Originally known as the Knights Hospitallers, their earliest duty was to protect and entertain pilgrims to the Holy Land and records show that in 1112 their monastery in Jerusalem was capable of housing as many as 2,000 guests in addition to providing accommodation for the sick. When they were turned out of Jerusalem they acquired the island of Rhodes and for a time were known as the

Knights of Rhodes. However, in 1530 they moved to Malta and became known as the Knights of Malta.

At the height of their power they were an immensely strong organisation, extremely wealthy and were responsible for building great castles such as the Krak des Chevaliers, barracks for their Knights, hospitals for the sick and rest houses for the pilgrims.

They established communities in a number of European countries which were responsible for providing recruits to the order and raising funds.

The order was suppressed in England by Henry VIII but in 1888 Queen Victoria granted a Royal Charter which constituted a restoration of the old religious and military order under the title of the Order of the Hospital of St. John of Jerusalem.

Knights Templars – The second of the great religious military orders arising out of the crusades for the protection of pilgrims and the defence of the Holy Sepulchre. The organisation was much the same as that of the Knights of St. John in their early days but because of the great corruption, vice and heresy which arose in connection with the order, accusations were levelled at it from all quarters.

In October 1307 the order was suppressed in France with considerable cruelty and a few years later it was suppressed in England but without acts of cruelty. The property of the order was handed over to the Knights of St. John.

Krak des Chevaliers – The great castle of the Knight's Hospitallers which was built some 25 miles inland north east of Tripoli. They were frequently attacked by Saladin

without success. It eventually fell in 1271 to another Sultan. It was immensely strong, having been built high on solid rock and no expense was spared in its beautiful internal decoration.

L

'Laissez Aller' – Let go. This was the command called by Heralds at a tournament as a signal for the Knights to charge.

Lists – The actual area where jousts and tournaments were held. The lists used at the famous tournament held at Smithfield in 1467 were 90 yards long by 80 yards wide surrounded by posts $7\frac{1}{2}$ feet high which were joined by heavy bars. This area was for a contest between only two knights and when contests involved a greater number of knights larger areas had to be used. At the Field of the Cloth of Gold (q.v.) the lists were 300 yards in length by 100 yards in width, this area being surrounded by a deep ditch to keep back spectators.

M

Magna Carta – The Great Charter is generally considered to be a document wrested from a tyrannical King by a united Baronage supposed to be the champions of the liberty of all individuals. Yet it was not intended to be a revolutionary document, but to provide for the preservation of ancient rights and privileges. It was worded so as to involve general principles and these made possible interpretations which had never occurred to the Barons.

In drawing up Magna Carta the counsellors and justices who framed it drew extensively on Henry I's Charter of 1100 which was a recognition of the national laws and which largely secured the rights of land owners whether of high or low estate.

There were 197 lay barons plus 39 ecclesiastical, or 236 in all. The lay Baronies were held by 45 barons who maintained 127 castles, thus a number of the barons held several baronies. The total of 236 was divided into 7,200 Knight's fees or Lordships which consisted of a manor or a tenure with sufficient income to support a Knight. Of the 45 lay barons only 24 were in revolt. These 24 barons, together with the Mayor of London composed the 25 Magna Carta sureties. The other 21 barons either remained neutral or sided with the King and were only interested in preserving their fiefs. Thus it is clear, the baronage was not united against King John and of the Knights only a small percentage was in revolt. As for the great mass of Englishmen there was no national feeling in that age; each man was bound by fealty to his Lord and followed his banner no matter how vacillating that may be.

On June 15th 1215 on the plain of Runnemede King John was forced by the barons to grant Magna Carta, which he ensealed but did not sign. However, this was not unusual because at the time many important nobles and even some Kings and Emperors could neither read nor write, hence it was more usual to enseal all documents rather than to append a signature.

In spite of his granting the char-ter King John had no intention of observing its clauses and he was supported by Pope Innocent the III who, in spite of earlier disagreements, sided with John and excommunicated both Magna Carta and Stephen Langton the Archbishop of Canterbury, who had sided with the barons in revolt. John died a year later to be succeeded by the young King Henry III in November 1216, and the charter was confirmed by William Marshal as regent and as guardian of the young King. It was in fact read in all the Churches in England twice yearly throughout the Middle Ages.

Mangonel – A siege engine designed to hurl stones high into the air against a fortified place, and it was also used actually for breaching the walls. It worked by torsion and had a long flexible beam which was fixed to twisted ropes. This was forced backwards and downwards and the missile was placed in a hole at the free end.

Mêlée – The name given to hand to hand fights between two teams of knights at a tournament.

Middle Ages – The period in history generally taken from the 5th to the 15th centuries. The name High Middle Age is generally taken to mean the period covered by the 13th and 14th centuries which embraced the principal age of chivalry.

Mine – A method used by besiegers to breach the wall of a castle or fortification. It generally consisted of digging under one corner of the structure being attacked and propping up the walls with stakes as the mine progressed. When a sufficiently large area had been uncovered the attackers withdrew, having first set fire to the stakes. When these burnt through they of course collapsed and the wall overhead fell, thus causing a breach through which the attackers entered the fortress.

Motte and Bailey – The name given to the early type of castle just prior to and immediately after the Norman conquest. Consisted of a small hill, sometimes natural and sometimes man made, on to which a stout wooden structure was built. The whole of the motte was surrounded by a deep ditch which became the forerunner of the moat.

O

Odo – Bishop of Bayeaux and half brother to William the Conquerer.

Though he was made a Bishop at approximately 15 years old his mind was filled with other than church matters. He was imprisoned by William I for his pride and tyranny and was later banished by William II. He took an extremely active part in the battle of Hastings in which he used a mace as his weapon thus salving his conscience in that a churchman must never shed blood, the mace being looked upon as a bruising weapon only.

Open Course – A joust between Knights run in the open with no barrier between. Sometime called Free Course.

Outremer – Literally meaning ' over seas ', a general name frequently used to cover the territories in which the crusades took place.

P

Pavilion – A gaily decorated and highly coloured tent used by a Knight at a tournament in which to put on his armour and to await his summons to fight.

Poitiers, Battle of – One of the Black Princes' great victories in France in which, with only 6,000 men, he defeated a vastly superior French army numbering some 50,000 soldiers. The principal attribute of the English army was its strict compliance with orders and its discipline throughout, which has been the means of bringing about a French defeat on so many occasions.

Portcullis – A strong grating, similar in design to a farmer's harrow, constructed of heavy wood and shod with metal, which slid down in grooves to close a castle gateway.

Postern – A small back gateway frequently found in a castle. It was designed as a means of exit which would probably be unknown to a besieging force and through which a messenger could be sent.

R

Richard I. 1189–1199 – Richard Coeur-de-Lion. Generally looked upon as one of the most glamorous of England's Kings. He was undoubtedly a magnificent fighter and of very strong physique yet he was one of the worst Kings England has ever known. He bled the country to finance the Crusade which he led, he was inordinately brave, yet he was cruel, greedy and vain. Of his ten years as King he spent less than nine months in England and then only to raise money, firstly for his Crusade and secondly for his expedition against France.

He married Berengaria of Navarre whilst on Crusade. She herself never even visited England.

Due largely to his quarrels with his allies Richard's crusading army gradually dwindled and it was also due to one of his quarrels that he spent so long in captivity on his return journey from the Crusade.

He died in France as the result of a wound received from a French archer.

Rolls of Arms – It was the custom in the early days, in order to record the presence of Knights at a particular siege, battle or tournament, to prepare a roll of arms consisting simply of the shield in colours beneath which was the name of the Knight who bore them. Many of these rolls have been preserved and are retained amongst the records of the College of Arms, where they provide valuable information from time to time.

S

Saint Albans, Battle of – There were two battles of this name both of which were fought during the Wars of the Roses. The first, which took place on the 22nd May 1455, was the opening battle of the war in which the Lancastrians were defeated. In the second occasion, on the 17th February 1461, the Lancastrians were victorious but completely threw away their advantage, because within a fortnight the Yorkist armies had taken London and Edward IV had been proclaimed King.

Saladin – The name by which a famous Sultan of Egypt and Syria and the most famous of the Saracen chiefs was known, his real name being Salah Ad-din Yusuf. In spite of all that has been said about him he was a particularly fine, generous and chivalrous man and though he displayed cruelty on many occasions these occasions were no more frequent than the acts of brutality ordered by Richard I who was Saladin's principal opponent.

Sandford, Francis – One of the early writers on Heraldry who dealt exclusively with the history of the Royal family in England and their armorial bearings. His work ' A Genealogical History of the Kings and Queens of England and Monarchs of Great Britain ' was first published at the end of the 17th century. The best edition of his work is that published in 1707.

Saracens – The general name given by the Christian armies to Arabs, Moors, Moslems, etc. Though they were invariably looked upon as being uncivilised and almost inhuman they were extremely skilful fighters, generally far more chivalrous than the crusaders and in their camps far more highly civilised than the Europeans were, even at home in their own countries.

Sergeant – The name used during the Middle Ages when referring to a non-knightly man at arms or trooper. In a few military orders it described an Esquire aspiring to Knighthood.

Siege Towers – Wooden towers constructed in the vicinity of the besieged fortress which were designed to raise numbers of the attacking troops to the height of the top of the wall to attack over the top of it or to a height above the wall from which archers could fire more effectively down on to the defenders.

Smithfield – A district of central London, north of the Thames and immediately outside the old city walls, which was used quite extensively for tournaments during the Middle Ages.

T

Tournaments – Apart from hunting, tournaments were the only sport available in the Middle Ages and even these could only be taken part in by the Nobility.

Tournaments were held on all possible occasions, such as coronations, births of Royal heirs, important marriages, etc., and on frequent occasions they were held with no particular cause to celebrate.

Originally the early tournaments were generally between teams of Knights, sometimes mounted, sometimes on foot, but although these were intended to be peaceful encounters it was not uncommon in the heat of the moment for blows to be struck in anger and many fatal casualties occurred.

In later years rules were produced and tournaments were held under strict control and on all principal occasions two or more Officers of Arms were present to act as controlling staff and masters of ceremony.

Prizes were awarded and at each tournament a ' Queen of the Tournament' was elected who, by her presence, virtually ensured that the Knights observed the laws of chivalry. It was she who presented the prizes at the end of the meeting.

The procedure was roughly as follows. On the day prior to the encounters beginning, the shields of all the participating Knights were displayed in a field near the lists by two or more of each Knight's retainers. The competing Knights then rode round the field touching the shield of all those to whom they issued a challenge. If the shield was touched with a sharp weapon the contest was to be fought with sharpened lances, if the shield was touched with blunt weapons then blunt weapons were used.

The encounters took place in an area known as the lists which varied in size according to the type of battle that was to be fought. In the case of the mêlée large areas were needed but in the later types of tournament when the strictest control was observed a barrier some five feet in height was constructed in the middle of the lists and the two Knights charged each other with the barrier on their left side. In this way, though the Knights could be wounded the horses were generally untouched.

Initially the principal object was to unhorse one's adversary but in later years a special type of brittle lance was employed which shivered (broke) on contact with the adversary's armour or shield. The points were scored by the number of lances shivered and each contest consisted of eight or ten courses.

A competitor was disqualified for various reasons, for example, for breaking the rules, or wounding his adversary's horse, or if he lost his helmet and so on.

Occasionally, where a severe quarrel had arisen between two knights and a challenge had been issued, by permission of the King the contest could be held 'to the death'. In these contests rules were even more strictly enforced and it was not uncommon, when one of the two contestants had been unhorsed, the King would call a halt and summon the two contestants to him. He would then issue summary punishment to the loser, such as banishment from the Kingdom, or he might order the two Knights to make up their quarrel declaring that honour was satisfied.

There were many particularly famous tournaments such as the two at Dunstable, the first in 1308 and the second in 1334 and that held in Smithfield in 1467 and at the **Field of the Cloth of Gold**. In addition there was a tournament area at Westminster where quite a number of tournaments were held at comparatively regular intervals.

Many attempts have been made in various European countries to renew the glamour of the tournament, perhaps the most famous being the abortive attempt by the Earl of Eglinton in 1839 which is so ably described by Ian Anstruther in 'The Knight and the Umbrella'.

Tower of London – One of the early castles built by William the Conqueror both to protect and intimidate the occupants of the city. Only part of the buildings are of Norman construction and many later styles are also represented. The original keep is what it now known as the White Tower.

The Tower of London has been occupied as a Royal Palace by all the English Kings and Queens up to the time of James I and it has been garrisoned continuously since it was first constructed.

W

War Cries – These were always used by the armies of the Middle Ages. Sometimes they were of national origin and on occasions have been a family battle cry. Many of them are recognisable today in the motto used in certain armorial bearings.

Westminster Tournament Roll – A well known pictorial record which is held by the College of Arms, London of the tournament held by Henry VIII at Westminster in February 1511. The tournament was held in honour of Queen Catherine of Aragon and the birth of their son Henry, Duke of Cornwall. The Roll is almost 60 feet long and nearly 15 inches wide comprising 35 sheets of vellum, illuminated in gold, silver and various colours.

APPENDIX A

SELECTED BIBLIOGRAPHY FOR FURTHER READING

Shield and Crest—Julian Franklyn
Armorial Insignia of the Kings and Queens of England—Williment
The Armorial Bearings of the Guilds of London—John Bromley
Complete Guide to Heraldry—Fox Davies
Boutells Heraldry—Scott-Giles
Armour and Weapons—Martin
Dictionary of Chivalry—Uden
Glossary of Heraldry—Parker
Orders of Chivalry—de la Bere
Mediaeval Armour, Costume and Weapons—Wagner, Durdik and Drobna
Heraldic Design—Child
A History of the Crusades—Runciman
Scots Heraldry—Innes of Learney
Armour and Blade—Ellacott
Castles and Fortresses—Sellman
Wills and their Whereabouts—Camp
Some Feudal Coats of Arms—Foster
Magna Carta, King John and the Barons—Bye
Battle of Agincourt—Nicolas
Heraldry in War—Cole
English Inn Signs—Larwood and Hotten
The Coat of Arms—The quarterly journal of The Heraldry Society
The Escutcheon—The quarterly journal of The Heraldry Society of
Australia